I0800111

Measuring the Man

The Writings of
FREDERICK DOUGLASS
on
ABRAHAM LINCOLN

Edited by Lucas E. Morel & Jonathan W. White

Copyright © 2025 by Lucas E. Morel and Jonathan W. White

Reedy Press
PO Box 5131
St. Louis, MO 63139, USA
reedypress.com

No part of this publication may be reproduced or transmitted in any form or by any means, electronic or mechanical, including photocopy, recording, or any information storage and retrieval system, without permission in writing from the publisher.

Permissions may be sought directly from Reedy Press at the above mailing address or via our website at reedypress.com.

Cover images: Frederick Douglass, taken in Portland, Maine, January 1864. Prints and Photographs Division, Library of Congress. Abraham Lincoln, January 1864. Lincoln Financial Foundation Collection, Allen County Public Library, Fort Wayne, Indiana.

Library of Congress Control Number: 2025943530

ISBN: 9781681066073

Printed in the United States of America

25 26 27 28 29   5 4 3 2 1

Praise for *Measuring the Man: The Writings of Frederick Douglass on Abraham Lincoln*

"In September 1862 Frederick Douglass castigated Abraham Lincoln for 'his pride of race and blood, his contempt for negroes and his canting hypocrisy.' Less than three years later the martyred president had earned Douglass's praise as 'emphatically the black man's President: the first to show any respect for their rights as men.' Lucas Morel's and Jonathan White's skillfully annotated anthology of Douglass's references to Lincoln in writings and speeches provides a barometer of the fluctuating progress of the antislavery cause during the Civil War, while the black leader's frequent postwar analyses of Lincoln's record anticipated the more nuanced interpretations by modern historians and biographers."

—James M. McPherson
Pulitzer Prize-winning author of *Battle Cry of Freedom: The Civil War Era*

"This collection tells a wonderful, thrilling, multi-dimensional, first-person story and should be in the bookshops of every Civil War, Lincoln, and Douglass site, as well as on so many syllabi. The relevance stretches from the added insight into Douglass to the overall lessons that it offers about social justice alliances, the difficulties between activism and party politics, and the importance of many, varied, and even critical voices for progress."

—Leigh Fought
Author of *Women in the World of Frederick Douglass*

"Few people defined the nineteenth-century United States like Abraham Lincoln and Frederick Douglass. Drawing on Douglass's writings and speeches, Lucas Morel and Jonathan White have scrupulously chronicled the orator's eagle-eyed scrutiny on and evolving thought regarding Lincoln—and have even uncovered previously-unknown letters from Douglass. Morel and White show Douglass moving between elation and despair, hope, and frustration. Their efforts show that the Civil War was both profoundly revolutionary and highly contingent. Viewing Lincoln through Douglass's eyes powerfully reminds us that the 'new birth of freedom' Lincoln celebrated in the Gettysburg Address was far from a certain outcome, and that it required both constant pressure and careful attention to political realities. This compilation is a service to students of the Civil War era and a model of editorial scholarship."

—Robert K. D. Colby
Author of *An Unholy Traffic: Slave Trading in the Civil War South*

Contents

Introduction

On February 6, 1863, Frederick Douglass walked onto the stage of the Cooper Union in New York City to deliver a speech "on the great questions of the day and of his race." The famous abolitionist implored white Americans to support black enlistment in the Union army. "Give them a chance," he repeated at least a half dozen times, for Douglass knew that black men could make the case for citizenship if they could prove their manhood and patriotism by risking their lives on the battlefield. Lincoln's Emancipation Proclamation had created an opportunity; now black men needed to seize it. The speech was greeted with loud cheers and applause by a "very large audience." When the *New-York Tribune* reported on it the following morning, the editors called Douglass "perhaps the most eloquent black man in America."[1]

A powerful and engaging speaker, Douglass made a lasting impression on those who heard him. "He stood there like an African prince, majestic in his wrath, as with wit, satire, and indignation he graphically described the bitterness of slavery and the humiliation of subjection to those who, in all human virtues and powers, were inferior to himself," recalled Elizabeth Cady Stanton.[2] By the time of the Civil War, people were thronging to hear him. When he delivered his "Mission of the War" speech in Portland, Maine, in January 1864, one spectator took note of the impressive array in the audience—"came officials of every grade, including mayor, ministers, consuls, and even Custom House men; came wealth, beauty, and fashion; came from the interior a hundred miles; came thankful for a place to stand while they listened two hours to a negro, who was to speak on a subject which they had heard discussed by the ablest men of the nation."[3] By 1864, Douglass had become one of the nation's most important and eloquent voices.

His rise to national prominence as an abolitionist orator coincided with the rise of Abraham Lincoln as the nation's premier antislavery politician. Beginning in 1858, with Lincoln's famed debates with Illinois Senator Stephen A. Douglas, Frederick Douglass began publishing his observations about the frontier lawyer ascending the ranks of the new Republican Party. Lincoln's rebuttals to the leading Democratic politician in the nation (and odds-on favorite to win the presidency in 1860) indicated to Douglass that "Slavery and Anti-Slavery are at the bottom of the contest."[4] He would continue to speak and write about Lincoln throughout his presidency and the decades that followed the assassination, when Douglass had many opportunities to eulogize "our beloved martyred President."[5] His measure of the man who would become the savior of the Union and emancipator of slaves presents a civic education of the highest order. Although Douglass and Lincoln never saw eye to eye on all political matters, Douglass's critiques and celebrations of Lincoln will enlighten readers as they consider two giants of American political oratory who addressed the greatest crisis to face the American republic.

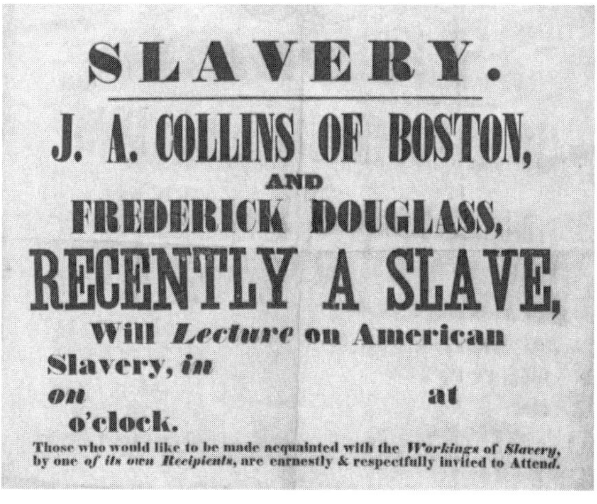

Undated broadside announcing a lecture on American slavery by Frederick Douglass, ca. 1841. Walter O. Evans Collection of Frederick Douglass and Douglass Family Papers, Beinecke Rare Book and Manuscript Library, Yale University

In compiling *Measuring the Man*, we have striven to gather every substantive comment written by Frederick Douglass about Abraham Lincoln. Many of these documents are well known, but never before have they been assembled into one collection that showcases the breadth, diversity, and development of Douglass's views about Lincoln. Several of these documents will be new to scholars of Douglass, Lincoln, and the Civil War. A few will transform the way we think about Douglass's opinion of Lincoln.

Throughout the war, Douglass corresponded with abolitionist friends in England who frequently published his letters in British newspapers. (Only five of these 13 letters have been previously anthologized.[6]) Although the recipients of these letters were rarely identified in the papers, we are confident that the letters published in the *Leeds Mercury* were sent to Julia Griffiths Crofts, one of Douglass's closest friends, most important collaborators, and staunchest financial supporters.[7] On May 19, 1865, she wrote him: "The lengthy extract I made from your last letter[8] . . . has been sent by me to the 'Leeds Mercury' & 'Wesleyan Times'—and was widely circulated in both journals. . . . Any *public* news you send me, is copied & sent off promptly to '*The Mercury*' & is *always* published the day after they get it."[9] Letters that appeared in the London *Inquirer* were likely sent to either Mary Browne Carpenter or her husband, Russell L. Carpenter. In one undated letter, Russell wrote, "I hope in a few days to send you an Inquirer containing extracts from your letter." In another, he added, "Unless any parts of your letters are marked *private*, or are obviously so in their nature, I take for granted that you have no objection to the publication of extracts, which I think may be generally useful."[10]

In his letters to these British correspondents, Douglass offered candid assessments of the situation in America that he never revealed in public speeches. For instance, in September 1864 he explained that both enslaved and free blacks would benefit from a prolonged war: "The hope of the slave is in the continuance of the war, and not in the abolition principles of the Northern people or Government. What the latter does is from necessity; when *that* ceases, abolition ceases."[11] A few days after Lincoln's assassination, in another previously unpublished letter, Douglass wrote, "For one, I have always looked with apprehension to the day of settlement. A reconstruction was, and still is, the great danger to the coloured race."[12] His anxieties would prove to be prescient. In the postwar period, the hard-won rights that black people had gained during the war and Reconstruction largely disappeared.

Douglass's most startling observations came in the wake of Lincoln's assassination on April 14, 1865. Five days after Lincoln's death, Douglass shared with Crofts that the assassination might actually help black people because Lincoln would have been too lenient toward the conquered white South. "I now think that even this dreadful crime," Douglass wrote, "though intended to strike down both the Government and the cause of the slave, will tend to the advantage of both." Lincoln had accomplished what was set before him—now Andrew Johnson would finish the work. "I think, too, that Mr. Johnson is, in many respects, better qualified for the work to come than was Mr. Lincoln," wrote Douglass, because Johnson "has lived all his life in a slave State, and better understands than Mr. Lincoln did the necessity of putting down not only slavery but the slave power."[13] However, Johnson's leniency toward ex-Confederates in 1865, as well as an interview between the two men on February 7, 1866, disabused Douglass of these notions, leading him to comment that at least Lincoln was "a progressive man—one who did not begin as a Moses and end as a Pharaoh."[14]

So jarring were some of Douglass's letters that some British readers did not believe they were genuine.[15] These new revelations of Douglass's opinions exhibit not just a high-minded abolitionist but also a political strategist seeking every way possible to move public opinion—on both sides of the Atlantic—to support the full enfranchisement of black Americans. In our comprehensive record of Douglass's thoughts on Lincoln, readers will trace the evolution of a master rhetorician assessing the words and deeds of a master politician.

Douglass had come a long way to get to this point. Born into slavery in Maryland in February 1818 as Frederick Augustus Bailey, he escaped to freedom 20 years later. Soon after the publication of his first autobiography, *Narrative of the Life of Frederick Douglass, an American Slave*, in 1845, Douglass had to flee the country because his notoriety made him liable to capture as a fugitive slave. He spoke on the abolition circuit for almost two years in England, Ireland, and Scotland and returned to the United States only after British and American friends secured his manumission by purchase. Douglass then edited an abolition newspaper, *The North Star*, and wrote and spoke almost daily in favor of abolition, equal rights, and ridding the nation of color prejudice. His indomitable spirit was matched by a fierce intelligence that produced three autobiographies, speeches, correspondence, and editorials that stand as lasting contributions to the progress of liberty in America. That intelligence also led him, a man who had every reason to hate his country, to become one of America's strongest defenders.

Douglass's journey to becoming one of the greatest abolition speakers in American history began as a personal one, when he decided to free himself from legal bondage. In his *Narrative*, Douglass famously recounted an incident when he resisted a flogging at the hands of a slave-breaker named Edward Covey: "Mr. Covey seemed now to think he had me, and could do what he pleased; but at this moment—from whence came the

Frederick Douglass, ca. 1853. Frontispiece of *My Bondage and My Freedom* (1855)

spirit I don't know—I resolved to fight; and, suiting my action to the resolution, I seized Covey hard by the throat; and as I did so, I rose." Douglass called it the "turning-point" of his "career as a slave" when he resolved that "however long I might remain a slave in form, the day had passed forever when I could be a slave in fact. I did not hesitate to let it be known of me, that the white man who expected to succeed in whipping, must also succeed in killing me."[16] In his second autobiography, *My Bondage and My Freedom* (1855), Douglass commented, "I had reached the point, at which I was *not afraid to die*. This spirit made me a freeman in *fact*, while I remained a slave in *form*."[17] (Notably, a fight was also central to Lincoln's rise to prominence.[18])

After escaping to the North, Douglass found a mentor in William Lloyd Garrison—a radical abolitionist who once burned the US Constitution in public while declaring it "a covenant with death, and an agreement with hell. . . . So perish all compromises with tyranny!"[19] Early in his career as an abolition speaker, Douglass adopted Garrison's views of the Constitution and the Union. "I have no love for America," he declared in 1847. "I have no patriotism. I have no country." He then asked, "What country have I? The institutions of this country do not know me, do not recognize me as a man." Given that American slavery could not exist without the cooperation of the northern free states, Douglass also detested the federal government: "I desire to see its overthrow as speedily as possible, and its Constitution shivered in a thousand fragments."[20]

He did not hold these positions for long. By July 1851, Douglass had become persuaded by political abolitionists like Lysander Spooner, William Goodell, and Gerrit Smith that a constitution that made no mention of "slavery"—and whose Preamble explicitly mentioned "justice" and "the blessings of liberty"—should be construed according to a plain reading of the text, not according to any secret, unwritten "intentions" of its framers.[21] In his most famous oration, "What to the Slave Is the Fourth of July?" (1852), Douglass called the Founding Fathers "great men" and "brave men," the principles of the Declaration of Independence "saving principles," and the Constitution "a Glorious Liberty Document." To his mind, the Garrisonian reading of the Constitution contradicted its Preamble and overlooked its "principles and purposes, entirely hostile to the existence of slavery."[22]

When rightly interpreted and enforced, Douglass argued, the Constitution was an antislavery document. The three-fifths compromise (article 1, section 2) "encourages freedom" because the southern states would gain more representation in Congress and the Electoral College if they abolished slavery. Douglass said the nonimportation clause (article 1, section 9), which permitted Congress to ban the importation of Africans after 20 years—which it did in 1808—"leans to freedom, not to slavery" because it "looked to the abolition of slavery rather than to its perpetuity." Finally, Douglass insisted that the "service or labor" clause, often called the fugitive slave clause (article 4, section 2), pertained to indentured servants and apprentices, not runaway slaves, since slaves "cannot owe service" to anyone.[23]

A constitution that never mentioned slavery also never mentioned race. Thirty years before Justice John Marshall Harlan's famous lone dissent in *Plessy v. Ferguson* (1896), Douglass observed that the Constitution "knows no distinction between citizens on account of color."[24] As Reconstruction waned in 1875, Douglass insisted, "The burden of our demand upon the American people shall simply be justice and fair play. We utterly repudiate all invidious distinctions, whether in our favor or against us, and ask only for a fair field and no favor."[25] Douglass boldly pronounced "race pride" a "false foundation" and "a positive evil" and the very "thing we are fighting against."[26] It was "our enemies," Douglass said, who sought "to deepen and widen the line of separation between the white and colored people of this country."[27] In his estimation, "*color* should not be a criterion of rights."[28]

When asked the misbegotten question, "What shall be done with the four million slaves if emancipated?" Douglass answered, "Let us alone. Do nothing with us, for us, or by us as a particular class." He thought "the broadest and bitterest of the black man's misfortunes is the fact that he is everywhere regarded and treated as an exception to the principles and maxims which apply to other men." If granted "simple justice, and an equal chance to live," Douglass had every confidence that black Americans would stand or fall just like everyone else. For a people who had been wronged for so long, Douglass pleaded, "we simply ask the right to bear the responsibility of our own existence."[29]

Because most white Americans revered the Declaration of Independence, Douglass implored them "to trust the operation of their own principles."[30] This meant governing according to the Constitution's true antislavery meaning. On the eve of the Civil War, Douglass argued that "the Constitution will afford slavery no protection when it shall cease to be administered by slaveholders." Once there is "a will in the people of America to abolish slavery, there is no word, no syllable in the Constitution to forbid that result."[31] (This constitutional view explains why Lincoln's supposed tardiness in dealing with slavery was so disappointing to Douglass.) In a public career that spanned half a century, Douglass joined a vanguard of black and white reformers in the struggle to align the nation's practices with its noblest professions.

Like Douglass, Lincoln called on Americans to live up to their nation's founding principles. "Let us re-adopt the Declaration of Independence," Lincoln pleaded in 1854, "and with it, the practices, and policy, which harmonize with it."[32] Like Douglass, Lincoln believed that slavery was immoral. "If slavery is not wrong," Lincoln wrote in 1864, "nothing is wrong. I can not remember when I did not so think, and feel."[33] And like Douglass, Lincoln thought that it was significant that the Constitutional Convention had deliberately kept the word "slave" out of the Constitution because James Madison "thought it wrong to admit in the Constitution the idea that there could be property in men."[34] As Lincoln put it, "At the framing and adoption of the constitution, they forbore to so much as mention the word 'slave' or 'slavery' in the whole instrument."[35] But in the 1850s, the similarities between these two men largely ended there. Lincoln never called himself an abolitionist, and therefore understood the antislavery mechanisms of the US Constitution somewhat differently than Douglass. Those differences explain why Douglass began the Civil War as one of Lincoln's fiercest critics.

Lincoln held the conventional view that, despite never using the words "slave" or "slavery," the three-fifths compromise, the fugitive slave clause, and the nonimportation clause were the result of compromises between states that wanted to hold onto slavery for the foreseeable future and states that did not want the federal government to strengthen slavery's grip on America. Ultimately, the Constitutional Convention determined that "to form a more perfect union" in 1787 required concessions to a minority of the slaveholding states—South Carolina and Georgia in particular. As Lincoln said, "I think that was the condition in which we found ourselves when we established this government. We had slavery among us, we could not get our Constitution unless we permitted them to remain in slavery, we could not secure the good we did secure if we grasped for more, and having by necessity submitted to that much, it does not destroy the principle that is the charter of our liberties."[36] Lincoln believed that the Founders could not have secured both national independence and emancipation at the same time. They nevertheless wrote certain principles into the nation's founding documents "for future use," thereby "constantly spreading and deepening its influence, and augmenting the happiness and value of life to all people of all colors everywhere."[37]

While Lincoln believed that the Constitution embodied certain compromises with slavery, he nevertheless maintained that the Constitution's text and operation in the early years of the republic indicated an antislavery principle. For example, of the nonimportation clause, Lincoln said, "In forming the Constitution they found the slave trade existing; capital invested in it; fields depending upon it for labor, and the whole system resting upon the importation of slave-labor. They therefore did not prohibit the slave trade at once, but they gave the power to prohibit it after twenty years. . . . Would they have done this if they had not thought slavery wrong?" Lincoln also pointed out that the founding generation "prohibited the spread of Slavery into Territories" through the Northwest Ordinance of 1787 and other laws, which showed "conclusively that they considered that the thing was wrong."[38]

Lincoln and Douglass diverged most sharply on the fugitive slave clause and the infamous Fugitive Slave Act of 1850. Believing that the "service or labor" clause did not pertain to runaway slaves, Douglass insisted that the Fugitive Slave Act was unconstitutional. Lincoln, by contrast, believed that the statute—odious as it was—was lawfully enacted and therefore must be enforced until it was repealed. (That said, in his first inaugural address he asked, "ought not all the safeguards of liberty known in civilized and humane jurisprudence to be introduced, so that a free man be not, in any case, surrendered as a slave?"[39] In practice, the law quickly became a dead letter.[40])

For the first year and a half of the war, Douglass criticized Lincoln for not emancipating slaves. Unlike Douglass, who believed abolition could be accomplished by an antislavery administration in Washington, Lincoln believed that the Constitution left the legality of slavery to the states. He therefore did not issue the Emancipation Proclamation until it could be justified as a war measure—a military necessity that was needed to defeat the Confederacy and restore the Union.

While Douglass rejoiced when Lincoln issued the Emancipation Proclamation on January 1, 1863, he renewed his criticism when Lincoln's administration did not treat black soldiers with equality (denying them equal pay as white soldiers, not commissioning black officers, and not retaliating against Confederates who committed war crimes against black Union soldiers). But three personal encounters transformed the way Douglass thought about Lincoln. Douglass was personally moved by Lincoln's genuine kindness and attentiveness when they met. Lincoln treated Douglass with dignity and respect; Douglass responded with gratitude and a change of heart. Eventually, Douglass came to appreciate the political realities that constrained Lincoln's decision making. Only by saving the Union *first* could Lincoln then free the slaves—much as the American Founders had needed to establish independence and the Union *first*, before they could work toward ridding the nation of slavery.

In a eulogy delivered three days after Lincoln's death—and published here for the first time—Douglass remarked with sadness, "It is not for me, I do not think that it is for any man, to attempt to measure the character of Mr. Lincoln. I feel his loss too deeply as a personal bereavement to do this, but I may, I will say, that I think in large measures Abraham Lincoln had done his work, and done it well."[41] Of course, Douglass had been measuring Lincoln since 1858—something he felt more comfortable admitting in 1876, on the 11th anniversary of Lincoln's assassination. "We saw him, measured him, and estimated him," Douglass said in his most famous speech about Lincoln, and "we came to the conclusion that the hour and the man of our redemption had somehow met in the person of Abraham Lincoln." Douglass never forgot his wartime criticisms, when he had judged Lincoln "cold, tardy, dull, and indifferent." But by 1876 he had come to appreciate Lincoln's approach to the war from a broader perspective—that of the "honest and comprehensive statesman." This gave Douglass a deeper understanding of just how much Lincoln had accomplished. Lincoln, it now seemed, was the one man who could achieve both Union and emancipation. And "measuring him by the sentiment of his country, a sentiment he was bound as a statesman to consult, he was swift, zealous, radical, and determined."[42]

For the rest of his life, Douglass would point Americans to Lincoln as a reminder of the promise of America. In the 1850s, Douglass had pointed Americans to the principles of the Declaration and Constitution; in the postwar period, he also pointed them to Lincoln, who now represented the nation's founding ideals.

When things looked bleak in the second half of the 19th century, Lincoln's legacy itself became an argument that Douglass marshalled in favor of equal citizenship for black Americans.

This book could not have been written without the support of many friends and colleagues. First, we thank Josh Stevens and his team at Reedy Press for their enthusiastic support of this project, especially Jaime Bourassa and Barbara Northcott. We also thank Kayden Miller of the Rochester Museum and Science Center, Maria Paxi of the Connecticut State Library, Emma MacDowell of Syracuse University, Michelle Krowl of the Library of Congress, and Daniel Worthington of the Papers of Abraham Lincoln for providing scans of documents. Todd Stephenson, Curt Witcher, and Jessie Cortesi of the Friends of the Lincoln Collection of Indiana and the Rolland Center for Lincoln Research at the Allen County Public Library graciously provided images from the Lincoln Financial Foundation Collection, as did Timothy Caspar of Hillsdale College and Kelsie Jankowski of Swan Galleries. Christopher Newport University students Charles Benfanti, Paiton Jones, Emily McKenna, Eden McMillan, Raechel Erler, Taylor Davis, Alanna Griffin, and Lainey Hostetler assisted with proofreading, and Charlie also took pictures of several Douglass letters in Buffalo. Elizabeth and Nathan Busch funded these wonderful students through CNU's Center for American Studies. Benjamin Lynerd suggested one of the sources. Finally, we thank Washington and Lee University, the Jack Miller Center, and CNU's Center for American Studies for providing financial assistance for publication expenses of a book that grew much longer than we'd initially anticipated.

Note on Method

In transcribing documents that originally appeared in newspapers, pamphlets, and books, we kept our transcriptions as close to the originals as possible, but for the sake of clarity we silently corrected minor typographical errors (such as replacing "Solmon Chase" with "Salmon Chase," correcting careless misspellings like "unrequitted," or inserting a correct word, like "future," when the typesetters mistakenly put "feature"). We silently inserted about a dozen commas and two periods; and we silently deleted about two dozen obviously misplaced punctuation marks. As some 19th-century publications did not use many paragraph breaks, we silently added about a dozen paragraph breaks to aid the reader. The typesetters at *Douglass' Monthly* frequently added an em dash at the end of a line if a sentence ended but they did not have room to start a new word. To avoid distraction, we silently deleted about two dozen of these em dashes. We rendered words in LARGE CAPS and SMALL CAPS as they appear in the original printed documents. Where newspapers used brackets to insert information, such as "[Cheers]" or an aside by Douglass, we used parentheses; our editorial insertions all appear in brackets. Finally, we retained British spelling in letters that were published in English newspapers even though Douglass would have originally used American spelling.

When transcribing Douglass's handwritten manuscripts, we kept our transcriptions as close to the originals as possible (including by retaining obvious errors in spelling and punctuation); however, we made a few minor interventions. Douglass's lowercase "i" and "e" are frequently indistinguishable other than a dot above the letter.

To assist the reader, we gave Douglass the benefit of the doubt and rendered words with those letters correctly, such as "grief" instead of "greif," "virtue" instead of "vertue," or "silence" instead of "selence." Missing punctuation and other interventions in our transcriptions of handwritten documents are made with brackets.

The Frederick Douglass Papers in the Manuscript Division at the Library of Congress are cited in the notes as "Douglass Papers." Quotations of Lincoln are taken from Roy P. Basler's *The Collected Works of Abraham Lincoln*, 9 vols. (New Brunswick, N.J.: Rutgers University Press, 1953), which is abbreviated *CWL* in the notes. Douglass frequently quoted Lincoln—especially the 1858 "House Divided" address, the Gettysburg Address, and the second inaugural address. We reproduced Douglass's quotations of Lincoln as he said them, which typically contained errors.

Part 1
Pre-Civil War Commentary

Douglass's pre-Civil War writings, running from June 1858 to May 1861, convey his first impressions of Lincoln during his rapid ascent to the presidency. The radical abolitionist set a high bar for the more moderate antislavery politics of the nation's first Republican president. Lincoln first drew the attention of Douglass with his "House Divided" speech, which Lincoln delivered upon accepting the nomination of the Illinois Republican Party to unseat his longtime Democratic rival, Senator Stephen A. Douglas. While Lincoln did not win the Senate seat, his debates with Douglas in 1858 made him a national figure among abolitionists and antislavery politicians. Along with Lincoln, Douglass worried that the Republican Party might be co-opted by Stephen Douglas as he fought with the Democratic president James Buchanan. But where Douglass argued that Congress should abolish slavery even in the states, Republicans like Lincoln thought the federal government had authority to ban slavery only in the federal territories. Nevertheless, Douglass affirmed Lincoln's prediction in his "House Divided" speech that either slavery or freedom would become national. As Douglass foretold in 1854: "The South must either give up slavery, or the North must give up liberty."[1]

After Lincoln's surprising nomination for the presidency by the Republican Party in May 1860, Douglass began offering more regular and detailed commentary on Lincoln and the prospects for federal abolition. In a private letter, Douglass told Gerrit Smith he would not support Lincoln, but publicly he called him "a radical Republican" and "a man of will and nerve."[2] When the Democratic Party fractured into northern and southern factions in June, dividing its support between Stephen Douglas of Illinois and Vice President John C. Breckinridge of Kentucky, Douglass predicted the Lincoln-Hamlin ticket would be elected in November.

However, late summer and fall found Douglass ambivalent about the prospects for abolition if Lincoln became president. On the one hand, he believed Lincoln's reputation as "an honest man" bode well for the presidential office, especially in the face of threats of secession and disunion by disgruntled southern Democrats. On the other hand, less than two months before the election, without mentioning Lincoln by name, he claimed the Republican "candidate" would "catch a negro while running for his liberty, or shoot him down while fighting for it."[3] Seeing in the Republican Party "neither will nor purpose to abolish slavery," Douglass announced plans to help "establish an abolition organization" pledged to ban slavery from states as well as territories. That effort produced the Abolition Political Party, which nominated Gerrit Smith for president and designated Douglass as a presidential elector at large.[4]

Despite Lincoln's victory in November, his commitment to enforcing the Fugitive Slave Act led Douglass to call him the "most powerful enemy" of the abolition movement. However, Douglass recognized that Lincoln had been elected because of "an *anti-slavery reputation*," and he credited the northern public's "startling courage" for standing up to threats of disunion, which had enabled the Slave Power to dictate national politics for far too long.[5] As Lincoln's inauguration approached, Douglass insisted on the president's power and obligation to prevent disunion. But if any concessions were made to seceding states, he preferred that "the Union perish, and perish forever."[6]

Douglass expressed great disappointment with Lincoln's inaugural address. He counted the many ways Lincoln would serve slaveholding interests while affirming few of the Republican Party's antislavery principles. An exasperated Douglass declared, "If we held the Constitution, as held by Mr. Lincoln, no earthly power could induce us to swear to support it."[7] Douglass did confess "a slight gleam of relief" in Lincoln's reminder that the Constitution guarantees the privileges and immunities of all American citizens regardless of where they travel in the United States. This followed Lincoln's suggestion that Congress revise the notorious Fugitive Slave Act so that "all the safeguards of liberty known in humane and civilized jurisprudence" might ensure "that a free man be not in any case surrendered as a slave."[8] Nevertheless, Douglass concluded warily that "our first modern anti-slavery President" may show himself "powerless for liberty, and only powerful for slavery."[9]

Douglass's prewar assessments took the measure of Lincoln by a strict abolition standard. He had hoped that Republicans would pronounce "Death to Slavery" throughout the United States instead of simply "No more Slave States." Nevertheless, he conceded that public opinion had yet to "be educated up to a higher standard of human rights and political morality."[10] Douglass sought to move Americans toward that higher standard by raising their expectations of Lincoln as the nation's first antislavery president.

Address Commemorating Emancipation in the British West Indies at Poughkeepsie, New York, August 2, 1858[11] (excerpts)

***New York Times*, August 3, 1858**

The contest going on just now in the State of Illinois is worthy of attention. STEPHEN A. DOUGLAS, the author of the Kansas-Nebraska bill,[12] is energetically endeavoring to hold his seat in the American Senate, and Mr. ABRAM LINCOLN is endeavoring as energetically to get that seat for himself. This, however, is only a partial view of the matter. The truth is, that Slavery and Anti-Slavery is at the bottom of the contest. . . . [Douglass here described the divisions between

Stephen Douglas and the southern wing of the Democratic Party, which wanted protection for slavery in the federal territories. He also mentioned how some eastern Republicans, like Horace Greeley, had contemplated joining forces with Douglas—something that infuriated Lincoln.]

It seems to me that the white DOUGLAS should occasionally meet his deserts at the hands of a black one. Once I thought he was about to make the name respectable, but now I despair of him, and must do the best I can for it myself. (Laughter.) I now leave him in the hands of Mr. LINCOLN, and in the hands of the Republican Party of Illinois, thanking both the latter, because they have nobly upheld and made prominent the principles of the Republican Party in Illinois, which seemed about to be compromised and sacrificed at the very heart of the Government.

The key-note of Republicanism in that State, at present, is given in the following extract from the great speech[13] of Mr. LINCOLN:

"We are now far into the fifth year since a policy was initiated with the avowed object and confident promise of putting an end to Slavery agitation.[14] Under the operation of that policy, that agitation has not only not ceased, but has constantly augmented. In my opinion it will not cease until a crisis shall have been reached and passed. 'A house divided against itself cannot stand.' I believe this Government *cannot endure permanently half Slave and half Free.* I do not expect the Union to be dissolved—I do not expect the house to fall—*but I do expect it will cease to be divided.* It will become all one thing, or all the other. Either the opponents of Slavery *will arrest the further spread of it*, and place it where the public mind shall rest in the belief *that it is in the course of ultimate extinction*; or its advocates *will push it forward till it shall become alike lawful in all the States*—old as well as new, North as well as South."

Well and wisely said. One system or the other must prevail. Liberty or Slavery must become the law of the land.

"The Chicago Nominations" (excerpts)
Douglass' Monthly, June 1860

The nomination of Mr. LINCOLN has taken the people of this part of the Country by surprise. The popular feeling in favor of Mr. SEWARD[15] was no where stronger, or more earnest, than in this part of the State. The people felt that he had a stronger claim upon his party than any other man, having done more to give that party shape, and to systematise the elements composing it, and to furnish it with ideas, than any other man in the nation. . . .

Mr. LINCOLN is a man of unblemished private character; a lawyer, standing near the front rank at the bar of his own State, has a cool, well balanced head; great firmness of will; is perseveringly industrious; and one of the most frank, honest men in political life. He cannot lay claim to any literary culture beyond the circle of his practical duties, or to any of the graces found at courts, or in diplomatic circles, but must rely upon his "good hard sense" and honesty of purpose, as capital for the campaign, and the qualities to give character to his administration. His friends cannot as yet claim for him a place in the front rank of statesmanship, whatever may be their faith in his latent capacities. His political life is thus far to his credit, but it is a political life of fair promise rather than one of rich fruitage.

It was, perhaps, this fact that obtained for him the nomination. Our political history has often illustrated the truth that a man may be too great a statesman to become President. The failure of Webster, Clay and Silas Wright[16] in the Presidential race, is in point here, and the success of Harrison, Polk, Taylor and Pierce,[17] tends to prove the same proposition.

If, therefore, Mr. LINCOLN possesses great capacities, and is yet to be proved a great statesman, it is lucky for him that a political exigency moved his party to take him on trust and before his greatness was ripe, or he would have lost the chance. But when once elected it will be no longer dangerous for him to develop great qualities, and we hope that in taking him on a "profession of his faith," rather than on the recommendations of his political life, his party will witness his continual "growth in grace," and his administration will redound to the glory of his country, and his own fame.

As to his principles, there is no reason why the friends of Mr. SEWARD should not heartily support him. He is a radical Republican, and is fully committed to the doctrine of the "irrepressible conflict."[18] In his debates with Douglas, he came fully up to the highest mark of Republicanism, and he is a man of will and nerve, and will not back down from his own assertions. He is not a compromise candidate by any means. Mr. BATES was to have played that part, with HORACE GREELEY for prompter.[19] But the Chicago Convention did not fall into the melting mood. GREELEY "piped unto them but they would not dance;" he mourned unto them, but they did not "lament," and his "betweenity" candidate fell flat between the two stools of Somewhere and Nowhere. Mr. GREELEY has the greatest passion for making political nominations from the ranks of his enemies of any man in America. His candidates are like the frogs bred along the Nile; the head begins to croak and show signs of life while the body is yet plain mud. So Mr. GREELEY is forever digging up some man for a candidate, whose head just begins to appear, while his whole body is yet enveloped in proslavery mud, and we are glad he was defeated.

The Presidential contest, this fall, is likely to be rather sharply defined. If Mr. DOUGLAS is put on the course, the old personal rivalry between him and Mr. LINCOLN will render the campaign especially spicy.

Illinois will form a sort of pivot, around which the waves of the political sea will sweep and dash with great force.

The nomination of BELL and EVERETT will tend to divert strength from the Democracy,[20] and give advantage to LINCOLN, but will have no great influence on the general result. Slavery propagandism, whether led by the vigorous and impulsive "little giant," or by the more staid and conservative BELL, will be the great enemy which the Republican party must meet.

For ourselves, we are sorry that the hosts of freedom could not have been led forth upon a higher platform, and have had inscribed upon their banners, "Death to Slavery," instead of "No more Slave States." But the people will not have it so, and we are compelled to work and wait for a brighter day, when the masses shall be educated up to a higher standard of human rights and political morality.

But as between the hosts of Slavery propagandism and the Republican party—incomplete as is its platform of principles—our preferences cannot hesitate.

While we should be glad to co-operate with a party fully committed to the doctrine of "All rights, to all men,"[21] in the absence of all hope of rearing up the standard of such a party for the coming campaign, we can but desire the success of the Republican candidates.

It will be a great work accomplished when this Government is divorced from the active support of the inhuman slave system. To pluck executive patronage out of the hands of the pliant tools of the whip and the chain; to turn the tide of the National Administration against the man-stealers of this country and in favor of even a partial application of the principles of justice is a glorious achievement, and we hope for its success.

Letter to Gerrit Smith, July 2, 1860 (excerpt)
Gerrit Smith Papers, Syracuse University

I cannot support Lincoln—but whether there is life enough in the Abolitionists to name a candidate I cannot say. I shall look to your letter for light to the pathway of duty.[22]

"The Democratic Party" (excerpts)
Douglass' Monthly, August 1860

This political organization is now hopelessly divided and broken up. . . . The condition of the scattered factions who still cling to the name of the party, makes it almost certain that ABRAHAM LINCOLN and HANNIBAL HAMLIN[23] will be President and Vice President of the United States in 1861.

Speech on the Twenty-Sixth Anniversary of Emancipation in the British West Indies, Geneva, New York, August 1, 1860 (excerpt)
Douglass' Monthly, September 1860

The slaveholders know that the day of their power is over when a Republican President is elected. The mobs gotten up to put down the Republican Conventions at Baltimore, Alexandria and Wheeling, the threats of violence offered to CASSIUS M. CLAY and his Republican associates at Kentucky, and the threats of dissolution of the Union in case of the election of LINCOLN, are tolerable endorsements of the anti-slavery tendencies of the Republican party; and for one, Abolitionist though I am, and resolved to cast my vote for an Abolitionist, I sincerely hope for the triumph of that party over all the odds and ends of slavery combined against it. I do not accord with those who prefer the defeat of the Republican party from a fear that it will serve slavery as faithfully as the Democratic party, or either branch of it. To do any thing of the kind would be to cut its own thread of existence.

Report by the Auburn *Journal* of the Emancipation Day Speech at Geneva, August 1, 1860 (excerpt)
Douglass' Monthly, October 1860

Mr. Douglass then took the stand, and occupied two hours in a speech of wonderful strength and power. His late trials and afflictions seem to have inspired him with unwonted energy and eloquence. His hatred of slavery seems to have been intensified. He showed the workings of slavery in all its ramified influences and cruelties, and did not fail to show the part the Sham Democracy of this country were acting in this matter. If his ambitious namesake [Stephen A. Douglas] had been present, and heard the black man, he would have found it necessary to leave the Presidential stump for a few days that he might apply a sufficient quantity of cabbage leaves to his blisters. While he regards the Republican party as failing fully to meet the demands of the Declaration of Independence, and to carry out the true measure and spirit of freedom, he concedes to that party all that there is that is hopeful in the land—that it is progressive with the age in the right direction, and he greatly desires to see the White House, at Washington, which has been so shamefully disgraced for the last four years, occupied for the next four years by an honest man—Abraham Lincoln.

"The Abolition Movement Re-Organized" (excerpts)
Douglass' Monthly, October 1860

Sentimental Abolitionism is abundant. It may well be met with in the pulpit, sometimes in the religious newspapers, and more frequently still we meet it in the meetings of the Republican party; yet among them all there is neither will nor purpose to abolish slavery. The Republican party, with all the professions of anti-slavery men attached to it, has no such *will*, no such *purpose*.

The very best that can be said of that party, is, that it is opposed to *forcing slavery into any Territory of the United States where the white people of that Territory do not want it*. . . . Even the sentiment[s] of the Republican party, as expressed by its leaders, have become visibly *thin* and *insipid* as the canvass has progressed. It promises to be about as good a Southern party as either wing of the old Democratic party. Its candidate is for slave-hunting at the North, and slaveholding at the South. He would catch a negro while running for his liberty, or shoot him down while fighting for it.[24]

Letter to Russell or Mary Carpenter, October 9, 1860 (excerpts)
London *Inquirer*, November 3, 1860

We are now in the thickest part of our electioneering excitement. Nothing like it has occurred since 1840, when the country was divided between [Martin] Van Buren and [William Henry] Harrison. Not even then was the country so deeply stirred; for then the question of slavery—the great overshadowing question of to-day—was not so fairly before the people as now. . . . [Douglass detailed the way "the slave power" had controlled the federal government over the previous 60 years and then concluded:] the arrogant and defiant attempt to legalise slavery by decisions of courts and party doctrines in all the States of the Union, north as well as south—have aroused a hostile spirit so strong and so general that there is the highest probability of a decided and lasting victory for freedom in the election to take place four weeks hence. . . . The election of Lincoln will ensure, I think, the election of Seward four years hence; and, notwithstanding that he has said some things which I hate, and some things quite equivocal and unworthy of him, I still recognise him as among the most formidable foes that we can marshal against the slave system, for he is a man who so manages as always to have a strong party to support his measures.

Rev. Russell L. Carpenter. *Bridport News*, January 22, 1892

"The Late Election"
Douglass' Monthly, December 1860

Our last monthly paper announced the probable election of ABRAHAM LINCOLN and HANNIBAL HAMLIN, the Republican candidates for President and Vice President of the U.S. What was then only speculation and probability, is now an accomplished fact. Pennsylvania, in her State election of October, it is true, had made this result, to a degree, certain; but there were efforts and appliances resorted to by the enemies of the Republican party, which could not fail to cause doubt and anxiety in the minds of the most sanguine. The deed is, however, now done, and a new order of events connected with the great question of slavery, is now fairly opening upon the country, the end whereof the most sagacious and far-sighted are unable to see and declare. No preceding election resembles this in its issues and parties, and none resembles it in the effects it has already produced, and is still likely to produce. It was a contest between sections, North and South, as to what shall be the principles and policy of the national Government in respect to the slave system of the fifteen Southern States. The broadest assertion of a right of property in man, holding such property equally innocent, sacred and legal under the Constitution, as property in houses, lands, horses, sheep, and horned cattle, and like the latter entitled to Congressional protection in all the Territories, and by parity of reasoning, in all the States of the American Union. The Southern candidate for the Presidency, Mr. BRECKINRIDGE,[25] fully represented this broad assertion of what Lord MANSFIELD[26] well declared to be so opposed to nature, that nothing short of positive law could support it, and BROUGHAM[27] denounced as the 'wild and guilty fantasy' of property in man. Mr. LINCOLN, the Northern Republican candidate, while admitting the right to hold men as slaves in the States already existing, regards such property as peculiar, exceptional, local, generally an evil, and not to be extended beyond the limits of the States where it is established by what is called positive law. We thus simply state the issue, more for the benefit of our trans-Atlantic friends and readers, than for those at home, who have heard and read little else during the last three or four months. The clamor now raised by the slaveholders about 'Northern aggression,' 'sectional warfare,' as a pretext of dissolving the Union, has this basis only: The Northern people have elected, against the opposition of the slaveholding South, a man for President who declared his opposition to the further extension of slavery over the soil belonging to the United States. Such is the head and front, and the full extent of the offense,[28] for which 'minute men' are forming, drums are beating, flags are flying, people are arming, 'banks are closing,' 'stocks are falling,' and the South generally taking on dreadfully.

By referring to another part of our present monthly, our respected readers will find a few samples of the spirit of the Southern press on the subject. They are full of intrigue, smell of brimstone, and betoken a terrific explosion. Unquestionably, 'secession,' 'disunion,' 'Southern Confederacy,' and the like phrases, are the most popular political watch words of the cotton-growing States of the Union. Nor is this sentiment to be entirely despised. If Mr. LINCOLN were really an Abolition President, which he is not; if he were a friend to the Abolition movement, instead of being, as he is, its most powerful enemy, the dissolution of the Union might be the only effective mode of perpetuating slavery in the Southern States—since if it could succeed, it would place slavery beyond the power of the President and his Government. But the South has now no such cause for disunion. The present alarm and perturbation will cease; the Southern fire-eaters will be appeased and will retrace their steps. There is no sufficient cause for the dissolution of the Union. Whoever lives through the next four years will see Mr. LINCOLN and his Administration attacked more bitterly for their pro-slavery truckling, than for doing any anti-slavery work. He and his party will become the best protectors of slavery where it now is, and just such protectors as slaveholders will most need. In order to defeat him, the slaveholders took advantage of the ignorance and stupidity of the masses, and assured them that LINCOLN is an Abolitionist. This,

Mr. LINCOLN and his party will lose no time in scattering to the winds as false and groundless. With the single exception of the question of slavery extension, Mr. LINCOLN proposes no measure which can bring him into antagonistic collision with the traffickers in human flesh, either in the States or in the District of Columbia. The Union will, therefore, be saved simply because there is no cause in the election of Mr. LINCOLN for its dissolution. Slavery will be as safe, and safer, in the Union under such a President, than it can be under any President of a Southern Confederacy. This is our impression, and we deeply regret the facts from which it is derived.

With an Abolition President we should consider a successful separation of the slave from the free States a calamity, greatly damaging to the prospects of our long enslaved, bruised and mutilated people; but under what may be expected of the Republican party, with its pledges to put down the slaves should they attempt to rise, and to hunt them should they run away, a dissolution of the Union would be highly beneficial to the cause of liberty. The South would then be a Sicily, and the North a Sardinia. Mr. LINCOLN would then be entirely absolved from his slave-hunting, slave-catching and slave killing pledges, and the South would have to defend slavery with her own guns, and hunt her negroes with her own dogs. In truth, we really wish those brave, fire-eating, cotton-growing States would just now go at once outside the Union and set up for themselves, where they could be got at without disturbing other people, and got away from without encountering other people. Such a consummation was 'one devoutly to be wished.'[29] But no, cunning dogs, they will smother their rage, and after all the dust they can raise, they will retire within the Union and claim its advantages.

What, then, has been gained to the anti-slavery cause by the election of Mr. LINCOLN? Not much, in itself considered, but very much when viewed in the light of its relations and bearings. For fifty years the country has taken the law from the lips of an exacting, haughty and imperious slave oligarchy. The masters of slaves have been masters of the Republic. Their authority was almost undisputed, and their power irresistible. They were the President makers of the Republic, and no aspirant dared to hope for success against their frown. LINCOLN'S election has vitiated their authority, and broken their power. It has taught the North its strength, and shown the South its weakness. More important still, it has demonstrated the possibility of electing, if not an Abolitionist, at least an *anti-slavery reputation* to the Presidency of the United States. The years are few since it was thought possible that the Northern people could be wrought up to the exercise of such startling courage. Hitherto the threat of disunion has been as potent over the politicians of the North, as the cat-o'-nine-tails is over the backs of the slaves. Mr. LINCOLN'S election breaks this enchantment, dispels this terrible night mare, and awakes the nation to the consciousness of new powers, and the possibility of a higher destiny than the perpetual bondage to an ignoble fear.

Another probable effect will be to extinguish the reviving fires of the accursed foreign slave trade, which for a year or two have been kindled all along the Southern coast of the Union. The Republican party is under no necessity to pass laws on this subject. It has only to enforce and execute the laws already on the statute book. The moral influence of such prompt, complete and unflinching execution of the laws, will be great, not only in arresting the specific evil, but in arresting the tide of popular demoralization with which the successful prosecution of the horrid trade in naked men and women was overspreading the country. To this duty the Republican party will be prompted, not only by the conscience of the North, but by what perhaps will be more controlling party interests.

It may also be conceded that the election of LINCOLN and HAMLIN, notwithstanding the admission of the former that the South is entitled to an efficient Fugitive Slave Law, will render the practice of recapturing and returning to slavery persons who have heroically succeeded, or may hereafter succeed in reaching the free States, more unpopular and odious, than it would have been had either DOUGLAS, BELL or BRECKINRIDGE been elected. Slaves may yet be hunted, caught and carried back to slavery, but the number will be greatly diminished, because of the popular disinclination to execute the cruel and merciless Fugitive Slave Law. Had LINCOLN been defeated, the fact would have been construed by slaveholders, and their guilty minions of the country, as strong evidence of the soundness of the North in respect to the alleged duty of hounding down and handing over the panting fugitive to the vengeance of his infuriated master. No argument is needed to prove this gain to the side of freedom.

But chief among the benefits of the election, has been the canvass itself. Notwithstanding the many cowardly disclaimers, and miserable concessions to popular prejudice against the colored people, which Republican orators have felt themselves required, by an intense and greedy desire of success, to make, they have been compelled also to recur to first principles of human liberty, expose the baseless claim of property in man, exhibit the hideous features of slavery, and to unveil, for popular execration, the brutal manners and morals of the guilty slavemasters. The canvass has sent all over the North most learned and eloquent men to utter the great truths which Abolitionists have for twenty years been earnestly, but unsuccessfully endeavoring to get before the public mind and conscience. We may rejoice in the dissemination of the truth by whomsoever proclaimed, for the truth will bear its own weight, and bring forth its own fruit.

Nevertheless, this very victory threatens and may be the death of the modern Abolition movement, and finally bring back the country to the same, or a worse state, than BENJ. LUNDY[30] and WM. LLOYD GARRISON found it thirty years ago. The Republican party does not propose to abolish slavery any where, and is decidedly opposed to Abolition agitation. It is not even, by the confession of its President elect, in favor of the repeal of that thrice-accursed and flagrantly unconstitutional Fugitive Slave Bill of 1850. It is plain to see, that once in power, the policy of the party will be only to seem a little less yielding to the demands of slavery than the Democratic or Fusion party, and thus render ineffective and pointless the whole Abolition movement of the North. The safety of our movement will be found only by a return to all the agencies and appliances, such as writing, publishing, organizing, lecturing, holding meetings, with the earnest aim not to prevent the extension of slavery, but to abolish the system altogether. Congress should be at once memorialized for the abolition of slavery in the District of Columbia, and the slave trade between the States. The same zeal, activity, energy and earnestness should be displayed in circulating petitions, as in the earlier stages of the movement. We have the pen, voice and influence of only one man, and that man of the most limited class; but with few or many, in whatever vicissitudes which may surround the cause, now or hereafter, we shall join in no cry, and unite in no demand less than the complete and universal *abolition* of the whole slave system. Slavery shall be destroyed.

"Dissolution of the American Union" (excerpts)
Douglass' Monthly, January 1861

The incoming President is elected to preside over the *United* States; and if any of them have been permitted, by the treachery and weakness of his predecessor, to break away from the Government, his business will be to bring them back, and see that the laws of the United States are duly extended over them, and faithfully executed. The coolest and wisest statesmen of the Republic deny the right of peaceful secession. They admit the right of revolution; but revolution in this country is rebellion, and rebellion is treason, and treason is levying war against the United States, with something more substantial than paper resolutions and windy declamations. There must be swords, guns, powder, balls, and men behind them to use them.

Now, when matters reach that point, South Carolina must conquer the United States, or the United States must conquer South Carolina. The right of South Carolina to secede, therefore, depends upon her ability to do so, and to stay so. If she can whip the Federal Government and scourge and keep it beyond her borders, and compel the United States to regard her as other than a revolted province, she can get out of the Union. But until she does all this, ABRAHAM LINCOLN is bound by his oath of office to regard her as one of the United States, and subject to the 'Union, the Constitution and the laws.'

Such every body knows to be the true legal view of secession; but the question comes—is there virtue enough in the Federal Government to enforce the law. When a poor slave escapes to Boston, and hides in the cellars and garrets of humane men, the U.S. Government is strong.[31] It can line the streets with soldiers, surround the granite Court House with chains, and convert the temple of justice into a prison to catch, hold and hurl the fugitive back into the house of bondage; but has that Government virtue enough to enforce the laws against the slaveholding, women-whipping rebels of Charleston? . . .

But to the dissolution of the Union, and its chance of success. Conquering a Federal army, and driving out all Federal officers, is not the only difficulty to be overcome. The slave population of South Carolina may at last prove the most serious check upon disunion. They are more than equal to the whites in number, and cannot have failed to learn something from passing events. All the precautions of their tyrant masters have not hid from them the fact that *they*, in some sort, have a direct interest in the controversy between the State and the Federal Government. It is more than probable that they have given Mr. LINCOLN credit for having intentions towards them far more benevolent and just than any he is known to cherish. His pledges to protect and uphold slavery in the States have not reached them; while certain dim, undefined, but large and exaggerated notions of his emancipating purposes have taken firm hold of them, and have grown larger and firmer with every look, nod and undertone of their oppressors. They were taught to look for freedom by the election of JOHN C. FREMONT.[32] He failed; but he so nearly succeeded, that hope was entertained that another trial would bring certain victory. That victory they have been taught to believe has now been achieved; that a friend of theirs is now about to take the reins of Government; that he is a '*Black Republican*;'[33] that his mission is to free the slaves. Let them learn that there is enmity between the State and the Federal Government, and that South Carolina has broken away from the Union to defeat their liberation from bondage; that ABRAHAM LINCOLN, the President, is on their side, and against their masters; that he has only been defeated in giving them their liberty by taking the State out of the Union, and it is easy to see that such impressions and ideas might burst forth and spread havoc and death among slaveholders to an extent never surpassed even in the annals of St. Domingo.[34] South Carolina, in such an event, would be more likely to fight her way back into the Union, than to fight her way out of it. Her salvation as a slave State might be made to depend upon Federal arms.

But will not the cotton States join South Carolina? They probably will; but the elements of weakness would be the same. South Carolina would only be presented on a larger scale: with her, those cotton States have to extinguish the life of the Federal Government within their limits, and keep that extinguished. This can only be done *by force, by treachery, or by negotiation*; and to neither will ABRAHAM LINCOLN succumb. To do so would be to put the razor to the throat of his party, write himself down a coward, make political platforms worse than a mockery, and to become the pliant tool of the very barbarism which he was elected to restrain, and 'place it where the public mind would rest in the belief in its ultimate extinction.'[35] He is pledged to the maintenance of the Union; and if he has the *will*, he will not lack the power to maintain it against all foes. But if the Union can only be maintained by new concessions to the slaveholders; if it can only be stuck together and held together by a new drain on the negro's blood; if the North is to forswear the exercise of all rights incompatible with the safety and perpetuity of slavery; that slavery shall be the only right, the only system superior to investigation, and superior to progress—we say, if this (and it is all demanded) be the price of the Union, then will every right minded man and woman in the land say, let the Union perish, and perish forever. As against compromises and national demoralization, welcome, ten thousand times over, the hardships consequent upon a dissolution of the Union.

"The New President"
Douglass' Monthly, March 1861

Of one satisfaction, one ray of hope amid the darkness of the passing hour, and the reign of doubt and distraction, we may now safely begin to assure ourselves. Before we can again speak to our respected readers through this channel, the long desired 4th of March will have come, LINCOLN will be inaugurated at Washington, and his policy declared. Whatever that policy may be towards the seceded and confederated States; whatever it may be towards Slavery, the ruling cause of our nation's troubles, it will at least be a great relief to know it, to rejoice in and defend it, if right, and to make war upon it if wrong. To know what it is, is now the main thing. If he is going to abandon the principles upon which he was elected, complement the South for being wrong, and censure himself and friends for being right, court treason and curse loyalty, desert his friends and cleave to his enemies, turn his back on the cause of Freedom and give new guarantees to the system of Slavery—whatever policy, whether of peace or war, or neither, it will be a vast gain at least to know what it is. Much of the present trouble is owing to the doubt and suspense caused by the shuffling, do-nothing policy of Mr. BUCHANAN.[36] No man has been able to tell an hour beforehand what to expect from that source. However well disposed he may have been, the slaveholding thieves and traitors about him have had him under their thumb from the beginning until now. Every man who wishes well to the country will rejoice at his out going, and feel that though he leaves the body politic weakened, and the nation's Constitution shattered, his out going, like the subsidence of some pestilence walking in darkness, is a cause for devout thanksgiving. A month longer in power, and perhaps, the epitaph of the American Republic might, if it may not now, be written, and its death consigned to the mouldy tombs of once great, but now extinct nations.

While not at all too confident of the incorruptible purity of the new President, (for we remember the atmosphere of Washington, and the subtle devices of the enemies of Liberty, among whom he has now gone,) still we hope something from him. His stately silence during these last tumultuous and stormy three months, his stern refusal thus far to commit himself to any of the much advocated schemes of compromise, his refusal to have concessions extorted from him under the terror instituted by thievish conspirators and traitors, the cool and circumspect character of his replies to the various speeches, some delicate, appropriate, and sensible, and some rudely curious and prying, made to him during his circuitous route to Washington, the modesty with which he has pushed aside the various compliments bestowed upon him, all prove that he has not won deceitfully the title of Honest Old Abe. True, indeed, he has made no immoderate promises to the cause of freedom. His party has made none. But what were small in Chicago, will be found large at Washington, and what were moderate in the canvass, have become much augmented by the frowning difficulties since flung in the way of their accomplishment by the movement for disunion. It was a small thing six months ago to say, as the Republican party did say, that the Union shall be preserved, but events have now transpired, which make this a very solemn matter to reduce to practice. Most things are easier said than done, and this thing belongs to the general rule. That declaration in the Chicago platform implied that those who uttered it, believed that this Government possesses ample power for its own preservation, and that those powers should be in their hands, faithfully wielded for that purpose. This, then, is the first question: Will Mr. LINCOLN boldly grapple with the monster of Disunion, and bring down his proud looks?

Will he call upon the haughty slave masters, who have risen in arms, to break up the Government, to lay down those arms, and return to loyalty, or meet the doom of traitors and rebels? He must do this, or do worse. He must do this, or consent to be the despised representative of a defied and humbled Government. He must do this, or own that party platforms are the merest devices of scheming politicians to cheat the people, and to enable them to crawl up to place and power. He must do this, or compromise the fundamental principle upon which he was elected, to wit, the right and duty of Congress to prohibit the farther extension of Slavery. Will he compromise? Time and events will soon answer this question. For the present, there is much reason to believe that he will not consent to any compromise which will violate the principle upon which he was elected; and since none which does not utterly trample upon that principle can be accepted by the South, we have a double assurance that there will be no compromise, and that the contest must now be decided, and decided forever, which of the two, Freedom or Slavery, shall give law to this Republic. Let the conflict come, and God speed the Right, must be the wish of every true-hearted American, as well as of that of an onlooking world.

"The Victors Conquered by the Vanquished—The Minority Ruling the Majority" (excerpt)
Douglass' Monthly, March 1861

Happily, up to this time, within twelve days of the inauguration of the Republican President, no word has fallen from the Leader of the party which can be construed into an abandonment of the principles upon which he was elected. So far so good; but how long this may remain the case, no man can tell. The atmosphere of the Capital has hitherto been fatal to the moral health of nearly all Northen men, and may prove so to that of Mr. Lincoln, though all our hopes are on the opposite side.

"The Inaugural Address"
Douglass' Monthly, April 1861

Elsewhere in the columns of our present monthly, our readers will find the Inaugural Address of Mr. Abraham Lincoln, delivered on the occasion of his induction to the office of President of the

United States. The circumstances under which the Address was delivered, were the most extraordinary and portentous that ever attended any similar occasion in the history of the country. Threats of riot, rebellion, violence and assassination had been freely, though darkly circulated, as among the probable events to occur on that memorable day. The life of Mr. LINCOLN was believed, even by his least timid friends, to be in most imminent danger. No mean courage was required to face the probabilities of the hour. He stood up before the pistol or dagger of the sworn assassin, to meet death from an unknown hand, while upon the very threshold of the office to which the suffrages of the nation had elected him. The outgoing Administration, either by its treachery or weakness, or both, had allowed the Government to float to the very verge of destruction. A fear, amounting to agony in some minds, existed that the great American Republic would expire in the arms of its newly elected guardian upon the very moment of his inauguration. For weeks and months previously to the 4th of March, under the wise direction and management of General SCOTT,[37] elaborate military preparations were made with a view to prevent the much apprehended outbreak of violence and bloodshed, and secure the peaceful inauguration of the President elect. How much the nation is indebted to General SCOTT for its present existence, it is impossible to tell. No doubt exists that to him, rather than to any forbearance of the rebels, Washington owes its salvation from bloody streets on the fourth of March. The manner in which Mr. LINCOLN entered the Capital was in keeping with the menacing and troubled state of the times. He reached the Capital as the poor, hunted fugitive slave reaches the North, in disguise, seeking concealment, evading pursuers, by the underground railroad, between two days, not during the sunlight, but crawling and dodging under the sable wing of night. He changed his programme, took another route, started at another hour, travelled in other company, and arrived at another time in Washington. We have no censure for the President at this point. He only did what braver men have done. It was, doubtless, galling to his very soul to be compelled to avail himself of the methods of a fugitive slave, with a nation howling on his track. It is hard to think of anything more humiliating. The great party that elected him fairly wilted under it. The act, in some sense, was an indication of the policy of the new Government—more cunning than bold, evading rather than facing danger, outwitting rather than bravely conquering and putting down the enemy. The whole thing looked bad, but it was not adopted without reason. Circumstances gave to an act which, upon its face, was cowardly and mean, the merit of wisdom, forethought and discretion.

Once in Washington, Mr. LINCOLN found himself in the thick atmosphere of treason on the one hand, and a cowardly, sentimental and deceitful profession of peace on the other. With such surroundings, he went to work upon his Inaugural Address, and the influence of those surroundings may be traced in the whole character of his performance. Making all allowance for circumstances, we must declare the address to be but little better than our worst fears, and vastly below what we had fondly hoped it might be. It is a double-tongued document, capable of two constructions, and conceals rather than declares a definite policy. No man reading it could say whether Mr. LINCOLN was for peace or war, whether he abandons or maintains the principles of the Chicago Convention upon which he was elected. The occasion required the utmost frankness and decision. Overlooking the whole field of disturbing elements, he should have boldly rebuked them. He saw seven States in open rebellion, the Constitution set at naught, the national flag insulted, and his own life murderously sought by slaveholding assassins. Does he expose and rebuke the enemies of his country, the men who are bent upon ruling or ruining the country?[38] Not a bit of it. But at the very start he seeks to court their favor, to explain himself where nobody misunderstands him, and to deny intentions of which nobody had accused him. He turns away from his armed enemy and deals his blows on the head of an innocent bystander. He knew, full well, that the grand objection to him and his party respected the one great question of slavery extension. The South want to extend slavery, and the North want to confine it where it is, "where the public mind shall rest in the belief of its ultimate extinction."[39] This was the question which carried the North and defeated the South in the election which made Mr. ABRAHAM LINCOLN President. Mr. LINCOLN knew this, and the South has known it all along; and yet this subject only gets the faintest allusion, while others, never seriously in dispute, are dwelt upon at length.

Mr. LINCOLN opens his address by announcing his complete loyalty to slavery in the slave States, and quotes from the Chicago platform a resolution affirming the rights of property in slaves, in the slave States. He is not content with declaring that he has no lawful power to interfere with slavery in the States, but he also denies having the least '*inclination*' to interfere with slavery in the States. This denial of all feeling against slavery, at such a time and in such circumstances, is wholly discreditable to the head and heart of Mr. LINCOLN. Aside from the inhuman coldness of the sentiment, it was a weak and inappropriate utterance to such an audience, since it could neither appease nor check the wild fury of the rebel Slave Power.

Any but a blind man can see that the disunion sentiment of the South does not arise from any misapprehension of the disposition of the party represented by Mr. LINCOLN. The very opposite is the fact. The difficulty is, the slaveholders understand the position of the Republican party too well. Whatever may be the honied phrases employed by Mr. LINCOLN when confronted by actual disunion; however silvery and beautiful may be the subtle rhetoric of his long-headed Secretary of State, when wishing to hold the Government together until its management should fall into other hands; all know that the masses at the North (the power behind the throne) had determined to take and keep this Government out of the hands of the slaveholding oligarchy, and administer it hereafter to the advantage of free labor as against slave labor. The slaveholders knew full well that they were hereafter to change the condition of rulers to that of being ruled; they knew that the mighty North is outstripping the

South in numbers, and in all the elements of power, and that from being the superior, they were to be doomed to hopeless inferiority. This is what galled them. They are not afraid that LINCOLN will send out a proclamation over the slave States declaring all the slaves free, nor that Congress will pass a law to that effect. They are no such fools as to believe any such thing; but they do think, and not without reason, that the power of slavery is broken, and that its prestige is gone whenever the people have made up their minds that Liberty is safer in the hands of freemen than in those of slaveholders. To those sagacious and crafty men, schooled into mastery over bondmen on the plantation, and thus the better able to assume the airs of superiority over Northern doughfaces,[40] Mr. LINCOLN'S disclaimer of any power, right or inclination to interfere with slavery in the States, does not amount to more than a broken shoestring! They knew it all before, and while they do not accept it as a satisfaction, they do look upon such declarations as the evidence of cowardly baseness, upon which they may safely presume.

The slaveholders, the parties especially addressed, may well inquire if you, Mr. LINCOLN, and the great party that elected you, honestly entertain this very high respect for the rights of slave property in the States, how happens it that you treat the same rights of property with scorn and contempt when they are set up in the Territories of the United States? If slaves are property, and our rights of property in them are to be so sacredly guarded in the States, by what rule of law, justice or reason does that property part with the attributes of property, upon entering into a Territory owned in part by that same State? The fact is, the slaveholders have the argument all their own way, the moment that the right of property in their slaves is conceded under the Constitution. It was, therefore, weak, uncalled for and useless for Mr. LINCOLN to begin his Inaugural Address by thus at the outset prostrating himself before the foul and withering curse of slavery. The time and the occasion called for a very different attitude. Weakness, timidity and conciliation towards the tyrants and traitors had emboldened them to a pitch of insolence which demanded an instant check. Mr. LINCOLN was in a position that enabled him to wither at a single blast their high blown pride. The occasion was one for honest rebuke, not for palliations and apologies. The slaveholders should have been told that their barbarous system of robbery is contrary to the spirit of the age, and to the principles of Liberty in which the Federal Government was founded, and that they should be ashamed to be everlastingly pressing that scandalous crime into notice. Some thought we had in Mr. LINCOLN the nerve and decision of an OLIVER CROMWELL;[41] but the result shows that we merely have a continuation of the PIERCES and BUCHANANS, and that the Republican President bends the knee to slavery as readily as any of his infamous predecessors.

Not content with the broadest recognition of the right of property in the souls and bodies of men in the slave States, Mr. LINCOLN next proceeds, with nerves of steel, to tell the slaveholders what an excellent slave hound he is, and how he regards the right to recapture fugitive slaves a constitutional duty; and lest the poor bondman should escape being returned to the hell of slavery by the application of certain well known rules of legal interpretation, which any and every white man may claim in his own case, Mr. LINCOLN proceeds to cut off the poor, trembling negro who had escaped from bondage from all advantages from such rules. He will have the pound of flesh, blood or no blood, be it more or less, a just pound or not.[42] The SHYLOCKS of the South, had they been after such game, might have exclaimed, in joy, an ABRAHAM come to judgment! But they were not to be caught with such fodder. The hunting down a few slaves, the sending back of a few LUCY BAGLEYS, young and beautiful though they be, to the lust and brutality of the slaveholders and slave-breeders of the Border States,[43] is to the rapacity of the rebels only as a drop of water upon a house in flames. The value of the thing was wholly in its quality. 'Mr. LINCOLN, you will catch and return our slaves if they run away from us, and will help us hold them where they are; what cause, then, since you have descended to this depth of wickedness, withholds you from coming down to us entirely? Indeed, in what respect are you better than ourselves, or our overseers and drivers who hunt and flog our negroes into obedience?' Again; the slaveholders have a decided advantage over Mr. LINCOLN, and over his party. He stands upon the same moral level with them, and is in no respect better than they. If we held the Constitution, as held by Mr. LINCOLN, no earthly power could induce us to swear to support it. The fact is, (following the lead of the Dred Scott decision, and all the Southern slaveholding politicians, with all the doughfaces of the North who have been engaged in making a Constitution, for years, outside of the Constitution of 1789,) Mr. LINCOLN has taken everything at this point in favor of slavery for granted. He is like the great mass of his countrymen, indebted to the South for both law and gospel.

But the Inaugural does not admit of entire and indiscriminate condemnation. It has at least one or two features which evince the presence or something like a heart as well as a head. Horrible as is Mr. LINCOLN'S admission of the constitutional duty of surrendering persons claimed as slaves, and heartily as he seems determined that that revolting work shall be performed, he has sent along with his revolting declaration a timid suggestion which, tame and spiritless as it is, must prove as unpalatable as gall to the taste of slaveholders. He says: 'In any law on this subject, ought not all the safeguards of liberty known in humane and civilized jurisprudence be introduced, so that a free man be not in any case surrendered as a slave.' For so much, little as it is, let the friends of freedom thank Mr. LINCOLN. This saves his Address from the gulf of infamy into which the Dred Scott decision sunk the Supreme Court of the United States. Two ideas are embraced in this suggestion: First, a black man's rights should be guarded by all the safeguards known to liberty and to humane jurisprudence; secondly, that slavery is an inhumane condition from which a free man ought by all lawful means to be saved. When we remember the prevailing contempt for the rights of all persons of African descent, who are mostly exposed to the operation of these slave-catching laws, and the strenuous efforts of the American Church and clergy to make slavery a divine relation, and especially blissful to our much hated variety of the human family, we are disposed to magnify and rejoice over even this slight recognition of rights, and this implied acknowledgment of the hatefulness of slavery. One of the safeguards of liberty is trial in open court. Another is the right of bringing evidence in one's own favor, and of confronting and questioning opposing witnesses. Another is the trial by a jury of our peers. Another is that juries are judges both of the law and the evidence in the case. There are other safeguards of liberty which we might specify, any one of which, faithfully applied, would not only make it difficult to surrender a free man as a slave, but would make it almost impossible to surrender any man as such. Thanking Mr. LINCOLN for even so much, we yet hold him to be the most dangerous advocate of slave-hunting and slave-catching in the land.

He has laid down a general rule of legal interpretation which, like most, if not all general rules, may be stretched to cover almost every conceivable villainy. '*The intention of the law-giver is the law*,' says Mr. LINCOLN. But we say that this depends upon whether the *intention* itself is lawful. If law were merely an arbitrary rule, destitute of all idea of right and wrong, the intention of the lawgiver might indeed be taken as the law, provided that intention were certainly known. But the very idea of law carries with it ideas of right, justice and humanity. Law, according to BLACKSTONE,[44] commands that which is right and forbids that which is wrong. A law authorizing murder is no law, because it is an outrage upon all the elements out of which laws originate. Any man called to administer and execute such a law is bound to treat such an edict as a nullity, having no binding authority over his action or over his conscience. He would have a right to say, upon the authority of the Supreme Court, that 'laws against fundamental morality are void;' that a law for murder is an absurdity, and not only from the purpose of all law and government, but wholly at war with every principle of law. It would be no avail in such a case to say that the 'intention of law-makers is the law.' To prove such an intention is only to destroy the validity of the law.

But the case is not murder, but simply the surrendering of a person to slavery who has made his or her escape from slavery into a free State. But what better is an act of this kind than murder? Would not Mr. LINCOLN himself prefer to see a dagger plunged to the hilt into the heart of his own daughter, than to see that daughter given up to the lust and brutality of the slaveholders of Virginia, as was poor, trembling LUCY BAGLEY given up a few weeks ago by the Republicans of Cleveland? What is slavery but a slow process of soul murder? What but murder is its chief reliance? How do slaveholders hold their slaves except by asserting their right and power to murder their slaves if they do not submit to slavery? Does not the whole slave system rest upon a basis of murder? Your money or your life, says the pirate; your liberty or your life, says the slaveholder. And where is the difference between the pirate and the slaveholder?

But the 'intention of the law is the law.' Well, suppose we grant it in the present case, that the intention of the law-maker is the law, and two very important questions arise—first, as to who were the makers, and, secondly, by what means are we required to learn their intentions? Who made the Constitution? The preamble to the Constitution answers that question. 'We, the people, do ordain and establish this Constitution.' The people, then, made the law. How stood their intention as to the surrender of fugitive slaves? Were they all agreed in this intention to send slaves to bondage who might escape from it? Or were only a part? and if a part, how many? Surely, if a minority only were of that intention, that intention could not be the law, especially as the law itself expresses no such intention. The fact is, there is no evidence whatever that any considerable part of the people who made and adopted the American Constitution intended to make that instrument a slave-hunting or a slaveholding instrument, while there is much evidence to prove the very reverse. DANIEL WEBSTER, even in his infamous 7th of March speech,[45] was sufficiently true to the letter of the Constitution, and to the history of the times in which the Constitution was framed and adopted, to deny that the Constitution required slaves to be given up, and quoted

Mr. James Madison in corroboration of his statement. This is Mr. Webster's language:—'It may not be important here to allude to that—I had almost said celebrated—opinion of Mr. Madison. You observe, sir, that the term slavery is not used in the Constitution. The Constitution does not require that fugitive slaves shall be delivered up; it requires that persons bound to service in one State escaping into another, shall be delivered up. Mr. Madison opposed the introduction of the term slave, or slavery, into the Constitution; for he said he did not wish to see it recognized by the Constitution of the United States of America, that there could be property in men.'

How sadly have the times changed, not only since the days of Madison—the days of the Constitution—but since the days even of Daniel Webster. Cold and dead as that great bad man was to the claims of humanity, he was not sufficiently removed from the better days of the Republic to claim, as Mr. Lincoln does, that the surrender of fugitive slaves is a plain requirement of the Constitution.

But here comes along a slight gleam of relief. Mr. Lincoln tremblingly ventures to *inquire* (for he is too inoffensive to the slaveholders to assert and declare, except when the rights of the black men are asserted and declared away) if it 'might not be well to provide by law for the enforcement of that clause in the Constitution which guarantees that the citizens of each State shall be entitled to all the privileges and immunities of citizens in the several States.'

Again we thank Mr. Lincoln. He has, however, ventured upon a hazardous suggestion. The man has not quite learned his lesson. He had not been long enough in Washington to learn that Northern citizens, like persons of African descent, have no rights, privileges or immunities that slaveholders are bound to respect.[46] To break open a man's trunk, to read the letters from his wife and daughters, to tar and feather him, to ride him on a rail and give him the alternative of being hanged or of leaving town the same hour, simply because he resides in a free State, is a privilege and immunity which our Southern brethren will not give up, though the requirement were made in every line of the

Constitution. Yet, we say, we are thankful. It is something even to have a sickly intimation that other American citizens, not belonging to the privileged slaveholding class, have rights which it '*might be well*' to secure by law, and that the mere fact of living in a free State ought not to subject the unfortunate traveler either to being whipped, hanged or shot. Yes, this is something to be thankful for and is more than any other American President has ever ventured to say, either in his Inaugural Speech or Annual Message. It is, perhaps, this latter fact that gives Mr. LINCOLN'S casual remark its chief importance. Hitherto our Presidents had pictured the South as the innocent lamb, and the greedy North as the hungry wolf, ever ready to tear and devour.

From slave-catching, Mr. LINCOLN proceeds to give a very lucid exposition of the nature of the Federal Union, and shows very conclusively that this Government, from its own nature and the nature of all Governments, was intended to be perpetual, and that it is revolutionary, insurrectionary and treasonable to break it up. His argument is excellent; but the difficulty is that the argument comes too late. When men deliberately arm themselves with the avowed intention of breaking up the Government; when they openly insult its flag, capture its forts, seize its munitions of war, and organize a hostile Government, and boastfully declare that they will fight before they will submit, it would seem of little use to argue with them. If the argument was merely for the loyal citizen, it was unnecessary. If it was for those already in rebellion, it was casting pearls before swine. No class of men in the country understand better than the rebels themselves the nature of the business on which they are engaged. They tell us this in the thousands of pounds of powder they have been buying, and the millions of money and arms they have been stealing. They know that unless the Government is a miserable and contemptible failure, destitute of every attribute of a Government except the name, that that Government must meet them on the field and put them down, or be itself put down. To parley with traitors is but to increase their insolence and audacity.

It remains to be seen whether the Federal Government is really able to do more than hand over some JOHN BROWN to be hanged, suppress a slave insurrection, or catch a runaway slave—whether it is powerless for liberty, and only powerful for slavery. Mr. LINCOLN says, 'I shall take care that the laws of the Union shall be faithfully executed in all the States'—that is, he will do so as '*as far as practicable*,' and *unless* the American people, his masters, shall, in some authoritative manner direct the contrary. To us, both these provisos had better have been omitted. They imply a want of confidence in the ability of the Government to execute its own laws, and opens its doors to all that border tribe who have nothing but smiles for the rebels and peace lecturers for the Government. The American people have placed the Government in the hands of ABRAHAM LINCOLN for the next four years, and his instructions are in the Constitution. He had no right to suppose that they will reverse those instructions in a manner to give immunity to traitors; and it was a mistake to admit such a possibility, especially in the presence of the very traitors themselves. But we are dwelling longer upon Mr. LINCOLN'S speech than we had intended, and longer than we are warranted either by the patience of our readers, or the extent of our space. The perusal of it has left no very hopeful impression upon our mind for the cause of our down-trodden and heart-broken countrymen. Mr. LINCOLN has avowed himself ready to catch them if they run away, to shoot them down if they rise against their oppressors, and to prohibit the Federal Government *irrevocably* from interfering for their deliverance.

With such declarations before them, coming from our first modern anti-slavery President, the Abolitionists must know what to expect during the next four years, (should Mr. LINCOLN not be, as he is likely to be, driven out of Washington by his rival, Mr. JEFF. DAVIS,[47] who has already given out that should Mr. LINCOLN attempt to do, what he has sworn to do—namely, execute the laws, fifty thousand soldiers will march directly upon Washington!). This might be taken as an empty threat on the part of the President of the

Confederated States, if we did not see with what steadiness, promptness and certainty the rebels have from the first executed all their designs, and fulfilled all their promises. A thousand things are less probable than that Mr. LINCOLN and his Cabinet will be driven out of Washington, and made to go out, as they came in, by the Underground Railroad. The game is completely in the hands of Mr. JEFFERSON DAVIS, and no doubt he will avail himself of every advantage.

"The Future of the Abolition Cause" (excerpt)
Douglass' Monthly, April 1861

The truth is, the South has no fear whatever of the North. They buy arms for the overthrow of the Government, and the Government seize the arms; the remedy is in the hands of the rebels. They have only to seize one or two old brigs belonging to New York merchants, to make the Government succumb. The bravest thing we ever did was to elect LINCOLN, and our meanest thing will be, as we certainly shall desert him, and leave him a potentate without power, a commander without a sword, the sport of traitors, and a hissing and byword to the surrounding world. The South is not afraid of us.

Report of Speech at Zion Church, Rochester, New York, April 28, 1861 (excerpt)
Douglass' Monthly, June 1861

He had been asked, "What are you colored men going to do?" He answered, let a few colored regiments go down South, and assist in setting their brothers free, and they could and would do this work effectively for our Government. He was ready to go; but this did not imply much courage, for he knew he would not be accepted. The South are wiser in their generation than the North. Black people are being made soldiers of at Montgomery.[48] They piled the sand-bags and raised the batteries which drove Major [Robert] Anderson from Sumter; but you Northerners are too aristocratic to march by the side of a "nigger." But the time may yet come when the President shall proclaim liberty through all the land.[49] The speaker argued that the Constitution granted this power to Congress. That great statesman, John Quincy Adams,[50] once told the chivalry to their faces that the power to set the slaves at liberty was clearly implied in the war-making power.

Report of Speech at Zion Church, Rochester, New York, May 5, 1861 (excerpts)

Douglass' Monthly, June 1861

Already, there is a visible change in the bearing of the Government at Washington. . . . Two weeks ago, the President was concerned for the safety of his soldiers [passing through Baltimore]. It will not be long before he will be concerned for the safety of the now persecuted loyal men and women in the State of Maryland. The President will, by and by, see that the United States Congress[51] gives him the right, and makes it his duty to take care that none are deprived of life or liberty, without due process of law; and that the citizens of each State shall enjoy all the rights and immunities of citizens of the several States. The first proclamation of Mr. Lincoln[52] was received with derision at the South. It is said that the cabinet of Jeff. Davis read it amid roars of laughter. They were intoxicated with their victory at Charleston. "Whom the Gods would destroy, they first make mad."[53]

"The Past and the Present" (excerpts)

Douglass' Monthly, May 1861

We are not disposed to deny that the usually cautious South, in thus reasoning from premise to conclusion, had a right to expect much from the spaniel-like servility which has been a prominent and disgraceful characteristic of the North. It would seem, after all, that the North has something more than 'a local habitation and a name,'[54] and that the Southern insolence and bravado have counted altogether too largely upon our constitutional proclivity to crush out liberty to 'save the Union.' Our new President and his Cabinet, as ardently as they desire Peace, are not content to accept as its condition, the proffered ultimatum of the rebels. The compromises manufactured to order by WEED, CORWIN & CO., look not only to a repeal of our Personal Liberty Bills,[55] &c., but they contemplate an abrogation of the fundamental principles of all legitimate civil government, the first, prime, sole law of social organization, the primal law of human relations. Mr. LINCOLN knows very well, that for him to adopt a policy which involves such abrogation, is to disband the Republican party, and cover himself with merited and imperishable infamy. It is to make the extension and perpetuation of slavery a fixed fact, and fling a solemn pall over the sanguine hopes of the eighteen hundred thousand men who placed him in power, firmly believing that he was the man for the hour.

We sincerely trust that the hopes which have been engendered by the disposition and determination of the new Administration to act firmly with the traitors and rebels of the seceded States, will not be blasted by any renewed attempts to 'compromise,' and 'concede,' and 'conciliate.' There is, in fact, but the one alternative—either to recognize the secession movement as a successful revolution, to be treated as such, or, as a causeless rebellion, to be promptly suppressed. Successful compromise is wholly out of the question. Indeed, the traitors with that impertinent coolness and diabolic candor peculiar to them, have repeatedly declared that they will listen to no compromises which acknowledge the right of the people of the free States to regard slavery as a moral and political evil, and thus to denounce it.

We cannot tell what a day or an hour may bring forth; but at the present moment, a peaceful settlement is scarcely within the range of human probability. THE DECISIVE BLOW MUST BE STRUCK. The question must be decided very shortly in one way or another. Our opinion is, that it is only necessary, in order to humble the haughty and defiant South, for Mr. LINCOLN to develop that inflexible Jacksonian firmness for which he has obtained credit; to show the South that he is in earnest, if need be, in *terrible* earnest; and that he will, at all hazards, enforce the laws. Let the South understand that *he* is President of the American Republic, and come weal, or come woe, he will, as such, exercise his authority. Then, and not till then, will there be an end to their pugnacious developments. But let him, BUCHANAN-like, tamper with the rapacious rebels, or show them any quarter, and he will eventually be driven by them from Washington, his inglorious Cabinet bearing him 'faithful company.'

We earnestly desire to see the South humbled. The 'high looks' of the lordly Assyrians must be 'brought low.'[56] The North has all things to hope for, and nothing to fear from such humility. We know something by experience of the character of slaveholders. To use a trite maxim, 'give them an inch and they will take an ell.' Refuse the ell, and they will rant, and bluster, and swear, in order to obtain it. So long as they can frighten an opponent, they act very frightfully. But let them understand that 'no one's afraid,' and they'll soon be in *statu quo!* For example: the 'Confederate' authorities have hitherto declared that [Maj. Robert] ANDERSON should not be supplied with provisions carried to Fort Sumter in the vessels of the United States. They had reason to believe that the attempt would not be made. They thus interpreted the Delphic utterances of the distinguished Premier. But now, when JEFF. DAVIS, the President of the new Confederacy, ascertains that the Administration is determined to re-enforce the forts, then, presto! change! he telegraphs, in eager haste to Charleston, 'not to fire on vessels carrying supplies to Fort Sumter.' This must have been humiliating, and from this letting down, Mr. LINCOLN should learn a lesson, if he has not done so already, and inflict upon the enemy such a chastisement as will give all to understand that there *is* a Government, and that we have at last a President who belongs to '*a healthy organization*.'[57] . . . [Douglass included a footnote here: "We must own that the rebels have been as good as their word, after all."]

Let the Administration, then, in its well directed efforts *to humble the South*, receive the cordial sympathy and co-operation of every well-wisher of his country, and of the world at large. The crisis has come, and it must be met manfully.

Part 2
Civil War Commentary: Pre-Emancipation

As the Civil War began, Douglass expressed one hope above all others for the commander-in-chief: fight the war to emancipate slaves. If a peacetime Constitution empowered the federal government to abolish slavery in states as well as territories, as Douglass suggested as early as 1851,[1] then a wartime Constitution gave Lincoln all he needed to abolish the cause and support of the rebellion. Douglass thought his hopes confirmed when Major General John C. Frémont declared martial law and emancipated slaves of rebels in the loyal but unruly border slave state of Missouri in August 1861. Frémont was the only Republican for whom Douglass had voted,[2] and now his proclamation did the two things Douglass thought Lincoln should have done from the outset of the war: free the slaves and put down the rebellion as forcefully as possible. When Lincoln ordered Frémont to modify the emancipation provision to apply only to slaves actually employed in rebellion (as stipulated by the First Confiscation Act of August 6, 1861), Douglass lamented that "the lawyer has prevailed over the warrior," and that the president "humbled and crippled him in the presence of his enemies."[3] A year would pass before Lincoln would publicly contemplate emancipation as a war measure.

That moment came on September 22, 1862, when Lincoln issued a Preliminary Emancipation Proclamation on the heels of the Battle of Antietam, which stopped General Robert E. Lee's invasion of Maryland. Douglass praised the proclamation for making emancipation a Union war aim. Although Douglass noted that the final proclamation would apply only to rebel-held territory, he drew attention to "one vital mistake"—namely, that Lincoln gave the Confederate states 100 days to return to the Union before the proclamation would take effect. Instead of waiting until January 1, 1863, the president should "at once strike the death blow of the rebellion by striking a death blow to slavery."[4]

Some of Douglass's harshest words for Lincoln came in response to an August 1862 meeting at the White House in which Lincoln encouraged black leaders to endorse the voluntary colonization of black Americans to alleviate racial strife in the United States.[5] Douglass was especially furious that Lincoln blamed black people for being the cause of the war. Here was yet another example of Lincoln's incapacity to do the right thing for the right reason and for the right people. Lincoln's public letter to *New-York Tribune* editor Horace Greeley a week later, which emphasized saving the Union and not destroying slavery as the aim of the war, also angered Douglass.

Douglass did not know that Lincoln had already decided in July to issue an emancipation proclamation, and that these were efforts to prepare the public for what was coming. Lincoln was already planning to free slaves in rebel-held territory "as a fit and necessary war measure for suppressing said rebellion."[6] Only by turning a humanitarian end—emancipation—into a constitutional means—preserving the Union—did Lincoln believe he could fulfill his oath to defend the Constitution. Lincoln and Douglass, the Republican and the radical, disagreed regarding what the federal government could do about slavery, and when and where it could do it. But on January 1, 1863, when Lincoln signed his famous edict, they finally agreed that the "slaves' liberation is the country's salvation."[7]

"Black Regiments Proposed" (excerpt)
Douglass' Monthly, May 1861

The measure recommended by 'Immaterial' meets our entire approval.[8] He speaks only what is passing in the minds of all thoughtful colored men of the North. If we are not seen in the present conflict, the fault is not with us, but with our circumstances. For the present, at least, we are between two fires. The slaveholders are willing to take free blacks to fight for slavery, but neither Mr. LINCOLN at Washington, nor Mr. DAVIS at Montgomery, wants us to fight for freedom; and if we fight, we must fight against the North as well as the South, ABRAHAM LINCOLN as well as JEFFERSON DAVIS. Mr. LINCOLN in his war proclamation assures the man stealers and pirates of the Cotton Confederacy that he shall not war upon their '*property*.' We all know that means that no attempt will be made to destroy slavery. Those of our number who have offered our services to the Government, have been coldly turned away, and in one instance, at Fort Pickens, sent back to slavery in irons to be whipped to death.

Our men are ready and eager to play some honorable part in the great drama of revolution now going forward; but we want to fight for freedom, and to know who we shall have to fight. Until another stage shall be reached in the progress of the war, we should be between two fires.

"The War and Slavery" (excerpts)
Douglass' Monthly, August 1861

In the late Message of our honest President, which purports to give an honest history of our present difficulties, no mention is, at all, made of slavery.[9] Any one reading that document, with no previous knowledge of the United States, would never dream from any thing there written that we have a slaveholding war waged upon the Government, determined to overthrow it, or so to reconstruct it as to make it the instrument of extending the slave system and enlarging its powers; while all here know that *that* is the vital and animating motive of the rebellion. The proclamation goes forth at the head of all our armies, assuring the slaveholding rebels that slavery shall receive no detriment from our arms. While fugitive slaves are not sent back just now to known rebels, the inducement is held out to all loyal slaveholders that they shall have their slaves sent back to them. While the slaveholders do not scruple to employ their slaves in the work of rebellion against the Government, our rulers at Washington steadily refuse to accept the aid of free colored citizens in defence of the Government. Thus do we belie and reject the issue presented to us in this contest. Thus do we refuse to see even what is impossible to hide from ourselves, that slavery is the cause of the war, and that its abolition is the true and only remedy for the war, and that all other remedies are but patch work, putting new wine into old bottles, and new cloth in old garments, and thus making the rent worse than before. Up to this time, slavery has lost nothing in point of doctrine, or principle, by the war, and no principle has been laid down by the Government which can necessarily give the soul-drivers of the South the least possible alarm for the safety of slavery. The impression which our Government seeks to make upon the slaveholders seems to be that slavery is safer in, than out of the Union. . . .

Nor are the people quite as far from this requirement of wisdom, justice and humanity, as at first sight it might seem. Though it is generally true that governments only move as they are moved upon by the people, they do sometimes find themselves moved by events which they cannot control, and when so moved in a just cause, they never move alone, but infallibly draw the people with them. Let but the Administration firmly occupy the ground pointed out by JOHN QUINCY ADAMS twenty years ago, that the war power of the Government gives power to abolish slavery, and assert the necessity of acting upon it, and tardy and blind as the people have seemed, they will go for it with startling unanimity and enthusiasm. Half the North but a few months ago denounced *coercion*, (*i.e.*,) the armed enforcement of the laws and the Constitution against slaveholding traitors and rebels. They would probably have yet been divided, had the Government remained undecided and in doubt. The moment the Government was resolved, the people were also resolved, and have so remained through good report and through evil report. The people at heart are against slavery. None other than a wolf's heart can be otherwise. All they want is a leader, with power and authority, and they are ready to follow where he leads. They are yet checked by supposed constitutional objections, and by practical difficulties. President LINCOLN, Secretaries SEWARD, CHASE, CAMERON and BLAIR,[10] have only to devise the mode of avoiding those difficulties of law and practice, and they will have the joyous support of the great heart of America, and the blessings of those ready to perish.

"The Progress of the War" (excerpts)
Douglass' Monthly, September 1861

The feeling is becoming general that a new element must be infused into the Government forces, and that unless a new turn is given to the conflict, and that without delay, we might as well remove Mr. LINCOLN out of the President's chair, and respectfully invite JEFFERSON DAVIS or some other slaveholding rebel to take his place. The conduct of the Government has been such as to weaken its friends, and in many respects to strengthen its enemies. . . . Witness the oft-repeated and shameless declaration of nearly all our Generals—doubtless with the approbation of the President himself—that slaves rising against the rebels for their liberty should be suppressed with an 'iron arm.'

"General Fremont's Proclamation to the Rebels of Missouri" (excerpt)
Douglass' Monthly, October 1861

For many days after the publication of FREMONT'S Proclamation,[11] the deepest anxiety existed throughout the country to learn whether that remarkable and startling document was the utterance of the Major-General, or that of the Cabinet at Washington—whether, if only from the former, the President would approve it or condemn it? Those who had confidence in the anti-slavery character and disposition of the Administration, unhesitatingly ascribed it to the wisdom, earnestness and courage that controls at Washington. While others, entertaining opposite impressions, openly predicted, what has since transpired, a pointed disapproval by the President of the main feature of FREMONT'S Proclamation. The suspense was truly painful, and attested the vast importance attached by the public to the measure. The action of FREMONT was the hinge, the pivot upon which the character of the war was to turn. It was whether the war should be waged against traitors only by the cunning technicalities of the crafty lawyer, or by the cannon and courage of the determined warrior.

Maj. Gen. John C. Frémont. Lincoln Financial Foundation Collection, Allen County Public Library, Fort Wayne, Indiana

Unhappily, as we think, for the country and for humanity, the lawyer has prevailed over the warrior. The President, of whom we would gladly speak naught but good, has interposed, most unseasonably, his Presidential authority, and placed a tame and worthless statute between the rebels and the merited chastisement which a brave and generous General had wisely prepared himself to inflict upon them. Many blunders have been committed by the

Government at Washington during this war, but this, we think, is the hugest of them all. The Government should have thanked their wise and intrepid General for furnishing them an opportunity to convince the country and the world of their earnestness, that they have no terms for traitors; that with them the heaviest blow is the wisest and best blow; and that the rebels must be put down at all hazards, and in the most summary and exemplary way. But, poor souls! instead of standing by the General, and approving his energetic conduct, they have humbled and crippled him in the presence of his enemies. The President interposes to cheapen the price of rebellion, and to let the rebels off on easier terms than that proposed by his faithful General.

We know not upon what maxim of political wisdom the Government has acted in this matter. The Cabinet is composed of reputed wise men, and the President is respected as honest and humane. But this policy is plainly one which can only dishearten the friends of the Government and strengthen its enemies. The *Times* newspaper of New York defends the anti-Fremont policy, by alleging that the rigor of that policy would drive the loyal slaveholders in Kentucky and Tennessee into the arms of the rebels. This assumption would have some weight did FREMONT'S Proclamation propose (as it does not) the liberation of the slaves of loyal masters. It strikes only at slaveholding rebels; and to suppose that loyal masters would be driven into disloyalty by the well-merited chastisement of slaveholding rebels, implies that, after all, there is a stronger bond existing between these loyal slaveholders and the slaveholding rebels, than subsists between the former and the Government. Taking this admission to be true, and what is the friendship of these so-called loyal slaveholders worth? The open hostility of these so-called loyal slaveholders is incomparably to be preferred to their friendship. They are far more easily dealt with and disposed of as enemies than as allies. From the beginning, these Border Slave States[12] have been the mill stone about the neck of the Government,[13] and their so-called loyalty has been the very best shield to the treason of the cotton States.

President LINCOLN says in his letter to Gen. FREMONT, that he accords with the general character of his Proclamation. One clause of it only is marked for disapproval, and that is the emancipating clause. Now mark! The Proclamation imposes that most dreaded of all descriptions of law, (except mob law,) martial law upon Missouri. The President approves that. The Proclamation proposes the confiscation of the property of the rebels. The President approves that. The Proclamation proposes that convicted rebels, within certain defined lines, *shall be shot.* The President approves that. The Proclamation proposes that the slaves of duly convicted traitors shall be liberated and treated as *free men.* Here's the rub; the President does not approve that.[14] Martial law, shooting, confiscation, with all their aggravation, are assented to; but liberation and freedom to the slave are vetoed by the President of the United States. The weakness, imbecility and absurdity of this policy are sufficiently manifest without a single word of comment.

"Fremont and Freedom—Lincoln and Slavery" (excerpt)
Douglass' Monthly, November 1861

In our number for the month of October, we recorded and commented on the pusillanimous and pro-slavery interference of President LINCOLN against the confiscation and liberation of the slaves held by those in arms against the Government in the State of Missouri. The friends of freedom and the Union had scarcely ceased to mourn this lamentable blunder, and the rebels to rejoice over it, when out came a still more disheartening rumor to the effect that FREMONT'S policy had not only been condemned by the Government, but that the Government was seriously debating the question of his removal from his command. At first, no body could believe that any such suicidal policy as that could have been entertained for a moment by the Government. But now, after weeks of telegrams "by authority," all calculated to impair the reputation of the young and vigorous anti-slavery General, there is no reason to doubt that FREMONT'S humiliation is fully determined upon, and that only a brief space is given him to save the Government the responsibility of his removal by his own resignation.[15]

Letter to Gerrit Smith, dated Rochester, New York, December 22, 1861 (excerpt)
Gerrit Smith Papers, Syracuse University

I have just read your letter to Thaddeus Stephens.[16] It is thus far the ablest paper—and the most thrilling—I have met with on the war—either from your pen or that of any other statesman. As you ply the knife to our rotten Government—I shudder with a feeling of something like despair of finding any sound place upon which to build a hope of national salvation. I am bewildered by the spectacle of moral blindness—infatuation and helpless imbecility which the Government of Lincoln presents. Is there no hope? I shall think there is not if all the Antislavery measures now before Congress are laid aside as was Lovejoys resolution on friday.[17] But go on, my Dear Sir, with your mighty work. Continue to fling the bright beams of truth upon the conduct of Cabinet and President and upon that of Congress. Your experience, knowledge, age, and position all give a right to speak in this mighty and momentous struggle—besides your pen is more powerful than ever—Your last letter is your best.

"The Slave Power Still Omnipotent at Washington" (excerpt)
Douglass' Monthly, January 1862

We confess that, while we would still hope that slavery is to receive its death wound from the present rebellion, we see nothing in the temper or disposition of our rulers in Washington to justify this hope. On the contrary, anti-slavery men have been, we think, most basely and scandalously betrayed on the vital and all-commanding question of the age. Our Government is not what it was elected to be, and LINCOLN this day shows himself to be about as destitute of any anti-slavery principle or feeling as did JAMES BUCHANAN, his predecessor. And as with the President, so with his Cabinet. It is idle to deceive ourselves; the friends of freedom are basely betrayed, and we might as well begin to familiarize the public mind with that fact, and begin to look for better material out of which to construct a future Cabinet. There is still no North at the Capital.

"War with England" (excerpt)
Douglass' Monthly, January 1862

There are, it is true, good men both in England and America, who are exerting all their influence to prevent a disaster so ruinous to both parties, as such a war would prove; but we cannot shut our eyes to what is passing before us.[18] Both countries are studded with the materials by which nations are hurled from peaceful security into the boiling abyss and fierce tumults of war. England is suffering at this moment untold calamities from the rebellion in this country. She sees that ABRAHAM LINCOLN at Washington is as sternly opposed to emancipation, as JEFF. DAVIS is sternly in favor of slavery, and that the cause of civilization has nothing to hope from either.

Speech on the War, Delivered in National Hall, Philadelphia, January 14, 1862 (excerpts)
Douglass' Monthly, February 1862

To what cause may we trace our present sad and deplorable condition? A man of flighty brain and flippant tongue will tell you that the cause of all our national troubles lies solely in the election of Abraham Lincoln to the Presidency of the Republic. To the superficial this is final. Before Lincoln there was peace; after Lincoln there was rebellion. It stands to reason that Lincoln and rebellion are related as cause and effect. Such is their argument; such is their explanation. I hardly need waste your time in showing the folly and falsehood of either. Beyond all question, the facts show that this rebellion was planned and prepared long before the name of Abraham Lincoln was mentioned in connection with the office he now holds, and that though the catastrophe might have been postponed, it could not have been prevented, nor long delayed. The worst of our condition is not to be sought in our disasters on flood or field. It is to be found rather in the character which contact with slavery has developed in every part of the country, so that at last there seems to be no truth, no candor left within us. We have faithfully copied all the cunning of the serpent, without any of the harmlessness of the dove, or the boldness of the lion.[19]

In dealing with the causes of our present troubles, we find in quarters, high and low, the most painful evidences of dishonesty. It would seem, in the language of Isaiah, that the whole head is sick, and the whole heart is faint, that there is no soundness in it.[20] After-coming generations will remark with astonishment this feature in this dark chapter in our national history. They will find in no public document emanating from the loyal Government, anything like a frank and full statement of the real causes which have plunged us in the whirlpool of civil war. On the other hand, they will find the most studied and absurd attempts at concealment. Jefferson Davis is reticent. He seems ashamed to tell the world just what he is fighting for. Abraham Lincoln seems equally so, and is ashamed to tell the world what he is fighting against. . . .

Witness the treatment of Fremont's proclamation. When that memorable document was given to the public, all truly loyal men felt that the Pathfinder of the Rocky Mountains had found the true path out of our national troubles. His words were few and simple, but strong enough to vibrate the heart of a continent. The weakness and imbecility of the letter of the President condemning that proclamation, have thus far characterized the whole war. Slavery has been, and is yet the shield and helmet of this accursed rebellion; but for this, its brains would have been out long ago. President, Government, and army, stand paralyzed in the presence of slavery. They are determined only to save the Union so far as they can save slavery. The President attests that he approved of the proclamation of Fremont generally, but disapproved of one feature of it. What was the proclamation generally? Why this: the establishment of martial law in Missouri. The President approved of that. What was it specially? Why, the confiscation and emancipation of all the slaves belonging to rebels. The President was in favor of martial law, in favor of shooting rebels, but was not in favor of freeing their slaves. In this brief letter to Fremont, we have the secret of all our misfortune in connection with rebellion.

Letter to Russell or Mary Carpenter, dated Boston, March 7, 1862 (excerpt)
London *Inquirer*, March 29, 1862

I am very much cheered this morning by the anti-slavery signs of the times. For the last six weeks clouds and darkness have seemed to overhang the immediate future of our cause. The policy of the Government at Washington seemed to aim at repressing all anti-slavery sentiment at the North, and so to manage the war as that slavery should receive no detriment. This policy is distinctly abandoned in a message just read before Congress from the President, calling upon Congress to co-operate with any of the Slave States in measures for gradual emancipation.[21] The President has presented the subject in the mildest possible terms, but all the more on that account do I trust to the radical character of his views concerning the necessity for putting away our great American abomination. I consider that we have fairly reached the turning point of the moral struggle involved in this terrible war.

"The War and How to End It," Lecture Delivered in Corinthian Hall, Rochester, New York, March 25, 1862 (excerpt)
Douglass' Monthly, April 1862

I thank all the powers, of earth and sky, that I am permitted to be a witness to this day's events. That slavery could always live and flourish in this country I have always known to be a foul and guilty heresy. That the vile system must eventually go down I have never doubted, even in the darkest days of my life in slavery. But that I should live to see the President of the United States deliberately advocating Emancipation was more than I ever ventured to hope.[22]

It is true that the President lays down his propositions with many qualifications some of which to my thinking, are unnecessary, unjust and wholly unwise. There are spots on the Sun. A blind man can see where the President's heart is. I read the spaces as well as the lines of that message, I see in them a brave man trying against great odds, to do right. An honest patriot endeavoring to save his country in its day of peril. It is the first utterance, and first utterances are not according to Carlyle[23] the most articulate and perfect. Time and practice will improve the President as they improve other men. He is tall and strong but he is not done growing, he grows as the nation grows. He has managed to say one good word, and to say it so distinctly that all the world may hear. He has dared to say that the highest interest of the country will be promoted by the abolition of slavery. And this, bear in mind, is not said in the bitterness of defeat, but when every morning brought news of glorious victories over the slaveholding rebels. The message comes at the call of no desperation. The time selected for sending it to Congress and the nation must be read with the document itself in order to appreciate its true significance.

Right upon the heels of the message comes the appointment of John C. Fremont, a man whose name thrills the young heart of America with every sentiment of honor, patriotism, and bravery. John C. Fremont carries his department in his name. He goes to free the mountains of rebels and traitors and the good wishes of all but traitors will go with him. Here is a new chapter of the war:

Fremont's proclamation was revised and modified by the President; Fremont was removed from his post when in the act of striking the foe. Calumny did its worst upon Fremont.[24]

Letter to Lt. Gen. Thomas Perronet Thompson,[25] dated Rochester, New York, April 7, 1862 (excerpt)
London *Inquirer*, May 3, 1862

The miserable diplomacy which controlled at Washington deprived the national cause of its chief glory in discarding the idea that the slaves might be freed by the war. During the first seven or eight months of the struggle we pursued a course which gave every advantage to the rebels. We could say that they were fighting for slavery, but could not say that we were fighting against it. It seemed to be our purpose to convince the rebels that they were labouring under a misapprehension of Northern opinion concerning slavery; that, though not the friends of slavery, we were not its enemies, and would hereafter, as heretofore, stand by the slave system.

"The National Unity" (excerpts)
Douglass' Monthly, July 1862

While we of the North have been waging one of the mightiest wars that ever shook a continent, for the suppression of rebellion and the establishment of national unity, our generals, and our people, are disunited on the most important element involved in that war. . . .

Nevertheless the great North is essentially in earnest for the Union, and the speedy suppression of the rebellion at any cost to slavery, and in the end this spirit will diffuse itself, overcome all factions, and unify all elements now opposed to the haggard front of this slaveholding rebellion. We are the more persuaded of this final result because of the testimony elsewhere borne of the anti-slavery feeling of the President.

"The Slaveholders Rebellion," An Address Delivered in Himrods Corners, Yates County, New York, July 4, 1862 (excerpts)

Douglass' Monthly, August 1862

THE CONDUCT OF THE WAR.

To-day we have to deal not with dead traitors, such as James Buchanan, Howell Cobb, Floyd, Thompson and others,[26] but with a class of men incomparably more dangerous to the country. They are our weak, paltering and incompetent rulers in the Cabinet at Washington and our rebel worshipping Generals in the field, the men who sacrifice the brave loyal soldiers of the North by thousands, while refusing to employ the black man's arm in suppressing the rebels, for fear of exasperating these rebels: men who never interfere with the orders of Generals, unless those orders strike at slavery, the heart of the Rebellion. These are the men to whom we have a duty to discharge to-day, when the country is bleeding at every pore, and when disasters thick and terrible convert this national festal day, into a day of alarm and mourning. I do not underrate the power of the rebels, nor the vastness of the work required for suppressing them. Jefferson Davis is a powerful man, but Jefferson Davis has no such power to blast the hope and break down the strong heart of this nation, as that possessed and exercised by ABRAHAM LINCOLN. With twenty millions of men behind him, with wealth and resources at his command such as might pride the heart of the mightiest monarch of Europe, and with a cause which kindles in every true heart the fires of valor and patriotism, we have a right to hold Abraham Lincoln, sternly responsible for any disaster or failure attending the suppression of this rebellion. I hold that the rebels can do us no serious harm, unless it is done through the culpable weakness, imbecility or unfaithfulness of those who are charged with the high duty, of seeing that the Supreme Law of the land is everywhere enforced and obeyed. Common sense will confess that five millions ought not to be a match for twenty millions. I know of nothing in the mettle of the slaveholder which should make him superior in any of the elements of a warrior to an honest

Northern man. One slaveholder ought not longer to be allowed to maintain the boast that he is equal to three Northern men: and yet that boast will not be entirely empty, if we allow those five millions much longer to thwart all our efforts to put them down. It will be most mortifyingly shown that after all our appliances, our inventive genius, our superior mechanical skill, our great industry, our muscular energy, our fertility in strategy, our vast powers of endurance, our overwhelming numbers, and admitted bravery, that the eight or ten rebel slave States, sparsely populated, and shut out from the world by our possession of the sea, are invincible to the arms, of the densely populated, and every way powerful twenty free States. I repeat, these rebels can do nothing against us, cannot harm a single hair of the national head, if the men at Washington, the President and Cabinet, and the commanding Generals in the field will but earnestly do their most obvious duty. I repeat Jeff. Davis and his malignant slaveholding Republic, can do this union no harm except by the permission of the reigning powers at Washington. . . .

This is already an old war. The statesmanship at Washington with all its admitted wisdom and sagacity, utterly failed for a long time to comprehend the nature and extent of this rebellion. Mr. Lincoln and his Cabinet will have by and by to confess with many bitter regrets, that they have been equally blind and mistaken as to the true method of dealing with the rebels. They have fought the rebels with the Olive branch. The people must teach them to fight them with the sword. They have sought to conciliate obedience. The people must teach them to compel obedience.

There are many men connected with the stupendous work of suppressing this slaveholding rebellion, and it is the right of the American people to keep a friendly and vigilant eye upon them all, but there are three men in the nation, from whose conduct the attention of the people should never be withdrawn: The first is President Lincoln, the Commander in chief of the army and navy. The single word of this man can set a million of armed men in motion: He can make and unmake generals, can lift up or cast down at will. . . .

THE POLICY OF THE ADMINISTRATION.

I come now to the policy of President Lincoln in reference to slavery. An Administration without a policy, is confessedly an administration without brains, since while a thing is to be done, it implies a known way to do it and he who professes his ability to do it, but cannot show how it is to be done, confesses his own imbecility. I do not undertake to say that the present administration has no policy, but if it has, the people have a right to know what it is, and to approve or disapprove of it as they shall deem it wise or unwise.

Now the policy of an administration can be learned in two ways. The first by what it says, and the second by what it does, and the last is far more certain and reliable, than the first. It is by what President Lincoln has done in reference to slavery, since he assumed the reins of government that we are to know what he is likely to do, and deems best to do in the premises.

We all know how he came into power. He was elected and inaugurated as the representative of the anti-slavery policy of the Republican party. He had laid down and maintained the doctrine that Liberty and Slavery were the great antagonistic political elements in this country. That the Union of these States could not long continue half free and half slave, that they must in the end be all free or all slave.

In the conflict between these two elements he arrayed himself on the side of freedom, and was elected with a view to the ascendancy of free principles. Now what has been the tendency of his acts since he became Commander in chief of the army and navy? I do not hesitate to say, that whatever may have been his intentions, the action of President Lincoln has been calculated in a marked and decided way to shield and protect slavery from the very blows which its horrible crimes have loudly and persistently invited. He has scornfully rejected the policy of arming the slaves, a policy naturally suggested and enforced by the nature and necessities of the war. He has steadily refused to proclaim, as he had the constitutional and moral right to proclaim, complete emancipation to all the slaves of rebels who should make their way into the lines of our army. He has repeatedly interfered with, and arrested the anti-slavery policy of some of his most earnest and reliable generals. He has assigned to the most important positions, generals who are notoriously pro-slavery, and hostile to the party and principles which raised him to power. He has permitted rebels to recapture their runaway slaves in sight of the capital. He has allowed General Halleck to openly violate the spirit of a solemn resolution by Congress forbidding the army of the United States to return the fugitive slaves to their cruel masters,[27] and has evidently from the first submitted himself to the guidance of the half loyal slave States, rather than to the wise and loyal suggestions of those States upon which must fall, and have fallen, the chief expense and danger involved in the prosecution of the war. It is from such action as this, that we must infer the policy of the Administration. To my mind that policy is simply and solely to reconstruct the union on the old and corrupting basis of compromise; by which slavery shall retain all the power that it ever had, with the full assurance of gaining more, according to its future necessities.

The question now arises, "Is such a reconstruction possible or desirable?" To this I answer from the depths of my soul, no. Mr. Lincoln is powerful, Mr. Lincoln can do many things, but Mr. Lincoln will never see the day when he can bring back or charm back, the scattered fragments of the Union into the shape and form they stood when they were shattered by this slaveholding rebellion. . . .

But it is asked, how will you abolish slavery. You have no power over the system before the rebellion is suppressed, and you will have no right or power when it is suppressed. I will answer this argument when I have stated how the thing may be done. The fact is there would be no trouble about the way, if the government only possessed the will. But several ways have been suggested. One is a stringent Confiscation Bill by Congress.[28] Another is by a proclamation by the President at the head of the nation. Another is by the commanders of each division of the army. Slavery can be abolished in any or all these ways. . . .

But a proclamation of Emancipation, says one, would only be a paper order. I answer, so is any order emanating from our Government. The President's proclamation calling his country men to arms, was a paper order. The proposition to retake the property of the Federal Government in the Southern States, was a paper order. Laws fixing the punishment of traitors are paper orders. All Laws, all written rules for the Government of the army and navy and people, are 'paper orders,' and would remain only such were they not backed up by force, still we do not object to them as useless, but admit their wisdom and necessity. Then these paper orders carry with them a certain moral force which makes them in a large measure self-executing. I know of none which would possess this self-executing power in larger measure than a proclamation of Emancipation. It would act on the rebel masters, and even more powerfully upon their slaves. It would lead the slaves to run away, and the masters to Emancipate, and thus put an end to slavery. The conclusion of the whole matter is this: The end of slavery and only the end of slavery, is the end of the war, the end of secession, the end of disunion, and the return of peace, prosperity and unity to the nation. Whether Emancipation comes from the North or from the South, from Jeff. Davis or from Abraham Lincoln, it will come alike for the healing of the nation, for slavery is the only mountain interposed to make enemies of the North and South.

"The Confiscation and Emancipation Law" (excerpt)
Douglass' Monthly, August 1862

At last there is some ground of hope for the slave, and for the country. Congress has passed a Confiscation law which extends to the slaves of rebels, and President LINCOLN has signed it. The measure is important or unimportant, significant or insignificant only as the President himself shall determine. The sole power of putting life into this law is vested in the President. He can make it effective and binding upon his generals or inoperative and void.

"What the People Expect of Mr. Lincoln"
Douglass' Monthly, August 1862

Mr. Lincoln should be informed that the people are becoming impatient for the execution of the important laws just passed by Congress. The Legislature has put a sword into the hands of the President, with the general approbation of the country, and every body is wondering why he delays to strike. Not one man in twenty throughout the free States disapproves of the passage of the Confiscation act, and those provisions of the new Militia act which authorises the President to employ men of the colored race in the service of the country and the suppression of the rebellion. Nobody expects that these laws are to remain a dead letter: they were not passed to be neglected and suffered to become obsolete.

On the steamers and on the railway trains which bring their thousands to this metropolis every morning, the first enquiry, as soon as the passengers furnish themselves with the morning papers, "Where is the President's proclamation bringing those who aid and encourage the rebellion within the penalties of the Confiscation act?[29] Where are the regulations which the President was to frame for the organization of the blacks in the service of the government?"[30]

A few days have made a decided and most important change to the views of a large class of persons who lately hesitated and doubted in regard to both these points—the policy of stripping the rebel population of their possessions and employing the colored race in any service which the exigencies of the Union require, to the extent of arming them against the rebels. Mr. Lincoln must hasten the publication of his proclamation and the framing of his rules for the employment of the blacks, or he will find himself halting at an immeasurable distance behind the public sentiment.

Such being the state of public opinion, it is clear that the true way to invigorate the spirit and put new life into the hopes of the nation is to do what it so ardently desires. No act which makes the fate of the rebellion more sure and speedy should be left undone. That vast resource which we have in the good will and ready aid of the colored population—a resource which we have heretofore left untouched—should be instantly brought to the aid of the government.

A shout of joy would raise from every true loyal neighborhood in the Union, if the assurance were but once given, in some solemn, authentic practical form, that the power given by the late acts of Congress would be used without reserve, to its utmost extent, in the defence of the Union; that the army would be provided, in every one of its departments, with the ablest leaders whom the times has produced; and that from every quarter the entire array of resources and means at our command would be gathered and flung upon the rebellion, to overwhelm and annihilate it. It is such a policy, and such a policy alone, that can make the work of recruiting for our volunteer army go on with spirit. It would have a better effect than heaps of gold offered in the shape of bounties.

"The President and His Speeches"
Douglass' Monthly, September 1862

The President of the United States seems to possess an ever increasing passion for making himself appear silly and ridiculous, if nothing worse. Since the publication of our last number he has been unusually garrulous, characteristically foggy, remarkably illogical and untimely in his utterances, often saying that which nobody wanted to hear, and studiously leaving unsaid about the only things which the country and the times imperatively demand of him. Our garrulous and joking President has favored the country and the world with two speeches, which if delivered by any other than the President of the United States, would attract no more attention than the funny little speeches made in front of the arcade by our friend John Smith, inviting customers to buy his razor strops. One of the speeches of the President was made at a war meeting in Washington in vindication of Mr. Stanton,[31] and in justification of himself against the charge that he had failed to send reinforcements to Gen. McClellan. Very little need be said of this first speech. In comparison with some speeches made on that occasion, the President's is short, but in comparison to the amount of matter it contains, it is tediously long, full of repetitions, and so remarkably careless in style that it reminds one strongly of the gossiping manner in which a loquacious old woman discusses her neighbor's and her own domestic affairs, and explaining herself so lucidly that her audience, after listening with all due patience, are in the end as well informed about the subject in question as before the exposition. In short, the speech does not prove anything except that the Secretary of War is not responsible, but that the President is responsible for the failure to send re-enforcements to General McClellan. We may at once have done with this speech, especially since the information it contains was explicitly given to the country full three weeks before its utterance at the War meeting in Washington.

The other and more important communication of the President it appears was delivered in the White House before a committee of colored men assembled by his invitation. In this address Mr. Lincoln assumes the language and arguments of an itinerant Colonization lecturer, showing all his inconsistencies, his pride of race and blood, his contempt for negroes and his canting hypocrisy.[32] How an honest man could creep into such a character as that implied by this address we are not required to show. The argument of Mr. Lincoln is that the difference between the white and black races renders it impossible for them to live together in the same country without detriment to both. Colonization, therefore, he holds to be the duty and the interest of the colored people. Mr. Lincoln takes care in urging his colonization scheme to furnish a weapon to all the ignorant and base, who need only the countenance of men in authority to commit all kinds of violence and outrage upon the colored people of the country. Taking advantage of his position and of the prevailing prejudice against them he affirms that their presence in the country is the real first cause of the war, and logically enough, if the premises were sound, assumes the necessity of their removal.

It does not require any great amount of skill to point out the fallacy and expose the unfairness of the assumption, for by this time every man who has an ounce of brain in his head—no matter to which party he may belong, and even Mr. Lincoln himself must know quite well that the mere presence of the colored race never could have provoked this horrid and desolating rebellion. Mr. Lincoln knows that in Mexico, Central America and South America, many distinct races live peaceably together in the enjoyment of equal rights, and that the civil wars which occasionally disturb the peace of those regions never originated in the difference of the races inhabiting them. A horse thief pleading that the existence of the horse is the apology for his theft or a highway man contending that the money in the traveler's pocket is the sole first cause of his robbery are about as much entitled to respect as is the President's reasoning at this point. No, Mr. President, it is not the innocent horse that makes the horse thief, not the traveler's purse that makes the highway robber, and it is not the presence of the negro that causes this foul and unnatural war, but the cruel and brutal cupidity of those who wish to possess horses, money and negroes by means of theft, robbery, and rebellion. Mr. Lincoln further knows or ought to know at least that negro hatred and prejudice of color are neither original nor invincible vices, but merely the offshoots of that root of all crimes and evils—slavery. If the colored people instead of having been stolen and forcibly brought to the United States, had come as free immigrants, like the German and the Irish, never thought of as suitable objects of property, they never would have become the objects of aversion and bitter persecution, nor would there ever have been divulged and propagated the arrogant and malignant nonsense about natural repellency and the incompatibility of races.

Illogical and unfair as Mr. Lincoln's statements are, they are nevertheless quite in keeping with his whole course from the beginning of his administration up to this day, and confirms the painful conviction that though elected as an anti-slavery man by Republican and Abolition voters, Mr. Lincoln is quite a genuine representative of American prejudice and negro hatred and far more concerned for the preservation of slavery, and the favor of the Border Slave States, than for any sentiment of magnanimity or principle of justice and humanity.

This address of his leaves us less ground to hope for anti-slavery action at his hands than any of his previous utterances. Notwithstanding his repeated declarations that he considers slavery an evil, every step of his Presidential career relating to slavery proves him active, decided, and brave for its support, and passive, cowardly, and treacherous to the very cause of liberty to which he owes his election.

This speech of the President delivered to a committee of free colored men in the capital explains the animus of his interference with the memorable proclamation of General Fremont. A man who can charge this war to the presence of colored men in this country might be expected to take advantage of any legal technicalities for arresting the cause of Emancipation, and the vigorous prosecution of the war against slaveholding rebels. To these colored people, without power and without influence, the President is direct, undisguised, and unhesitating. He says to the colored people: I don't like you, you must clear out of the country. So too in dealing with anti-slavery Generals the President is direct and firm. He is always brave and resolute in his interferences in favor of slavery, remarkably unconcerned about the wishes and opinions of the people of the north; apparently wholly indifferent to the moral sentiment of civilized Europe; but bold and self-reliant as he is in the ignominious service of slavery, he is as timid as a sheep when required to live up to a single one of his anti-slavery testimonies. He is scrupulous to the very letter of the law in favor of slavery, and a perfect latitudinarian as to the discharge of his duties under a law favoring freedom.

When Congress passed the Confiscation Bill, made the Emancipation of the slaves of rebels the law of the land, authorized the President to arm the slaves which should come within the lines of the Federal army, and thus removed all technical objections, everybody who attached any importance to the President's declarations of scrupulous regard for law, looked at once for a proclamation emancipating the slaves and calling the blacks to arms. But Mr. Lincoln, formerly so strict and zealous in the observance of the most atrocious laws which ever disgraced a country, has not been able yet to muster courage and honesty enough to obey and execute that grand decision of the people. He evaded his obvious duty, and instead of calling the blacks to arms and to liberty he merely authorized the military commanders to use them as laborers, without even promising them their freedom at the end of their term of service to the government, and thus destroyed virtually the very object of the measure. Further, when General Halleck issued his odious order No. 3, excluding fugitive slaves from our lines, an order than which none could be more serviceable to the slaveholding rebels, since it was a guarantee against the escape of their slaves, Mr. Lincoln was deaf to the outcry and indignation which resounded through the north, and west, and saw no occasion for interference, though that order violated a twice adopted resolution of Congress. When General McClellan employed our men guarding rebel property and even when Gen. Butler committed the outrage paralleled only by the atrocities of the rebels—delivering back into bondage thousands of slaves—Mr. Lincoln again was mute and did not feel induced to interfere in behalf of outraged humanity.

The tone of frankness and benevolence which he assumes in his speech to the colored committee is too thin a mask not to be seen through. The genuine spark of humanity is missing in it, no sincere wish to improve the condition of the oppressed has dictated it. It expresses merely the desire to get rid of them, and reminds one of the politeness with which a man might try to bow out of his house some troublesome creditor or the witness of some old guilt. We might also criticize the style adopted, so exceedingly plain and coarse threaded as to make the impression that Mr. L. had such a low estimate of the intelligence of his audience, as to think any but the simplest phrases and constructions would be above their power of comprehension. As Mr. Lincoln however in all his writings has manifested a decided awkwardness in the management of the English language, we do not think there is any intention in this respect, but only the incapacity to do better.

Letter to Julia Griffiths Crofts, dated Rochester, New York, September 22, 1862 (excerpts)
Leeds Mercury, October 9, 1862

Slavery still exists in America. Men still defend it with pen and tongue, as well as sword. The moral sentiment of the country is still corrupt and deeply pro-slavery, while our weak Government is largely under the dominion of the slave power. The slave is still in his galling chains. The justice and mercy of our country and the world are now, as ever, appealed to for deliverance. The fact that we are still in danger of settling our controversy with the South without emancipating the slave, and possibly by giving new guarantees to human bondage makes continued anti-slavery effort more important than ever. . . .

I have been strongly urged by a member of the American Government to lend my influence to the new scheme of colonisation. I have no doubt that my acceptance of that scheme would greatly redound to my personal advantage; but, for the sake of my people, whose prospects it tends to blight, *I spurn the bribe.*[33]

"Emancipation Proclaimed"
Douglass' Monthly, October 1862

Common sense, the necessities of the war, to say nothing of the dictates of justice and humanity have at last prevailed. We shout for joy that we live to record this righteous decree. *Abraham Lincoln*, President of the United States, Commander-in-Chief of the army and navy, in his own peculiar, cautious, forbearing and hesitating way, slow, but we hope sure, has, while the loyal heart was near breaking with despair, proclaimed and declared: "THAT ON THE FIRST OF JANUARY, IN THE YEAR OF OUR LORD ONE THOUSAND, EIGHT HUNDRED AND SIXTY-THREE, ALL PERSONS HELD AS SLAVES WITHIN ANY STATE OR ANY DESIGNATED PART OF A STATE, THE PEOPLE WHEREOF SHALL THEN BE IN REBELLION AGAINST THE UNITED STATES, SHALL BE THENCEFORWARD AND FOREVER

FREE."[34] "Free forever" oh! long enslaved millions, whose cries have so vexed the air and sky, suffer on a few more days in sorrow, the hour of your great deliverance draws nigh! oh! ye millions of free and loyal men who have earnestly sought to free your bleeding country from the dreadful ravages of revolution and anarchy, lift up now your voices with joy and thanksgiving, for with freedom to the slave will come peace and safety to your country. President Lincoln has embraced in this proclamation the law of Congress passed more than six months ago, prohibiting the employment of any part of the army and naval forces of the United States, to return fugitive slaves to their masters, commanded all officers of the army and navy to respect and obey its provisions. He has still further declared his intention to urge upon the Legislature of all the slave States not in rebellion the immediate or gradual abolishment of slavery. But read the proclamation, for it is the most important of any to which the President of the United States has ever signed his name.

Opinions will widely differ as to the practical effect of this measure upon the war. All that class at the North who have not lost their affection for slavery will regard the measure as the very worst that could be devised, and as likely to lead to endless mischief. All their plans for the future have been projected with a view to a reconstruction of the American Government upon the basis of compromise between slaveholding and non-slaveholding States. The thought of a country unified in sentiments, objects and ideas, has not entered into their political calculations, and hence this newly declared policy of the Government, which contemplates one glorious homogeneous people, doing away at a blow with the whole class of compromisers and corrupters, will meet their stern opposition. Will that opposition prevail? Will it lead the President to reconsider and retract? Not a word of it. Abraham Lincoln may be slow, Abraham Lincoln may desire peace even at the price of leaving our terrible national sore untouched, to fester on for generations, but Abraham Lincoln is not the man to reconsider, retract and contradict words and purposes solemnly proclaimed over his official signature.

The careful, and we think, the slothful deliberation which he has observed in reaching this obvious policy, is a guarantee against retraction. But even if the temper and spirit of the President himself were other than what they are, events greater than the President, events which have slowly wrung this proclamation from him may be relied on to carry him forward in the same direction. To look back now would only load him with heavier evils, while diminishing his ability, for overcoming those with which he now has to contend. To recall his proclamation would only increase rebel pride, rebel sense of power and would be hailed as a direct admission of weakness on the part of the Federal Government, while it would cause heaviness of heart and depression of national enthusiasm all over the loyal North and West. No, Abraham Lincoln will take no step backward. His word has gone out over the country and the world, giving joy and gladness to the friends of freedom and progress wherever those words are read, and he will stand by them, and carry them out to the letter. If he has taught us to confide in nothing else, he has taught us to confide in his word. The want of Constitutional power, the want of military power, the tendency of the measure to intensify Southern hate, and to exasperate the rebels, the tendency to drive from him all that class of Democrats at the North, whose loyalty has been conditioned on his restoring the union as it was,[35] slavery and all, have all been considered, and he has taken his ground notwithstanding. The President doubtless saw, as we see, that it is not more absurd to talk about restoring the union, without hurting slavery, than restoring the union without hurting the rebels. As to exasperating the South, there can be no more in the cup than the cup will hold, and that was full already. The whole situation having been carefully scanned, before Mr. Lincoln could be made to budge an inch, he will now stand his ground. Border State influence, and the influence of half-loyal men, have been exerted and have done their worst. The end of these two influences is implied in this proclamation. Hereafter, the inspiration as well as the men and the money for carrying on the war will come from the North, and not from half-loyal border States.

The effect of this paper upon the disposition of Europe will be great and increasing. It changes the character of the war in European eyes and gives it an important principle as an object, instead of national pride and interest. It recognizes, and declares the real nature of the contest, and places the North on the side of justice and civilization, and the rebels on the side of robbery and barbarism. It will disarm all purpose on the part of European Government to intervene in favor of the rebels and thus cast off at a blow one source of rebel power. All through the war thus far, the rebel ambassadors in foreign countries have been able to silence all expression of sympathy with the North as to slavery. With much more than a show of truth, they said that the Federal Government, no more than the Confederate Government, contemplated the abolition of slavery.

But will not this measure be frowned upon by our officers and men in the field? We have heard of many thousands, who have resolved that they will throw up their commissions and lay down their arms, just so soon as they are required to carry on a war against slavery. Making all allowances for exaggeration there are doubtless far too many of this sort in the loyal army. Putting this kind of loyalty and patriotism to the test will be one of the best collateral effects of the measure. Any man who leaves the field on such a ground will be an argument in favor of the proclamation, and will prove that his heart has been more with slavery than with his country. Let the army be cleansed from all such pro-slavery vermin, and its health and strength will be greatly improved. But there can be no reason to fear the loss of many officers or men by resignation or desertion. We have no doubt that the measure was brought to the attention of most of our leading Generals, and blind as some of them have seemed to be in the earlier part of the war, most of them have seen enough to convince them that there can be no end to this war that does not end slavery. At any rate, we may hope that for every pro-slavery man that shall start from the ranks of our loyal army, there will be two anti-slavery men to fill up the vacancy, and in this war one truly devoted to the cause of Emancipation is worth two of the opposite sort.

Whether slavery will be abolished in the manner now proposed by President Lincoln, depends of course upon two conditions, the first specified and the second implied. The first is that the slave States shall be in rebellion on and after the first day of January 1863, and the second is we must have the ability to put down that rebellion. About the first there can be very little doubt. The South is thoroughly in earnest and confident. It has staked everything upon the rebellion. Its experience thus far in the field has rather increased its hopes of final success than diminished them. Its armies now hold us at bay at all points, and the war is confined to the border States slave and free. If Richmond were in our hands and Virginia at our mercy, the vast regions beyond would still remain to be subdued. But the rebels confront us on the Potomac, the Ohio, and the Mississippi. Kentucky, Maryland, Missouri, and Virginia, are in debate on the battle fields and their people are divided by the line which separates treason from loyalty. In short we are yet, after eighteen months of war, confined to the outer margin of the rebellion. We have scarcely more than touched the surface of the terrible evil. It has been raising large quantities of food during the past summer. While the masters have been fighting abroad, the slaves have been busy working at home to supply them with the means of continuing the struggle. They will not [missing word?] down at the bidding of this Proclamation, but may be safely relied upon till January and long after January. A month or two will put an end to general fighting for the winter. When the leaves fall we shall hear again of bad roads, winter quarters and a spring campaigns [*sic*]. The South which has thus far withstood our arms will not fall at once before our pens. All fears for the abolition of slavery arising from this apprehension may be dismissed. Whoever, therefore, lives to see the first day of next January, should Abraham Lincoln be then alive and President of the United States, may confidently look in the morning papers for the final proclamation, granting freedom, and freedom forever, to all slaves within the rebel States.

On the next point nothing need be said. We have full power to put down the rebellion. Unless one man is more than a match for four, unless the South breeds braver and better men than the North, unless slavery is more precious than liberty, unless a just cause kindles a feebler enthusiasm than a wicked and villainous one, the men of the loyal States will put down this rebellion and slavery, and all the sooner will they put down that rebellion by coupling slavery with that object. Tenderness towards slavery has been the loyal weakness during the war. Fighting the slaveholders with one hand and holding the slaves with the other, has been fairly tried and has failed. We have now inaugurated a wiser and better policy, a policy which is better for the loyal cause than an hundred thousand armed men. The Star Spangled banner is now the harbinger of Liberty and the millions in bondage, inured to hardships, accustomed to toil, ready to suffer, ready to fight, to dare and to die, will rally under that banner wherever they see it gloriously unfolded to the breeze. Now let the Government go forward in its mission of Liberty as the only condition of peace and union, by weeding out the army and navy of all such officers as the late Col. Miles,[36] whose sympathies are now known to have been with the rebels. Let only the men who assent heartily to the wisdom and the justice of the anti-slavery policy of the Government, be lifted into command; let the black man have an arm as well as a heart in this war, and the tide of battle which has thus far only waved backward and forward, will steadily set in our favor. The rebellion suppressed, slavery abolished, and America will, higher than ever, sit as a queen among the nations of the earth.

Now for the work. During the interval between now and next January, let every friend of the long enslaved bondman do his utmost in swelling the tide of anti-slavery sentiment, by writing, speaking, money and example. Let our aim be to make the North a unit in favor of the President's policy, and see to it that our voices and votes, shall forever extinguish that latent and malignant sentiment at the North, which has from the first cheered on the rebels in their atrocious crimes against the union, and has systematically sought to paralyze the national arm in striking down the slaveholding rebellion. We are ready for this service or any other, in this, we trust the last struggle with the monster slavery.

"Address to Our Readers and Friends in Great Britain and Ireland" (excerpt)

Douglass' Monthly, October 1862

From the first hour of our slaveholding rebellion, you, not less clearly than ourselves, saw that the only way to restore this country to permanent peace, is the complete abolition of slavery. Knowing that whatever disguises the rebels might assume for effect, in Europe or elsewhere, the one cause of their resort to arms against the Government was the desire, and the purpose by that means, to strengthen and perpetuate slavery, you have believed with us that no peace could be lasting which should leave this, the prime motive of the rebellion still existing. The conviction of the necessity and the duty of national Emancipation has increased with every step in the progress of the war. From Radical abolitionists and moderate Republicans, to loyal democrats, this conviction has rolled on until it has reached the American Cabinet, and the President has at last proclaimed his purpose to act upon it, and Emancipate the slaves of all States which shall be in rebellion on the first day of January 1863. Our arguments, appeals and entreaties combining with events, have at last moved the Government to this high duty, and opened up to the downtrodden millions the hope of speedy deliverance from a bondage whose horrors and crimes no pen can describe.

From the 22d of September 1862, in the second year of the rebellion, the American Government entered upon a new career. For sixty years that Government had been on the side of slavery and inflexibly opposed to the emancipation of slaves, at home or abroad, whether in the West Indies, in Central America or in Mexico. Wherever there was an effort made to emancipate the African slaves, the face of our Government had been sternly against that effort, and wherever tyranny to that race needed an approving smile it might look with confidence to the American Government. Its flag had been the shelter of slavetrading pirates, and its shores the sure refuge of slaveholding filibusters, while all the power of its diplomacy had been systematically flung into the scale against humanity and civilization. Even under our present Administration, while slavery was in arms against the Government, so controlling was its influence that no denunciation of slavery could be tolerated in any department of the national service. The secretary of State, himself long distinguished for his anti-slavery sentiments, strangely forbade all allusion to slavery, in the communications of our ministers to foreign countries. Our Generals in the field freely offered the aid of the loyal army to the slave States, in putting down their slaves, should they avail themselves of the opportunity afforded by the rebellion to rise and assert their Liberty. With a fierce alacrity which extorted a cry of shame from Christendom our loyal army officers acted the degrading part of bloodhounds to ferret out and return trembling slaves, who had sought their protection, to infuriated rebel masters, to be whipped and otherwise tortured to death. Others to divest the slaves of all hope of freedom through the war, ordered that no slaves should be allowed within their lines. For any General to distinguish himself by any act of humanity to the negro, was the surest way to incur the displeasure of the Government and to secure his own humiliation. So that even our Republican Government under ABRAHAM LINCOLN, though elected on the strength of anti-slavery sentiment and warred upon as such by slaveholding rebels has been in fact, during nearly the whole course of its existence, a bulwark of slavery.

Now, to the gladness and joy of all who wish well to the country and sympathise with the sorrows of the enslaved negro, all is changed. The 22d of September is the beginning of a new dispensation in America. The Proclamation of President Lincoln is the first chapter of a new history. The object of the Government is no longer to preserve, but to destroy slavery, no longer to recapture fugitive slaves, but to set them at Liberty, no longer to prevent slaves from rising against their cruel masters, but to see that nothing is done for such prevention. Already the war has put an end to slave hunting in the Northern States. The Underground Railroad lays idle and useless, and its agents out of employment. The depot kept by us on this road is no longer necessary, for those of our Southern Brethren who reach here, are safe from pursuit. The funds which you have occasionally sent to us for the use of this road are no longer needed for that object, and it is but a plain duty to tell you so. What we can do in the way of finding employment for those of our brethren from bondage when newly arrived here from the South we shall do, giving them food, shelter, and advice, but the sending them to Canada, may now be abandoned as a needless expense.

"The Slave Democracy Again in the Field" (excerpt)
Douglass' Monthly, November 1862

We are profoundly grateful for the President's Proclamation, but it contained in itself one vital mistake, full of mischief to the cause of the country. The space given to rebels for repentance, is taken advantage of to strengthen the great transgression. Had Mr. LINCOLN made his proclamation of freedom, absolute and immediate instead of conditional and prospective, all hope of arresting his beneficent work by reviving the pro-slavery Democratic party of the North would have disappeared. Now, however, there is time upon which to base a hope of defeating his policy. Vastly better would it be for the country if Mr. Lincoln should even now alter this feature of his policy and at once strike the death blow of the rebellion by striking a death blow to slavery. Mr. Lincoln has no right to postpone the salvation of his country. If it is necessary to put down slavery as a military measure, two months hence, if the rebellion shall then exist it is right and imperative to abolish slavery now. Delay gives all the advantages of the situation to the enemy. It enables him to put his slaves beyond our reach and affords space to organize opposition in the North to defeat this very measure. Necessity is in its nature immediate, and brooks no unavoidable delay. What it demands, it demands now. The rebellion is as bad to-day as it will be on the first of January 1863. Why then withhold the blow which is needed to bring the gigantic evil to a speedy and permanent end? Why give the rebels time to prepare for the blow, and their special friends at the

North time to arrest the loyal arm and bring the Government under the brutal and tyrannical power of the lords of the lash?

Letter to Julia Griffiths Crofts, dated Rochester, New York, November 11, 1862[37] (excerpt)

Leeds Mercury, December 4, 1862

One of the most hopeful events in the cause of the slave, and for the cause of the country, which I can now communicate is that General [George B.] McClellan, of whom you know my opinion, has been at last remanded from the command of the Potomac army and his command given to General [Ambrose] Burnside, a friend to the slave, and in earnest in his efforts to put down the rebellion. I have from the first urged the removal of McClellan, believing him at least a friend to the traitors, and wholly unfit to lead the armies of the Union and liberty against the slaveholders. Thank God, this view of the man has now been adopted at Washington. But is there not something providential in the retention of this man McClellan so long at the head of the army? Had his place been filled by an earnest man, with the means at his command, the rebellion might have been crushed in its infancy, and slavery might have lived to entail horrors on the slave and to insult Heaven yet a long time. For the policy of the Government through one year and a half of the war was to suppress the rebellion without disturbing the relation of master and slave. How the wisdom of the crafty has been confounded and the counsels of the ungodly brought to nought![38] The Government now sees, what you and I have long seen, that the salvation of the country depends upon the salvation of the slave. Day and night, with pen and tongue, I have endeavoured to bring this view to the attention of my countrymen. They now begin to see and speak the same thing. Heaven be thanked we live to see this day.

Do not be alarmed lest the elections, which have generally been unfavourable to the administration, should have a repressive tendency to the anti-slavery policy.[39] On the other hand, I think they will stir up the administration to a still more vigorous anti-slavery policy. Two explanations may be given of the victory of the Democrats. The first is that a larger number of anti-slavery Republicans volunteered for the war, and are now in the army, than of Democrats. Another is that a good many Republicans had become disgusted with the want of vigour displayed in the protraction of the war, and held the administration, as they had a right to do, responsible for the slipshod manner of fighting the rebels. They had poured out their treasures only to be squandered upon selfish contractors. They had sent their sons only to die in trenches by fever; and they were sick of the whole thing, and wanted a change. It will not prove a check-rein to "Old Abraham," but a whip to drive him on. He, very possibly, undertook, in the beginning, to slight his friends, and to take counsel of his enemies, in the hope of attaching them to his administration. The thing has turned out precisely as all such folly turns out. At the moment of trial, these half friends, who followed him, not from principle, but only for the five loaves and the two fishes,[40] deserted him, and combined to drive him from power. I should have been glad to have had the election go otherwise, especially in this State (N.Y.). Wadsworth is a noble man; Seymour the representative of slavery, whisky, and all that is 'mobocratic.'

Nevertheless, I am in a very serene state of mind about the defeat of my party, and believe, after all, it, in the end, will turn out for the best. It certainly will if it leaves our Republican administration to follow up the good work they have begun by throwing overboard that Jonah of our national ship, General McClellan. They have promoted Democrats and degraded Republicans, and this is their reward. It will do them good. This reaction is not against the anti-slavery policy, but against the miserable reaction and lifelessness of the administration.

"The Slave's Appeal to Great Britain" (excerpt)
The Independent (New York), November 20, 1862

I am now fulfilling my appointed mission in making on the slaves' behalf this appeal to you.

I am grateful for your benevolence, jealous for your honor, but chiefly now I am concerned, lest, in the present tremendous crisis of American affairs, you should be led to adopt a policy which may defeat the now proposed emancipation of my people, and forge new fetters of slavery for unborn millions of their posterity. You are now more than ever urged, both from within and from without your borders, to recognize the independence of the so-called Confederate States of America. I beseech and implore you, resist this urgency. You have nobly resisted it thus long. You can, and I ardently hope you will, resist it still longer. The proclamation of emancipation by President Lincoln will become operative on the first day of January, 1863. The hopes of millions, long trodden down, now rise with every advancing hour. Oh! I pray you, by all your highest and holiest memories, blast not the budding hopes of these millions by lending your countenance and extending your potent and honored hand to the blood-stained fingers of the impious slaveholding Confederate States of America.

"January First 1863," final week of December 1862
Douglass' Monthly, January 1863

The first of January, which is now separated from us only by a few days and hours, is properly looked forward to with an intense and all surpassing interest, by all classes of the American people and from the most opposite reasons and motives. The slave hopes to gain his liberty, the slaveholder fears the loss of Slaves, and northern doughfaces fear the loss of political power. It is a pivotal period in our national history—the great day which is to determine the destiny not only of the American Republic, but that of the American Continent. Far off in the after coming centuries, some Gibbon[41] with truthful pen, will fix upon that date, as the beginning of a glorious rise, or of a shameful fall of the great American Republic. Unquestionably, for weal or for woe, the first of January is to be the most memorable day in American Annals. The fourth of July was great, but the first of January, when we consider it in all its relations and bearings, is incomparably greater. The one had respect to the mere political birth to a nation, the last concerns the national life and character, and is to determine whether that life and character shall be radiantly glorious with all high and noble virtues, or infamously blackened, forevermore, with all the hell darkened crimes and horrors which attach to Slavery—it is whether our national life shall be to ourselves and the world, a withering curse or a benediction of all national blessedness for ages to come. We may well stay before it and amplify it. It is an occasion which can happen but seldom in the life of any nation. It is not the creation of individual design and calculation, but the grand result of stupendous all controlling wide sweeping national events. Powerful as Mr. Lincoln is, he is but the hands of the clock. He cannot change the pivotal character of the day. The word has gone forth—and no system of balancing, of props here, or weight there, can possibly anchor the national ship in anything like a stationary position after the first day of January. From that day her ample form will swing round, her towering sails will be swelled by the trade winds of the Almighty and she will either be wafted off gloriously to the open sea, on a prosperous voyage, or furiously driven by rebellious gales upon the sharp and flinty rocks only to mark the place of danger to other and aftercoming voyagers. We repeat, there is no escape. The tide is reached which must be taken at the flood. For the present the Angel of Liberty has one ear of the nation and the demon of Slavery the other. One or the other must prevail on the first of January. The national head swings, pendulum like, now to the one side and now to the other. Alas, no man can tell which will prevail—and we are compelled to wait, hope, labour and pray.

It is of but little use to speculate as to probabilities, when events are at the door which will dispel all doubt and make all certain—yet we may even now glance at the probable effects which may be looked for as certain to follow any one of the other three courses open to the President of the United States on the first of January. We say *three courses* although in a radical point of view there are but *two*. One is the issuing, according to promise, of his proclamation abolishing slavery in all the States and parts of States which shall be in rebellion on the first of January and the second is, not to issue it at all. Any postponement, any apology—any plan of compromise which saves the guilty neck of slavery one hour beyond the first of January, will be in effect a suppression of the proclamation altogether. And now supposing that Mr. Lincoln shall fail, supposing that the hour comes and the man is missing, what will be the effect upon him? Thus far the loyal north has trusted him, less for his ability than his honesty. They have supported him with patience rather than enthusiasm. His word though clumsily uttered has been esteemed his bond, good for all, and more than all it has promised. But what, as we have already said, if the President fails in this trial hour, what if he now listens to the demon slavery—and rejects the entreaties of the Angel of Liberty? Suppose he cowers at last before the half loyal border Slave States, which have already nearly ruined his administration, and have been of more service to Richmond than to Washington from the beginning—withholds his proclamation of freedom—disappoints the just hopes of his true friends, dispels the fear and dismay of his enemies—and thus gives a new lease of life to the slaveholder's rebellion? Where then will stand Mr. Abraham Lincoln? We know not what will become of him. The North has been so often betrayed and trifled with that it has become unsafe to predicate anything spirited, resolute and decided on her part. But this we will say, if Mr. Lincoln shall thus trifle with the wounds of his bleeding country—thus fiddle, while the cold earth around Fredericksburg is wet with the warm blood of our patriot soldiers—every one of whom was slain by slaveholding rebels, he will be covered with execrations as bitter and as deep as any that ever settled upon the head of any perjured tyrant ancient or modern. His name would go down in history scarcely less loathsome than that of Nero. Such a course, on the part of Mr. Lincoln would justly make him the distrust and scandal of his friends, the scorn of the world and the contempt of his enemies. Henceforth none but fools will believe in him, and his protestations of honesty and patriotism will be hailed but as the deceitful utterances of another Iago.[42]

To the country, a failure to issue the Emancipation proclamation would prove the most stunning and disastrous blow received during the war. It would well nigh break the loyal heart of the nation, and fill its enemies North and South, with a demoniacal enthusiasm. Missouri, with its noble German population and Western Virginia, both sternly endeavoring against terrible odds of treachery and danger, to throw off the system of bondage would fall paralysed in the presence of their exulting foes, while the loyal North and West would feel that they had fought and bled in vain. The most hopeful of all our prophets would wilt in despair. For who could trust to presidential promises or in any arm or department of Government when the central pillar had fallen? Who but a fool can believe that any grace shown the rebels at this moment after nearly two years of patience will not be construed into conscious weakness, into a base and cowardly spirit, as another proof of the unfitness of the Northern round heads[43] to rule, and of the necessity of rebel dominion? The natural and inevitable effect of the suppression or postponement of the proclamation will be to cheer the hopes and intensify the determination and efforts of the rebels to break up and destroy the Union. Mr. Lincoln might threaten in the event of continued resistance, to send out another decree on the fourth of July 1863, but the North would gain no hope from it and the South would be caused no fear by it for the moral constitution of the Government more solemn than all paper ones would be broken down beyond repair.

But on the other hand let the President promptly on the morning of the first of January, with the truthful steadiness and certainty of the movement of the heavenly bodies send forth his glorious proclamation of Liberty, and a shout like the voice of many waters will rise to heaven from three millions of robbed and plundered bondmen, while a groan of despair, will [be] heard in every rebel hall South of Mason and Dixon's line. It will add four millions to the strength of the Union with a single dash of the pen, establish the moral power of the Government, kindle anew the enthusiasm of the friends of freedom, number the days of Northern doughfaceism, strengthen the hearts of our brave troops in the field, convince the world of our sincerity, give a fuller meaning to the declaration of Independence, and put peace forever between the conscience and the patriotism of the people.

> When a deed is done for freedom, through the broad earth's
> aching breast
> Runs a thrill of joy prophetic trembling on from East to West.[44]

But will that deed be done? Oh! that is the question. There is reason both for hope and fear. The promise is yet unretracted, the rebels are still in arms, bold, active, unyielding, strong and defiant. There is not a sign of weakness on all the Southern horizon, at this writing. Their army is said to be shoeless, coatless, hatless, tentless, blanketless, half starved and deserting, but this is on paper. On the field they tell a different story especially in all the Great Battles of Virginia, and we hope for Emancipation none the less, because this is so. The being in rebellion was the ground for the promised proclamation. This ground within nine days of the first of January holds good. Not a single rebel State has grounded its weapons since the twenty second of September. Thus far the President is dared to do his worst, thus far the villainy of the South is a spur to the virtue of the North, and affords reason to hope that we shall have the promised proclamation of freedom to all the Inhabitants of the rebel States.

On the 22d of September, as we have said, the President declared that he would issue, on the first of January 1863, a proclamation of Emancipation Abolishing Slavery in all the Slave States which should then be in rebellion. But alas, he made these a burden of what should have been a joy. He reached that point like an ox under the yoke, or a Slave under the lash, not like the uncaged eagle spurning his bondage and soaring in freedom to the skies. His words kindled no enthusiasm. They touched neither justice nor mercy. Had there been one expression of sound moral feeling against Slavery, one word of regret and shame that this accursed system had remained so long the disgrace and scandal of the Republic, one word of satisfaction in the hope of burying slavery and the rebellion in one common grave, a thrill of joy would have run round the world, but no such word was said, and no such joy was kindled. He moved but was moved by necessity. Emancipation—is put off—it was made future and conditional—not present and absolute.

While, however, there are grounds for supposing that President Lincoln will duly issue his proclamation on the morning of the first of January, the absence of all mention of purpose to do so, in his recent message,[45] his reported saying that the rebellion is already substantially suppressed, his parleying with the border State men, his avowed readiness to change his opinion, whenever he should be convinced, the tremendous pressure likely to be brought to bear upon him, by the conservators of slavery, the apparent lack in him of any vital hostility towards slavery, the declared motives for the measure being only military, not moral or political necessity, the democratic pro-slavery gains obtained at the North since the 22d of September,[46] the space given in his late message to compensated Emancipation, all served to cast a doubt upon the promised and hoped for proclamation, which only the event can remove or confirm. So stands the case within one week of the first of January. The suspense is painful, but will soon be over. Our paper shall wait for the day and the deed, that it may carry especially to our transatlantic readers the result whatever it may be.

Part 3
Civil War Commentary: Post-Emancipation

Douglass's observations of the wartime president prior to the Emancipation Proclamation emphasized the need to turn the war for the Union into a war for abolition. With slavery the cause and support of the southern rebellion, Douglass thought slavery should be a target of the Union military, and he believed Lincoln was too deferential to what Douglass called the "half loyal" border slave states.[1] He also consistently called for black men to be allowed to join the fight, predicting just a few weeks into the war that black soldiers would be required eventually. Lincoln's resistance to both ideas led Douglass to worry that on January 1, 1863, the president would find some reason to postpone or even cancel his announced plan to free the slaves in rebel territory.

After Lincoln issued his Emancipation Proclamation, slaves in rebellious states now had the nation's military to protect them. The rule of law would now be the friend of freedmen and freedwomen, not their enemy. As Douglass put it to Julia Griffiths Crofts, "The master fights against law. The slave fights for law."[2] Douglass rejoiced that Lincoln's emancipation policy would expand the rights of black Americans in a practical way, authorizing their service to defend the nation even as they defended their own freedom.

Douglass lamented that the proclamation did not apply to slavery in all the states, but he prophesied that slavery's fall in the rebel states would have a domino effect on the loyal border slave states. To those who argued that Lincoln's edict was only ink on paper because it applied only to areas where the Union military lacked control, Douglass half conceded the critique. But he hastened to add that the Declaration of Independence was also just ink on paper until made a material fact by victory in war. The proclamation would need to be "backed up by force" to take effect, which was all the more reason for Lincoln to enlist black Americans in the fight.[3]

The Year of Jubilee found Douglass giving speeches at a breakneck pace, seeking to consolidate northern support for equal citizenship for black Americans once the war was over. In his mind, the best chance for complete equality after the war was to secure justice for black Americans during the war, while loyal white Americans still required their help to preserve the Union. Most important was the right to vote, which Douglass championed throughout the war, into Reconstruction, and up to the ratification of the 15th amendment in 1870. Without the vote, Douglass explained, slaves to individual masters would be emancipated "only to become the slaves of the community at large."[4] On several occasions he criticized Lincoln for not publicly supporting black voting rights, unaware that Lincoln was working behind the scenes on this issue.[5]

When black men finally began serving in the Union army, Douglass's demand of the president was no different than his demand before emancipation—complete equality. As every person should be accorded equality before the law, so too should every black soldier be equally compensated, equally promoted for exemplary service, and equally defended by the president if captured. (Official Confederate policy was to execute or enslave black soldiers who were captured on the battlefield, treating them as slaves in insurrection rather than as prisoners of war.[6]) Several months would pass before Douglass saw progress on these fronts, moving him to grieve that "nothing of justice, liberty or humanity can come to us except through tears and blood."[7]

On August 10, 1863, Douglass showed up at the White House, uninvited, to press Lincoln to ensure equal rights for black soldiers and to protect them from Confederate atrocities. While Douglass was not completely satisfied with Lincoln's responses to these concerns, he was gratified that Lincoln treated him with dignity and respect. A year later, on August 29, 1864, Lincoln invited Douglass to the White House to discuss a plan to free as many slaves as possible before Lincoln was out of office. (The war was going so badly for the Union that Lincoln thought he would not be reelected and that a Democrat would succeed him and rescind the Emancipation Proclamation.) Douglass later stated that this meeting revealed Lincoln's genuine concern for black freedom—that emancipation was not simply about military necessity but Lincoln's sincere desire to rid the nation of slavery.[8]

Nevertheless, Douglass was still disappointed in Lincoln for not doing enough for blacks in the army and in the reconstructed states. On September 1, 1864, he again shared with a British abolitionist that Lincoln was "not my first or even second choice for the Presidency during the next four years," but he pledged "to promote the election of Mr. Lincoln, or rather to defeat [the Democratic nominee, George B.] McClellan, in November." Douglass added that a prolonged war would actually be best for the freedpeople: "The hope of the slave is in the continuance of the war, and not in the abolition principles of the Northern people or Government. What the latter does is from necessity; when *that* ceases, abolition ceases."[9] This shocking remark, shared privately with a British friend, underscores that for Douglass, the primary goal of the war was always black liberation and equal citizenship. To win the war without winning equal rights would sorely disappoint the hopes of black America.

Only by January 1865 was Douglass confident that slavery would end with the war. But as he cheered the news of the fall of Richmond in April 1865, he warned that black people would be hated by whites in the South even more than they had been before the war. Living among their former oppressors, black Americans would require the full complement of civil and political rights. For the next three decades, Douglass would draw on the name of the soon-to-be "martyred President" in his appeals for racial justice and equality in post-Civil War America.[10]

"Truth and Error," Report of Speech at Metropolitan Hall, Chicago, January 19, 1863 (excerpt)

Chicago Tribune, January 20, 1863 [11]

A fatal blow had at last been struck at the root of the gigantic evil. The President's proclamation had given the slaves the *legal* right to liberty. Now they could obtain their personal freedom without trampling upon civil laws. Instead of rising up as insurrectionists, in opposition to law, they could rise up in obedience to law. It was a proud thought that the first man to put the knife of military power to the throat of this vile monster, was an Illinoisan.

At last the edict of freedom had gone forth, and the people were prepared to sustain it and carry it out. The speaker had a great deal of confidence in the virtue of the North, but still more in the villainy of the South. He thanked Abe Lincoln for what he had done towards destroying slavery, and he also felt grateful to Jeff. Davis.

Letter to Samuel J. May,[12] dated Rochester, New York, January 28, 1863 (excerpt)

Sara A. Thomson-Kinney Papers, Connecticut State Library

I am just home from a fortnights tour in the west as far as Chicago—and am to be off again in a day or two on a similar tour in Connecticut where as elsewhere powerful efforts are making to turn the current of sentiment against the Emancipation proclamation. The work before the Abolitionists is now to make the north a unit in favour of that great measure—and if possible to carry it beyond it. The slaves' liberation is the country's salvation. So I preach in all the congregations—and the people hear me gladly. To have lived to see this truth so generally acknowledged is a great and precious privilege. God bless Abraham Lincoln, bless the old and faithful Abolitionists and bless you, My Dear Sir, who have contributed your full share to this grand result.

Letter to Julia Griffiths Crofts, dated Rochester, New York, January 28, 1863 (excerpt)
Leeds Mercury, February 16, 1863

Within the past month I have travelled more than two thousand miles, often leaving the platform and proceeding directly to the railway, to ride all night after speaking, in order to reach my next appointment. In this way I have travelled to Chicago from Boston, taking my route through the States of New York, Pennsylvania, Ohio, Indiana, and Michigan.

You will naturally ask why this flying about just now more than usual? I answer *the country needs it.* The President has issued his proclamation, and has now fairly committed the Government to liberty—made the cause of the slave the cause of the country—welcomed the black man to a place under the star-spangled banner—given him a country, or the hope of a country—stimulated his patriotism, and in doing all this has roused against the Government all that is pro-slavery and disloyal at the North.

A tremendous effort is being made just now to defeat the policy of freedom, now inaugurated, and to drag the nation down to the 'hole of the pit,' from which we have been for years labouring to extricate it. They are endeavouring more than ever to poison the minds of men against the man of colour, and to stir up all the latent prejudices against him. Some of my friends here are pleased to think that my labours on the platform are especially needed to co[u]nteract the malign influence of the pro-slavery Democrats, and there is no end to the calls I have to address public meetings. Of course, while life and health are vouchsafed to me, I cannot be silent when required to speak for the dumb and defenceless. Hence I am abroad doing my utmost in this grand pivotal period in the history of the nation.

How much better and wiser are the works and ways of Providence than our calculations concerning the end of slavery! Having since 1850 (when the Fugitive Slave Law was passed) given up hope for the peaceful abolition of slavery in this country, I had about made up my mind that freedom could only come through blood, and that a succession of insurrections would take place, wherein scenes would occur which would rouse the indignation of the whole world against the negro. That the slave system would come to an end by bloodshed—here, I was right—but that it would come in a lawless and disorderly way—here I was wrong.

I thought the slave would be the rebel; but lo! it is the master. The master fights against law. The slave fights for law. Vastly better for us is it that we fight for country and government as well as for liberty. This brings the North to help us instead of hindering us. It compels the North to fight for us as the best means of fighting for themselves. You will have noticed how nearly all the views I have insisted upon concerning even our generals in the field, as well as the true policy of the war, have been gradually adopted by the Government; so that now we are clearly engaged in a war for liberty.

I wish you could have been a witness with me of the scenes in Boston on the first of January. The jubilee celebration would have touched your heart deeply—'joy and gladness, thanksgiving and the voice of melody'[13] broke forth from the coloured people and their friends that day—all felt that they saw and heard on that New Year's day what they never expected to see and hear in this life. The past month has been a month of jubilee. Celebrations have been held in all the large towns and cities of the North. I have been on hand at many of them, and have sung and shouted myself hoarse. I have never held larger meetings, and I am sure I never did better service to the cause of the slave. Tell the Doctor that I can now almost equal a Yorkshireman in singing 'The year of jubilee is come!'[14]

The South are determined and desperate, but they cannot hold out against the North.

"The Proclamation and a Negro Army," Address Delivered at the Cooper Union, New York City, February 6, 1863 (excerpts)
New-York Tribune, February 7, 1863[15]

I congratulate you, upon what may be called the greatest event of our nation's history, if not the greatest event of the century. In the eye of the Constitution, the supreme law of the land, there is not now, and there has not been, since the 1st day of January, a single slave lawfully deprived of Liberty in any of the States now recognized as in Rebellion against the National Government. In all those States Slavery is now in law, as in fact, a system of lawless violence, against which the slave may lawfully defend himself. (Cheers.)

In the hurry and excitement of the moment, it is difficult to grasp the full and complete significance of President Lincoln's proclamation. The change in the attitude of the Government is vast and startling. For more than sixty years the Federal Government has been little better than a stupendous engine of Slavery and oppression, through which Slavery has ruled us, as with a rod of iron. The boast that Cotton is King was no empty boast. Assuming that our Government and people will sustain the President and his Proclamation, we can scarcely conceive of a more complete revolution in the position of a nation. England, no longer ruled by a king, the Pope turned Protestant, Austria—a Republic, would not present a greater revolution. I hail it as the doom of Slavery in all the States. I hail it as the end of all that miserable statesmanship, which has for 60 years juggled and deceived the people, by professing to reconcile what is irreconcilable. No politician need now hope to rise to power, by crooking the pregnant hinges of the knee to Slavery. We part company forever with that amphibious animal called a Northern man with Southern principles. Color is no longer a crime or a badge of bondage. At last the out-spread wings of the American Eagle afford shelter and protection to men of all colors, all countries, and all climes, and the long oppressed black man may honorably fall or gloriously flourish under the star-spangled banner. (Applause.) I stand here tonight not only as a colored man and an American, but, by the express decision of the Attorney-General of the United States, as a colored citizen, having, in common with all other citizens, a stake in the safety, prosperity, honor, and glory of a common country.[16] (Cheering.) We are all liberated by this proclamation. Everybody is liberated. The white man is liberated, the black man is liberated, the brave men now fighting the battles of their country against rebels and traitors are now liberated, and may strike with all their might, even if they do by thus manfully striking hurt the Rebels, at their most sensitive point. (Applause.)

I congratulate you upon this amazing change—this amazing approximation toward the sacred truth of human liberty. All the space between man's mind and God's mind, says Parker,[17] is crowded with truths that wait to be discovered and organized into law for the better government of society. Mr. Lincoln has not exactly discovered a new truth, but he has dared, in this dark hour of national peril, to apply an old truth, long ago acknowledged in theory by the nation—a truth which carried the American people safely through the war for independence, and one which will carry us, as I believe, safely through the present terrible and sanguinary conflict for national life, if we shall but faithfully live up to that great truth. (Cheers.)

Born and reared as a slave, as I was, and wearing on my back the marks of a slave-driver's lash, as I do, it is natural that I should value the Emancipation Proclamation for what it is destined to do for the slaves. I do value it for that. It is a mighty event for the bondman, but it is a still mightier event for the nation at large, and mighty as it is for both, the slave and the nation, it is still mightier when viewed in its relation to the cause of truth and justice throughout the world. It is in this last character that I prefer to consider it. There are certain great national acts, which by their relation to universal principles, properly belong to the whole human family, and Abraham Lincoln's Proclamation of the 1st of January, 1863, is one of these acts. Henceforth shall that day take rank with the Fourth of July. (Applause.) Henceforth it becomes the date of a new and glorious era in the history of American liberty. Henceforth it shall stand associated in the minds of men, with all the stately steps of mankind, from the regions of error and oppression, which have lifted them from the trial by poison and fire to the trial by Jury—from the arbitrary will of a despot to the sacred writ of habeas corpus—from abject serfdom to absolute citizenship. It will stand in the history of civilization with Catholic Emancipation, with the British Reform Bill, with the repeal of the Corn Laws,[18] and with the noble act of Russian liberty, by which twenty millions of serfs, against the clamors of haughty tyrants, have been released from servitude. (Loud cheering.) Aye! It will stand with every distinguished event which marks any advance made by mankind from the thraldom and darkness of error to the glorious liberty of truth. I believe in the millennium—the final perfection of the race, and hail this Proclamation, though wrung out under the goading lash of a stern military necessity, as one reason of the hope that is in me. Men may see in it only a military necessity. To me it has a higher significance. It is a grand moral necessity.

> "Thrice is he armed who hath his quarrel just,
> And he but naked, though wrapped up in steel.
> Whose conscience with injustice is corrupted."[19]

The conscience of the North has been troubled during all this war. It has seen the inconsistency of fighting for Slavery. It has seen the absurdity of killing the Rebel, while asserting the Rebels' right to the slave. It has seen the folly of fighting the Rebels with our soft white hands, and keeping back our iron black hands. (Cheers). . . .

Let Slavery go down with the war, and let labor cease to be fettered, chained, flogged, and branded. Let it be paid honest wages for honest work, and then we shall see as never before, the laborers in all sections of this country rising to respectability and power. (Cheers.) That this war is to abolish Slavery I have no manner of doubt. The process may be long and tedious, but the event will come at last. It is among the undoubted certainties of the future. (Cheering.)

It is objected to the Proclamation of Freedom, that it only abolishes Slavery in the Rebel States. To me it seems a blunder that Slavery was not declared abolished everywhere in the Republic. Slavery everywhere[20] endangers the National cause, and should perish everywhere. (Loud applause.) But even in this omission of the Proclamation the evil is more seeming than real. When Virginia is a free State, Maryland cannot be a slave State. When Missouri is a free State, Kentucky cannot be a slave State. (Cheers.) Slavery must stand or fall together. Strike it at either extreme—either on the head or at the heel, and it dies. A brick knocked down at either end of the row brings every brick in it to the ground. (Applause.) You have heard the story of the Irishman who paid the price of two spurs—but refused to carry away but one; on the ground, as he said, that if he could make one side of his horse go, he would risk the other. (Laughter and cheering.) So I say, if we can strike down Slavery in the Rebel States, I will risk the downfall of Slavery in the Border States. (Cheering.)

It is again objected to this Proclamation that it is only an ink and paper proclamation. I admit it. The objector might go a step further, and assert that there was a time when this Proclamation was only a thought, a sentiment, an idea—a hope of some radical Abolitionist—for such it truly was. But what of it? The world has never advanced a single inch in the right direction, when the movement could not be traced to some such small beginning. . . . Greater than all, our own Declaration of Independence was at one time but ink and paper. (Cheering.) The freedom of the American colonies date from no particular battle during the war. No man can tell upon what particular day we won our national independence. But the birth of our freedom is fixed on the day of the going forth of the Declaration of Independence. In like manner, aftercoming generations will celebrate the first of January as the day which brought liberty and manhood to the American slaves. (Loud cheers.) How shall this be done? I answer: That paper Proclamation must now be made iron, lead and fire, by the prompt employment of the negro's arm in this contest. (Great applause.) I hold that the Proclamation, good as it is, will be worthless—a miserable mockery—unless the nation shall so far conquer its prejudice as to welcome into the army full-grown black men to help fight the battles of the Republic. (Renewed applause.) . . .

The colored man only waits for honorable admission into the service of the country. They know that who would be free, themselves must strike the blow, and they long for the opportunity to strike that blow. Thus far, however, the colored men of the Free States, and for the most part, of the Slave States, have had their military ardor chilled by the contempt with which their offer to serve their country has been refused. . . .

If I could speak loud enough to be heard by the Government at Washington I should say, have a care, have a care, lest you let slip the last moment when your call for help can be answered. You have wronged us long and wronged us greatly, but it is not yet too late to retrieve the past. We still stand ready to serve you, and will do it with a will, at the first sound of your war-trumpet. (Cheers.) I know the colored men of the North; I know the colored men of the South. They are ready to rally under the stars and stripes at the first tap of the drum. Give them a chance; stop calling them "niggers," and call them soldiers. (Applause.) Give them a chance to seek the bauble reputation at the cannon's mouth.[21] Stop telling them they can't fight, and tell them they can fight and shall fight, and they will fight, and fight with vengeance. Give them a chance. . . . Away with prejudice, away with folly, and in this death struggle for liberty, country, and permanent security, let the black, iron hand of the colored man fall heavily on the head of the slaveholding traitors and rebels and lay them low. Give them a chance! Give them a chance. I don't say they are great fighters. I don't say they will fight better than other men. All I say is, give them a chance.

I feel that we are living in a glorious time. I felt so on the first of January, and have been feeling so ever since. I felt whiter, and I have combed my hair with less difficulty. (Cheers and laughter.) You had a grand time here, and we had a grand time at Boston. We had two machines running—at Music Hall and Tremont Temple—more than three thousand at each. You want to know what the colored people think. I will tell you how joyfully they received the Proclamation of Abraham Lincoln. We were not all colored either; but we all seemed to be about of one color that day. We met in good spirits at 10 o'clock expecting before the adjournment to have the Proclamation. We had waited on each speaker keeping our eye on the door. No

Proclamation. The President said we would meet again at two when he had no doubt we should have read the Proclamation. We met again but no Proclamation. We did not know whether to shout or hold our peace but we adjourned again with the understanding that it was on the wires and we should certainly see it in the evening. But no Proclamation came. We went on until 11 o'clock and I said, we won't go home till morning. By and by Judge [Thomas] Russell went to one of the newspaper offices and obtained a slip containing the Proclamation. I never saw enthusiasm before. I never saw joy before. Men, women, young and old, were up; hats and bonnets were in the air, and we gave three cheers for Abraham Lincoln and three cheers for about[22] everybody else. Some prayed and some sang, and finally we adjourned from that place to meet in the Rev. Mr. Grimes' Church;[23] that good old soul (laughter) and we continued greeting them till 3 o'clock. There was shouting and singing, "Glory, Hallelujah," "Old John Brown," "Marching On," and "Blow Ye, the Trumpet Blow!"—till we got up such a state of enthusiasm that almost anything seemed to be witty—and entirely appropriate to the glorious occasion. . . . The feeling of the whole of this black congregation—for it was mainly black—was that they were ready to offer their services at any moment this Government should call for them. And I want to assure you, and the Government, and everybody, that we are ready, and we only ask to be called into this service. What a glorious day when Slavery shall be no more in this country, when we have blotted out this system of wrong, and made this United States in fact and in truth what it is in theory—The Land of the Free and the Home of the Brave. (Loud applause.)

Rev. Leonard A. Grimes, pastor of Twelfth Baptist Church in Boston, raised money to free Anthony Burns in 1854 and helped raise the 54th Massachusetts Infantry in 1863. Prints and Photographs Division, Library of Congress

"The Enlistment of Colored Men," Address at a Mass Meeting Held at National Hall, Philadelphia, July 6, 1863 (excerpts) Philadelphia *North American and United States Gazette*, July 8, 1863

The case presented in the present war, and the light in which every colored man is bound to view it, may be stated thus. There are two governments struggling now for the possession of and endeavoring to bear rule over the United States—one has its capital in Richmond, and is represented by Mr. Jefferson Davis, and the other has its capital at Washington, and is represented by "Honest Old Abe."[24] These two governments are to-day face to face, confronting each other with vast armies, and grappling each other upon many a bloody field, north and south, on the banks of the Mississippi, and under the shadows of the Alleghenies. Now, the question for every colored man is, or ought to be, what attitude is assumed by these respective governments and armies toward the rights and liberties of the colored race in this country; which is for us and which against us?[25]

Now, I think there can be no doubt as to the attitude of the Richmond or confederate government. . . .

Now, what is the attitude of the Washington government towards the colored race? What reasons have we to desire its triumph in the present contest? . . . Events more mighty than men, eternal Providence, all-wise and all-controlling, have placed us in new relations to the government and the government to us. What that government is to us to-day, and what it will be tomorrow, is made evident by a very few facts. Look at them, colored men. Slavery in the District of Columbia is abolished forever; slavery in all the territories of the United States is abolished forever; the foreign slave trade, with its ten thousand revolting abominations, is rendered impossible; slavery in ten States of the Union is abolished forever; slavery in the five remaining States is as certain to follow the same fate as the night is to follow the day. The independence of Hayti is recognized; her Minister sits beside our Prime Minister, Mr. Seward, and dines at his table in Washington,[26] while colored men are excluded from the cars in Philadelphia; showing that a black man's complexion in Washington, in the presence of the Federal government, is less offensive than in the city of brotherly love. Citizenship is no longer denied us under this government.

Under the interpretation of our rights by Attorney General Bates, we are American citizens. We can import goods, own and sail ships, and travel in foreign countries with American passports in our pockets; and now, so far from there being any opposition, so far from excluding us from the army as soldiers, the President at Washington, the Cabinet and the Congress, the generals commanding the whole army of the nation unite in giving us one thunderous welcome to share with them in the honor and glory of suppressing treason and upholding the star-spangled banner. The revolution is tremendous, and it becomes us as wise men to recognize the change, and to shape our action accordingly.[27]

Letter to Maj. George L. Stearns,[28] August 1, 1863
Douglass' Monthly, August 1863

ROCHESTER, August 1st, 1863.

MAJOR G. L. STEARNS:—MY DEAR SIR—

Having declined to attend the meeting to promote enlistments, appointed for me at Pittsburgh, in present circumstances, I owe you a word of explanation. I have hitherto deemed it a duty, as it certainly has been a pleasure, to cooperate with you in the work of raising colored troops in the free states, to fight the battles of the Republic against the slaveholding rebels and traitors. Upon the first call you gave me to this work, I responded with alacrity. I saw, or thought I saw, a ray of light, brightening the future of my whole race as well as that of our war-troubled country, in arousing colored men to fight for the nation's life. I continue to believe in the black man's arm, and still have some hope in the integrity of our rulers. Nevertheless, I must for the present leave to others the work of persuading colored men to join the Union Army. I owe it to my long abused people, and especially to those already in the army, to expose their wrongs and plead their cause. I cannot do that in connection with recruiting.

When I plead for recruits, I want to do it with all my heart, without qualification. I cannot do that now.

The impression settles upon me that colored men have much overrated the enlightenment, justice and generosity of our rulers at Washington. In my humble way I have contributed somewhat to that false estimate. You know that when the idea of raising colored troops was first suggested, the special duty to be assigned them, was the garrisoning of forts and arsenals in certain warm, unhealthy and miasmatic localities in the South. They were thought to be better adapted to that service than white troops. White troops, trained to war, brave and daring, were to take fortifications, and the blacks were to hold them and keep them from falling again into the hands of the rebels. Three advantages were to arise out of this wise division of labor. 1st. The spirit and pride of white troops was not to waste itself in dull and monotonous inactivity in fort-life. Their arms were to be kept bright by constant use. 2dly. The health of white troops was to be preserved. 3dly. Black troops were to have the advantage of sound military training, and be otherwise useful at the same time that they should be tolerably secure from capture by the rebels, who early avowed their determination to enslave and slaughter them in defiance of the laws of war. Two out of the three advantages were to accrue to the white troops. Thus far, however, I believe that no such duty as holding fortifications has been committed to colored troops. They have done far other and more important work than holding fortifications. I have no special complaint to make at this point, and I simply mention it to strengthen the statement that from the beginning of this business it was the confident belief among both the colored and white friends of colored enlistments that President Lincoln as Commander-in-Chief of the army and navy would certainly see to it that his colored troops should be so handled and disposed of as to be but little exposed to capture by the rebels, and that—if so exposed—as they have repeatedly been from the first, the President possessed both the disposition and the means for compelling the rebels to respect the rights of such as might fall into their hands.

The piratical proclamation of President Davis, announcing Slavery and assassination to colored prisoners, was before the country and the world. But men had faith in Mr. Lincoln and his advisers. He was silent, to be sure, but charity suggested that being a man of action rather than words, he only waited for a case in which he should be required to act. This faith in the man enabled us to speak with warmth and effect in urging enlistments among colored men. That faith, my dear Sir, is now nearly gone.[29] Various occasions have arisen during the last six months for the exercise of his power in behalf of the colored men in his service. But no word comes from Mr. Lincoln or from the War Department, sternly assuring the Rebel Chief that inquisitions shall yet be made for innocent blood. No word of retaliation when a black man is slain by a rebel in cold blood. No word was said when free men from Massachusetts were caught and sold into slavery in Texas. No word is said when brave black men who according to the testimony of both friend and foe, fought like heroes to plant the star-spangled banner on the blazing parapets of Fort Wagner, and in so doing were captured, some mutilated and killed, and others sold into slavery. The same crushing silence reigns over this scandalous outrage as over that of the slaughtered teamsters at Murfreesboro. The same as over that at Millikens Bend and Vicksburg. I am free to say, my dear sir, that the case looks as if the confiding colored soldiers had been betrayed into bloody hands by the very Government in whose defense they were heroically fighting.

I know what you will say to this; you will say; "wait a little longer, and after all, the best way to have justice done to your people is to get them into the army as fast as possible." You may be right in this; my argument has been the same, but have we not already waited, and have we not already shown the highest qualities of soldiers, and on this account deserve the protection of the Government for which we are fighting? Can any case stronger than that before Charleston ever arise? If the President is ever to demand justice and humanity, for black soldiers, is not this the time for him to do it? How many 54ths[30] must be cut to pieces, its mutilated prisoners killed, and its living sold into Slavery, to be tortured to death by inches before Mr. Lincoln shall say: "Hold, enough!"

You know the 54th. To you, more than to any one man belongs the credit of raising that Regiment. Think of its noble and brave officers literally hacked to pieces while many of its rank and file have been sold into slavery, worse than death, and pardon me if I hesitate about assisting in raising a fourth Regiment until the President shall give the same protection to them as to white soldiers.

With warm and sincere regards,

FREDERICK DOUGLASS.

Since writing the foregoing letter, which we have now put upon record, we have received assurances from Major Stearns, that the Government of the United States is already taking measures which will secure for the captured colored soldiers, at Charleston and elsewhere, the same protection against slavery and cruelty, extended to white soldiers. What ought to have been done at the beginning, comes late, but it comes. The poor colored soldiers have purchased this interference dearly. It really seems that nothing of justice, liberty or humanity can come to us except through tears and blood.[31]

"The Commander-in-Chief and His Black Soldiers"
Douglass' Monthly, August 1863

Whatever else may be said of President Lincoln, the most malignant Copperhead[32] in the country cannot reproach him with any undue solicitude for the lives and liberties of the brave black men, who are now giving their arms and hearts to the support of his Government. When a boy, on a slave plantation, the saying was common: "Half a cent to kill a negro and half a cent to bury him." The luxury of killing and burying could be enjoyed by the poorest members of Southern society, and no strong temptation was required to induce white men thus to kill and bury the black victims of their lust and cruelty. With a Bible and pulpit affirming that the negro is accursed of God, it is not strange that men should curse him, and that all over the South there should be manifested for the life and liberty of this description of man, the utterest indifference and contempt. Unhappily the same indifference and contempt for the lives of colored men is found wherever slavery has an advocate or treason an apologist. In the late terrible mobs in New York[33] and elsewhere, the grim features of this malice towards colored men was everywhere present. Beat, shoot, hang, stab, kill, burn and destroy the negro, was the cry of the crowd. Religion has cursed him and the law has enslaved him, and why may not the mob kill him? Such has been our national education on this subject, and that it still has power over Mr. Lincoln seems evident from the fact, that no measures have been openly taken by him to cause the laws of civilized warfare to be observed towards his colored soldiers. The slaughter of blacks taken as captives, seems to affect him as little as the slaughter of beeves for the use of his army.

More than six months ago Mr. Jefferson Davis told Mr. Lincoln and the world, that he meant to treat blacks not as soldiers but as felons. The threat was openly made, and has been faithfully executed by the rebel chief. At Murfreesboro twenty colored teamsters in the Federal service, were taken by the rebels, and though not soldiers, and only servants, they were in cold blood—every man of them—shot down. At Millikens Bend, the same black flag with its death's head and cross-bones was raised. When Banks[34] entered Port Hudson he found white federal prisoners, but no black ones. Those of the latter taken, were no doubt, in cold blood put to the sword. To-day, news from Charleston tells us that negro soldiers taken as prisoners will not be exchanged, but sold into slavery—that some twenty of such prisoners are now in their hands. Thousands of negroes are now being enrolled in the service of the Federal Government. The Government calls them, and they come. They freely and joyously rally around the flag of the Union, and take all the risks, ordinary and extraordinary, involved in this war. They do it not for office, for thus far, they get none; they do it not for money, for thus far, their pay is less than that of white men. They go into this war to affirm their manhood, to strike for liberty and country. If any class of men in this war can claim the honor of fighting for principle, and not from passion, for ideas, not from brutal malice, the colored soldier can make that claim preeminently. He strikes for manhood and freedom, under the forms of law and the usages of civilized warfare. He does not go forth as a savage with tomahawk and scalping knife, but in strict accordance with the rules of honorable warfare. Yet he is now openly threatened with slavery and assassination by the rebel Government—and the threat has been savagely executed.

What has Mr. Lincoln to say about this slavery and murder? What has he said? Not one word. In the hearing of the nation he is as silent as an oyster on the whole subject. If two white men are threatened with assassination, the Richmond Rebels are promptly informed that the Federal Government will retaliate sternly and severely. But when colored soldiers are so threatened, no word comes from the Capitol. What does this silence mean? Is there any explanation short of base and scandalous contempt for the just rights of colored soldiers?

For a time we tried to think that there might be solid reasons of state against answering the threats of Jefferson Davis—but the Government has knocked this favorable judgment from under us, by its prompt threat of retaliation in the case of the two white officers at Richmond who are under sentence of death. Men will ask, the world will ask, why interference should be made for those young white officers thus selected for murder, and not for the brave black soldiers who may be flung by the fortunes of war into the hands of the rebels? Is the right to "life, liberty and the pursuit of happiness" less sacred in the case of the one than the other?

It may be said that the black soldiers have enlisted with the threat of Jefferson Davis before them, and they have assumed their position intelligently, with a full knowledge of the consequences incurred. If they have, they have by that act shown themselves all the more worthy of protection. It is noble in the negro to brave unusual danger for the life of the Republic, but it is mean and base in the Republic if it rewards such generous and unselfish devotion by assassination, when a word would suffice to make the laws of war respected, and to prevent the crime. Shocking enough are the ordinary horrors of war, but the war of the rebels toward the colored men is marked by deeds which well might "shame extremest hell."[35] And until Mr. Lincoln shall interpose his power to prevent these atrocious assassinations of negro soldiers, the civilized world will hold him equally with Jefferson Davis responsible for them.

The question is already being asked: Why is it that colored soldiers which were first enlisted with a view to "Garrison forts and arsenals, on the Southern coast," where white men suffer from climate, should never be heard of in any such forts and arsenals? Was that a trick? Why is it that they who were enlisted to fight the fevers of the South, while white soldiers fight the rebels, are now only heard of in "forlorn hopes," in desperate charges, always in the van, as at Port Hudson, Milliken Bend, James Island and Fort Wagner? Green colored recruits are called upon to assume the position of veterans. They have performed their part gallantly and gloriously, but by all the proofs they have given of their patriotism and bravery we protest against the meanness, ingratitude and cruelty of the Government, in whose behalf they fight, if that Government remains longer a silent witness of their enslavement and assassination. Having had patience and forbearance with the silence of Mr. Lincoln a few months ago, we could at least imagine some excuses for his silence as to the fate of colored troops falling by the fortunes of war into the hands of the rebels, but the time for this is past. It is now for every man who has any sense of right and decency, to say nothing of gratitude, to speak out trumpet-tongued in the ears of Mr. Lincoln and his Government and demand from him a declaration of purpose, to hold the rebels to a strict account for every black federal soldier taken as a prisoner. For every black prisoner slain in cold blood, Mr. Jefferson Davis should be made to understand that one rebel officer shall suffer death, and for every colored soldier sold into slavery, a rebel shall be held as a hostage. For our Government to do less than this, is to deserve the indignation and the execration of mankind.

Report of Speech at Fifteenth Avenue Presbyterian Church, Washington, DC, August 10, 1863
New-York Tribune, August 13, 1863

The black orator, Frederick Douglass, spoke to a large audience in the Fifteenth-street Church on Monday evening on the prospective overthrow of the Slaveholders' Rebellion and the redemption of his race. He referred with gratitude to the kind attention which President Lincoln[36] and leading members of the Cabinet had extended to him, and said that the revolution in Northern sentiments and prejudices is hardly less than that going forward on Southern plantations. He said the time had at last come when the colored people could honorably offer themselves to the Government, and that in rising in defense of their country now, they were, in a very literal sense, rising in defense of themselves—in marching upon the Rebels and Slavery, they were really asserting their manhood, striking down their disabilities, and laying siege to the base citadels of prejudice in the North. Self-respect and safety called them as loudly as patriotism. Douglass said he had been commissioned by the President to assist in the organization of his people for the war.

Copy of Letter to Maj. George L. Stearns, August 12, 1863
Abraham Barker Collection on the Free Military School for Applicants for the Command of Colored Regiments, Historical Society of Pennsylvania

Head Quarters 1210 Chestnut St
Phila Aug 12th 1863

Maj Geo L Stearns.
A.A.G. USV &c[37]
Dear Sir,

According to your request I paid a flying visit to Washington. I spent the entire day (Monday) in calling upon the Heads of Depts there and other influential persons[.] I had the good fortune, early in the morning after reaching there, of meeting with Senator Pomeroy[38] who at once offered to accompany me and facilitate my mission.

First I called on Secty Stanton at the War Department who kindly granted me an interview of about thirty minutes which must be considered a special privalege in view of the many pressing demands upon his time and attention. His manner was cold and business like throughout but earnest.

I at once gave him in brief my theory of the elements of negro character which should be had in view in all measures for raising colored troops. I told him that the negro was the victim of two extreme opinions. One claimed for him too much and the other too little. That it was a mistake to regard him either as an angel or a demon. He is simply a man and should be dealt with purely as such[.] That a certain percentage of negroes were brave and others cowardly. That a part were ambitious and aspiring and another part quite otherwise and that the theory in practice of Government in raising colored troops should conform to these essential facts. The Secty instantly inquired in what respect the present conditions of colored enlistments conflicted with the views I had expressed. I answered "In the unequal pay accorded to colored soldiers and in the fact that no incentive was given to the ambition of colored soldiers and that the regulations confined them to the dead level of privates or non-commissioned officers[."]

In answer the Secty went into an interesting history of the whole subject of the employment of Colored Troops briefly mentioning some of the difficulties and prejudices to be surmounted[.] Gave a history of the bill drawn up by himself giving equal pay, the same rations, the same uniforms, and equipments, to colored troops as to White, and spoke with much apparent regret. his[39] bill, though passed in the House was defeated in the Senate on what he considered quite an insufficient reason alleging that the President already possessed necessary powers to employ colored troops.

I told Mr Stanton that I held it to be the duty of Colored men to fight for the Government even though they should be offered but subsistance and arms considering that we had a cause quite independent of pay or place. But he quickly responded "That he was in favor of giving the same pay to black as to white soldiers and also of making merit the criterion of promotion further stating his readiness to grant commissions to any reported to him by their superior officers for their capacity or bravery.["] The conclusion of our conversation was, That Gen Thomas[40] was now vigorously engaged in organizing colored troops on the Mississippi and that he (the Secty) wished me to report to Gen Thomas and cooperate with him in raising said troops. I told the Secty that I was already at work under the direction of Major Stearns and that I thought that he would still need my services. But the Secty thought I had better report as aforesaid, adding that he would send me the sufficient papers immediately. Thus you see, My dear Sir, that you have sent me to Washington to some purpose. Mr Stanton was very imperative in his manner, and I did not know but that you had suggested this prompt employment of me, from the fact that you inquired as to my willingness to go South in this work. My interview with Mr Stanton was free from compliments of every kind. There was nothing from him to me, nor from me to him, but I felt myself stopped in regard to your own efficient services not so much from his manner as from what I knew to be your own wishes—

From the War Office I went directly to the White House[.] Saw for the first time the President of the United States. Was received cordially and saw at a glance the justice of the popular estimate of his qualities expressed in the prefix "*Honest*" to the name of Abraham Lincoln. I have never seen a more transparent countenance[.] There was not the slightest shadow of embarrassment after the first moment. The drift of my communication to the President, except that I thanked him for extending Equal protection to Colored Prisoners of War, was much the same as that to the Secty of War. I desired only to say so much as to furnish a text for a discourse from Mr Lincoln himself. In this I was quite successful for the President instantly upon my ceasing to speak proceeded with an earnestness and fluency of which I had not suspected him, to vindicate his policy respecting the whole slavery question and especially that in reference to employing colored troops.

I need not here repeat his views[.] One remark, however, of his was of much significance[.] He said he had frequently been charged with tardiness, hesitation and the like, especially in regard to issuing his retaliatory proclamation. But had he sooner issued that proclamation such was the state of public popular prejudice that an outcry would have been raised against the measure[.] It would be said "Ah! We thought it would come to this. White men were to be killed for negroes.["] His general view was that the battles in which negroes had distinguished themselves for bravery and general good conduct was the necessary preparation of the public mind for his proclamation. But the best thing said by the President was "I have been charged with vacillation even by so good a man as Jno. Sherman of Ohio,[39] but" said he "I think the charge cannot be sustained[.] No man can say that having once taken the position I have contradicted it or retreated from it[.]" This remark of the President I took as an assurance that whoever else might abandon his anti-slavery policy President Lincoln would stand firm to his. My whole interview with the President was gratifying and did much to assure me that slavery would not survive the War and that the Country would survive both Slavery and the War. I am very sorry[,] my Dear Sir, not to see you before leaving[.] I should be glad to have a line from you if convenient before I leave Rochester.

With Great Respect and Regard
Your Ob^t^ Servant.
(Signed) *Fred^k^ Douglass*

Letter to Mary Carpenter, ca. September 1863[42] (excerpt)
London *Inquirer*, October 10, 1863

It is now nearly one month since I went to Washington, had a talk with the Secretary of War, and with the President of the United States. They gave me a respectful hearing. I went there to urge upon them the impolicy and injustice of asking and requiring colored men to fight the battles of their country for less pay than white men receive, and to protest against the rule which deprives the colored soldier of all hope of

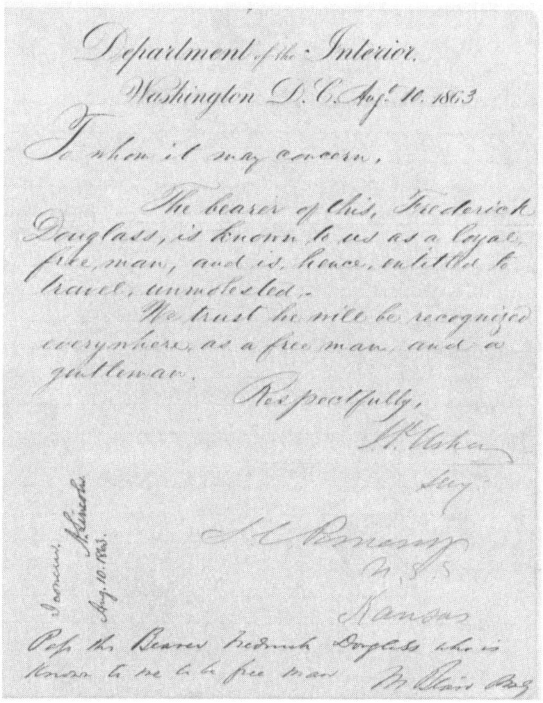
Department of the Interior.
Washington D.C. Aug. 10. 1863

To whom it may concern,

The bearer of this, Frederick Douglass, is known to us as a loyal, free, man, and is, hence, entitled to travel, unmolested.

We trust he will be recognized everywhere, as a free man, and a gentleman.

Respectfully,
J.P. Usher
Secy
S.C. Pomeroy
U.S.
Kansas

Pass the Bearer Frederick Douglass who is known to me to be free man M Blair PMG

I concur. A. Lincoln
Aug. 10. 1863.

John P. Usher and Samuel C. Pomeroy letter to Whom it May Concern, August 10, 1863, stating that Douglass "is known to us as a loyal, free, man, and is, hence, entitled to travel, unmolested." They added: "We trust he will be recognized everywhere, as a free man, and a gentleman." Lincoln endorsed the letter the same day: "I concur." However, Douglass was frustrated that he was being offered a pass as a private citizen rather than as a commissioned officer. Frederick Douglass National Historic Site

promotion. They heard me, as I have said, respectfully, and I may add, with assurances that the next Congress would blot out these discriminations, and give the colored soldier the same pay that is given to white ones. Finally the subject turned upon myself, and as I avowed my willingness to serve the State in any way that my services could be made available, the Secretary of War promptly said he would give me a commission to assist Adjutant-General Thomas in organising coloured troops in the South-West. I agreed to go at once, and left for home to arrange my affairs for the purpose; but thus far no commission has reached me, and I now doubt if any will reach me. They now want me to go simply as a private person, without any commission. This I am not quite prepared to do, for many reasons. It was all well enough to work for the Government here in the free States without a regular commission, where I am known, and to some extent respected, where I run no risk of capture by the enemy; but to go into the very heart of the slave country, with enemies all around me, liable at any moment to kill me or take me prisoner, I want the protection that a Government would give me; for if taken without such a commission

I should have no protection whatever. On the principles acted upon by our army and by the laws of war, the rebels would be justified in treating me as a spy, to be hanged or shot at their pleasure. In asking me to go without the United States' uniform, the Government asks me to go in the detestable and dangerous character of a spy. I will do no such thing; and am therefore now at home, and for the moment without any settled activity.

Address to the American Anti-Slavery Society, Philadelphia, December 4, 1863 (excerpts)

Henry M. Parkhurst, ed., *Proceedings of the American Anti-Slavery Society, at its Third Decade, Held in the City of Philadelphia, Dec. 3d and 4th, 1863* (New York: American Anti-Slavery Society, 1864)

For twenty-five years, Mr. President, you know that when I got as far South as Philadelphia, I felt that I was rubbing against my prison wall, and could not go any further. I dared not go over yonder into Delaware. Twenty years ago, when I attended the first decade meeting of this Society, as I came along the vales and hills of Gettysburg, my good friends, the anti-slavery people along there warned me to remain in the house during the day-time, and travel in the night, lest I should be kidnapped, and carried over into Maryland. My good friend, Dr. FUSSELL,[43] was one of the number who did not think it safe for me to attend an Anti-Slavery meeting along the borders of this State. I can go down there now. I have been down there to see the President; and as you were not there, perhaps you may like to know how the President of the United States received a black man at the White House. I will tell you how he received me—just as you have seen one gentleman receive another (great applause); with a hand and a voice well-balanced between a kind cordiality and a respectful reserve. I tell you I felt big there! (Laughter.) Let me tell you how I got to him; because everybody can't get to him. He has to be a little guarded in admitting spectators. The manner of getting to him gave me an idea that the cause was rolling on. The stairway was crowded with applicants. Some of them looked eager; and I have no doubt some of them had a purpose in being there, and wanted to see the President for the good of the country! They were white; and as I was the only dark spot among them, I expected to have to wait at least half a day; I had heard of men waiting a week; but in two minutes after I sent in my card, the messenger came out, and respectfully invited "Mr. DOUGLASS" in. I could hear, in the eager multitude outside, as they saw me pressing and elbowing my way through, the remark, "Yes, damn it, I knew they would let the nigger through," in a kind of despairing voice—a Peace Democrat, I suppose. (Laughter.) When I went in, the President was sitting in his usual position, I was told, with his feet in different parts of the room, taking it easy. (Laughter.) Don't put this down, Mr. Reporter, I pray you; for I am going down there again to-morrow! (Laughter.) As I came in and approached him, the President began to rise, (laughter,) and he continued rising until he stood over me (laughter); and, reaching out his hand, he said, "Mr. DOUGLASS, I know you; I have read about you, and Mr. SEWARD has told me about you"; putting me quite at ease at once.

Now, you will want to know how I was impressed by him. I will tell you that, too. He impressed me as being just what every one of you have been in the habit of calling him—an honest man. (Applause.) I never met with a man, who, on the first blush, impressed me more entirely with his sincerity, with his devotion to his country, and with his determination to save it at all hazards. (Applause.) He told me (I think he did me more honor than I deserve) that I had made a little speech, somewhere in New York, and it had got into the papers, and among the things I had said was this: That if I were called upon to state what I regarded as the most sad and most disheartening feature in our present political and military situation, it would not be the various disasters experienced by our armies and our navies, on flood and field, but it would be the tardy, hesitating, vacillating policy of the President of the United States; and the President said to me, "Mr. DOUGLASS, I have been charged with being tardy, and the like"; and he went on, and partly admitted that he might seem slow; but he said, "I am charged with vacillating; but, Mr. DOUGLASS, I do not think that charge can be sustained; I think it cannot be shown that when I have once taken a position, I have ever retreated from it." (Applause.) That I regarded as the most significant point in what he said during our interview. I told him that he had been somewhat slow in proclaiming equal protection to our colored soldiers and prisoners; and he said that the country needed talking up to that point. He hesitated in regard to it, when he felt that the country was not ready for it. He knew that the colored man throughout this country was a despised man, a hated man, and that if he at first came out with such a proclamation, all the hatred which is poured on the head of the negro race would be visited on his administration. He said that there was preparatory work needed, and that that preparatory work had now been done. And he said, "Remember this, Mr. DOUGLASS; remember that Milliken's Bend, Port Hudson and Fort Wagner are recent events; and that these were necessary to prepare the way for this very proclamation of mine." I thought it was reasonable, but came to the conclusion that while ABRAHAM LINCOLN will not go down to posterity as ABRAHAM the Great, or as ABRAHAM the Wise, or as ABRAHAM the Eloquent, although he is all three, wise, great and eloquent, he will go down to posterity, if the country is saved, as Honest ABRAHAM (applause); and going down thus, his name may be written any where in this wide world of ours side by side with that of WASHINGTON, without disparaging the latter. (Renewed applause.)

But we are not to be saved by the captain, at this time, but by the crew. We are not to be saved by ABRAHAM LINCOLN, but by that power behind the throne, greater than the throne itself. You and I and all of us have this matter in hand. . . . We are fighting for unity; unity of idea, unity of sentiment, unity of object, unity of institutions, in which there shall be no North, no South, no East, no West, no black, no white, but a solidarity of the nation, making every slave free, and every free man a voter. (Great applause.)

"The Mission of the War," Address Delivered at the Cooper Union, New York City, January 13, 1864 (excerpts)
New-York Tribune, January 14, 1864

It is true we have the Proclamation of January, 1863. It was a vast and glorious step in the right direction. But unhappily, excellent as that paper is—and much as it has accomplished temporarily—it settles nothing. It is still open to decision by courts, canons and Congresses. I have applauded that paper and do now applaud it, as a wise measure—while I detest the motive and principle upon which it is based. By it the holding and flogging of negroes is the exclusive luxury of loyal men.

Our chief danger lies in the absence of all moral feeling in the utterances of our rulers. In his letter to Mr. Greeley[44] the President told the country virtually that the abolition or non-abolition of Slavery was a matter of indifference to him. He would save the Union with Slavery or without Slavery. In his last Message he shows the same moral indifference, by saying as he does say that he had hoped that the Rebellion could be put down without the abolition of Slavery.[45]

When the late Stephen A. Douglas uttered the sentiment that he did not care whether Slavery were voted up or voted down in the Territories, we thought him lost to all genuine feeling on the subject, and no man more than Mr. Lincoln denounced that sentiment as unworthy of the lips of any American statesman. But to-day, after nearly three years of a Slaveholding Rebellion, we find Mr. Lincoln uttering substantially the same heartless sentiments. Douglas wanted Popular Sovereignty; Mr. Lincoln wants the Union. Now did a warm heart and a high moral feeling control the utterances of the President, he would welcome, with joy unspeakable and full of glory, the opportunity afforded by the Rebellion to free the country from the matchless crime and infamy. But policy, policy, everlasting policy, has robbed our statesmanship of all soul-moving utterances. . . .

I have now given, very briefly, some of the grounds of danger. A word as to the grounds of hope. The best that can be offered is, that we have made progress—vast and striking progress—within the last two years.

President Lincoln introduced his administration to the country as one which would faithfully catch, hold, and return runaway slaves to their masters. He avowed his determination to protect and defend the slaveholder's right to plunder the black laborer of his hard earnings. Europe was assured by Mr. Seward that no slave should gain his freedom by this war. Both the President and the Secretary of State have made progress since then. . . .

The Rebellion has been a rapid educator. Congress was the first to respond to the instinctive judgment of the people, and fixed the broad brand of its reprobation upon slave-hunting in shoulder-straps. Then came very temperate talk about confiscation, which soon came to be pretty radical talk. Then came propositions for Border-State, gradual, compensated, colonized Emancipation. Then came the threat of a proclamation, and then came the proclamation. Meanwhile the negro had passed along from a loyal spade and pickax to a Springfield rifle.

Hayti and Liberia are recognized. Slavery is humbled in Maryland,[46] threatened in Tennessee,[47] stunned nearly to death in Western Virginia,[48] doomed in Missouri,[49] trembling in Kentucky,[50] and gradually melting away before our arms in the rebellious States.

The hour is one of hope as well as danger.

Report of "The Mission of the War" Address Delivered at the Cooper Union, New York City, January 13, 1864 (excerpt)
New York Times, January 14, 1864

He had hoped that Slavery and rebellion would find a common grave without further discussion, but found that the Proclamation settled nothing permanently. It may yet be negatived by Congress, the Supreme Court, or by cannon. He detested its principles. It says to rebels, we will take your slaves, but to loyal men, you may keep yours. It should have stricken Slavery everywhere. The President was brought to it with reluctance, as may be found in his letter to Mr. Greeley. I have been to see the President—a man in a low condition, meeting a high one. Not Greek meeting Greek,[51] exactly, but railsplitter meeting nigger. Perhaps you would like to know how I, a negro, was received at the White House by the President of the United States. Why, precisely as one gentleman would be received by another. (Applause.) He extended me a cordial hand, not too warm or too cold. I had previously in a speech attacked him for his tardiness and vacillation. Without alluding especially to this speech, he defended himself against the charge of vacillation. "Mr. Douglass, ('he addressed me as *Mr.* Douglass,' added the speaker laughingly,) when I take a position, I think no man can say I retreat from it." Like the rest of us, however, he has often been restrained by policy from doing what he felt to be a virtue; and that should be done.

Report of "The Mission of the War" Address Delivered at the Cooper Union, New York City, January 13, 1864 (excerpt)
New York Herald, January 14, 1864

He did not like the proclamation of Mr. Lincoln, because it said to take the slaves from the traitors in the South, but to leave them with loyal men. He did not like that. He had tried to impress it on the President, but it did no good. He hardly believed the President though, for he knew him too well—he had been to see him. (Cheers and laughter.) It was no Greek meeting Greek when they met—(more laughter)—but it was a rail splitter meeting a nigger. (Boisterous laughter.) Probably some of them would like to know how "the black man was received at the White House?" He received me, continued the speaker, for all the world just as you see one gentleman receive another—(shouts of laughter)—with the hand and the voice of welcome; not too cordially nor too coldly, but just the right thing; and I made myself quite at home in his presence. One thing I told him then which I now tell you; and it was, that if I were called upon to point out the most discouraging feature of the present situation, it would not be any of the distress experienced by flood and field by our forces, but it would be the tardiness, and hesitation and vascillation of the President of the United States. Mr. Lincoln did not, of course, admit that this came from me, but went on at once to defend himself from the charges brought—and there was one charge he did not defend himself from at all. He admitted that he was slow, but would not allow it to be understood that he was vascillating. He said to me, with great earnestness, "Mr. Douglass, I don't think that charge can be sustained." Think of the President of the United States addressing a black man as Mr. Douglass. (Laughter.) He moved his hands back and forth as he said, "Vascillation," says he, "I don't think that can be sustained, sir." (Laughter.) Says he, "When I take a position I think no man can say that I ever retreat." (Cheers.) But his warm heart and high feelings, the speaker continued to say, did not control Mr. Lincoln's utterances. It was policy, policy, prudence, prudence with him. So it was we were trying to crush every noble utterance, but doing from necessity what we knew in our heart of hearts to be a great virtue, and as such was demanded to be done.

Letter to Julia Griffiths Crofts, dated Rochester, New York, March 23, 1864[52] (excerpts)
Leeds Mercury, April 22, 1864

I have never worked harder, and I think never more successfully, than this winter. Co-operating with the mighty events which are still sweeping on with resistless force, I have been endeavouring to persuade the people to come fully up to the demands of justice, and to abandon all temporising schemes for getting out of their present troubles, knowing, as I do, that if the people of this country shall now, when in the fierce heat and light of the furnace of affliction, fail to do full justice to the negro, it may be centuries before they can again be brought up to that measure. The light that begets a disregarded conviction can never be sufficient to beget a similar one. Every time the metal is put in the crucible it becomes harder, and only melts under an intenser heat. The American people are now pretty generally convinced that they must do something with the coloured man—what that something shall be is now the important question. He cannot be, as formerly, an absolute slave. All seem to admit that;

but shall he be an absolute free man? I say, yes—in the fullest sense. I advocate making him a part of the American people—a legal voter, and eligible to any and every office, from postmaster to President. Some say I ask too much; but even those who say so have nothing but prejudice with which to meet my arguments. . . .

I see, by the London *Times*, that the attempt of General Banks to establish in the far South a system of serfdom instead of slavery, is attracting deserved attention.[53] Heaven grant that the civilized world may thunder its protest against this shameless enormity! Hitherto we have commended the cause of the North to the people of Europe by affirming that ours is the cause of liberty and progress. We shall deserve the execration of good men everywhere if, after winning British and European sympathy on that ground, we shall shamelessly turn our backs upon our professed principles, and go back to a system long since blotted out by every Christian Power save Russia, and which even she is now blotting out. You, on your side of the Atlantic, can do vast and important service, by keeping a wakeful eye upon our affairs and the course of events here, and by administering a word of timely admonition when you see us halting between truth and error. . . .

Slavery in all its forms, and the slave power, whether supported by slavery or serfdom, is the deadly enemy of the peace, prosperity, and happiness of the country. You are, no doubt, anxious to know, as I am, when this terrible civil strife will end. I wish I could tell you. I have no expectation that it will be before next November. The rebels, I think, may be relied on to fight until after the Presidential election, in the hope of helping their Northern friends, the 'Copperheads,' to elect McClellan,[54] with whom they will find it easy to make terms in case he is elected. There is, however, at present, a very poor chance for any Copperhead candidate.

Letter to Mary Carpenter, ca. June 1864[55] (excerpt)
London *Inquirer*, August 13, 1864[56]

The more you can say of the swindle by which our Government claims the respect of mankind for abolishing slavery—at the same time that it is practically re-establishing that hateful system in Louisiana, under General Banks—the better. I have not readily consented to the claims set up in the name of anti-slavery for our Government, but I have tried to believe all for the best. My patience and faith are not very strong now. The treatment of our poor black soldiers—the refusal to pay them anything like equal compensation, though it was promised them when they enlisted; the refusal to insist upon the exchange of coloured prisoners, and to retaliate upon rebel prisoners when coloured prisoners have been slaughtered in cold blood, although the President has repeatedly promised thus to protect the lives of his coloured soldiers, have worn my patience quite threadbare. The President has virtually laid down this as the rule of his statesmen: Do evil by choice, right from necessity. You will see that he does not sign the Bill adopted by Congress restricting the organisation of State Governments only to those States where there is a loyal majority. His plan is to organise such Governments wherever there is one-tenth of the people loyal!—an entire contradiction of the constitutional idea of Republican Government.[57] I see no purpose on the part of Lincoln and his friends to extend the elective franchise to the coloured people of the South, but the contrary. This is extremely dishonourable. No rebuke of it can be too stinging from your side of the water. The negro is deemed good enough to fight for the Government, but not good enough to vote or enjoy the right to vote in the Government. We invest with the elective franchise those who with broad blades and bloody hands have sought the life of the nation, but sternly refuse so to invest those who have done what they could to save the nation's life. This discrimination becomes more dishonourable when the circumstances are duly considered. Our Government asks the negro to espouse its cause; it asks him to turn against his master, and thus fire his master's hate against him. Well, when it has attained peace, what does it propose? Why this, to hand the negro back to the political power of his master, without a single element of strength to shield himself from the vindictive spirit sure to be roused against the whole coloured race.

Letter to Russell or Mary Carpenter, dated Rochester, New York, September 1, 1864 (excerpt)
London *Inquirer*, October 8, 1864

There has never been a time, during all this war, when the Confederates might not have saved slavery by simply laying down their arms. They might do it now. The hope of the slave is in the continuance of the war, and not in the abolition principles of the Northern people or Government. What the latter does is from necessity; when *that* ceases, abolition ceases. Mr. Lincoln's Proclamation becomes void the very moment Federal relations are established, and the necessity for it ceases. It is a part of the military proceedings against the rebellion, and dies with the rebellion. Those slaves only who shall then be found within our lines, at the close of the war, may rationally hope to be free, unless the war shall be a war of extermination.

While at Washington, a few days ago, President Lincoln invited me to see him, and gave me a lengthened interview. Much of the good impression I had received of the President, at our interview last year, had been removed by what I thought his culpable failure to pay and protect his coloured soldiers, and his refusal to permit coloured men to vote in the States reconstructed under his auspices. I had also held him responsible for the course of General Banks in Louisiana, which amounted to a re-enslavement of the coloured people of that State. Going to Washington with such an account against Mr. Lincoln, I certainly had no intention of seeking an interview with him, being quite content with my public denunciations of the wrong of which I thought him guilty, and now think him guilty in part. But the President sought the interview, and I consented. I am glad I did. I found him at least five years older in appearance than last year. The number and depth of the lines on his face tell of intense and wearing anxiety. His enemies speak of him as a thoughtless joker; they do him great wrong; he is a most thoughtful man. He is not my first or even second choice for the Presidency during the next four years; yet I shall rejoice greatly if a worse do not come in his place. General McClellan, his competitor, is a bitterly pro-slavery man; should he be elected he will place everything as before the rebellion, as far as he can do so. Much noise is now made over this General, and if the election could take place to-morrow he might possibly be elected; but there remains full two months yet to canvass his merits, and I predict that his prospects will diminish by degrees and grow beautifully less as the canvass proceeds. If the South could only get into the Union before election day, McClellan would undoubtedly be our next President. During all the war he has supported an unsullied reputation with the rebels. They liked him when they fought him, and seemed to regret when he left the field,—said he was the only general the Federals could boast. But the South will not be in time to vote for McClellan, and for this, and many other reasons, I hardly think he can be elected. Nevertheless, the friends of freedom may be compelled to bestir themselves, or they will be defeated. They had last year an advantage of three hundred thousand votes over the Democrats; it is a vast advantage, and hard to overcome, but the times are full of change. After intense action there is reaction, and we may see a reaction here. In any event the contest lies between Lincoln and McClellan. Fremont can get no votes, and will, I think, be withdrawn from the canvass by his friends. He is the fittest man, but has the fewest supporters; and though one man in the right is a majority against the whole world wrong,—at the polls, numbers rule. A candidate without a party may be sublime, but he cannot be successful. I am now-a-days taking a more practical view of things than formerly, and hence I shall be found doing all I can—it is not much—to promote the election of Mr. Lincoln, or rather to defeat McClellan, in November.

Letter to William Lloyd Garrison, dated Rochester, New York, September 17, 1864 (excerpt)

The Liberator, September 23, 1864

You were pleased to remark in the last number of the *Liberator*, (heading it with "Frederick Douglass on President Lincoln,") that the secessionist newspapers in Great Britain are publishing with exultation a letter recently addressed by Mr. Douglass to an English correspondent [the ca. June 1864 letter to Mary Carpenter]; and you further favor your readers with an extract from the same letter, which criticises in plain terms the policy of the present Administration towards the colored people of the country.

I am sure you will allow me space in the columns of the *Liberator*, (not to qualify, not to take back any charge, statement, or argument contained in that letter, not even to find fault with its publication here or elsewhere,—though it was flung off in haste, and was not written for publication, but for the eyes of the esteemed friend to whom it was addressed,) to remove an inference respecting my present political course, which may possibly and will probably be drawn from the extract in question.

In the first place, it is proper to state that that letter was not written recently as you mistakenly allege, but three months ago, and was in no wise intended to be used against the present Administration in the canvass and issues as now made up between the great parties, and especially by the disloyal and slavery perpetuating nominations placed before the country by the Chicago convention. Since the date of those nominations, we are met by a new state of facts, and new considerations have arisen to guide and control the political action of all those who are animated by a sincere desire to see justice, liberty, and peace permanently established in this rebellion and slavery cursed land. While there was, or seemed to be, the slightest possibility of securing the nomination and election of a man to the Presidency of more decided anti-slavery convictions and a firmer faith in the immediate necessity and practicability of justice and equality for all men, than have been exhibited in the policy of the present Administration, I, like many other radical men, freely criticized, in private and in public, the actions and the utterances of Mr. Lincoln, and withheld from him my support. That possibility is now no longer conceivable; it is now plain that this country is to be governed or misgoverned during the next four years, either by the Republican party represented in the person of Abraham Lincoln, or by the (miscalled) Democratic party, represented by George B. McClellan. With this alternative clearly before us, all hesitation ought to cease, and every man who wishes well to the slave and to the country should at once rally with all the warmth and earnestness of his nature to the support of Abraham Lincoln and Andrew Johnson,[58] and to the utter defeat and political annihilation of McClellan and Pendleton;[59] for the election of the latter, with their known antecedents, declared sentiments, and the policy avowed in the Chicago platform, would be the heaviest calamity of all these years of war and blood, since it would upon the instant sacrifice and wantonly cast away everything valuable, purchased so dearly by the precious blood of our brave sons and brothers on the battlefield for the perfect liberty and permanent peace of a common country.

Let me say one other word. I would never give intentionally the slightest joy to the enemies of human liberty. My rule is to do that *least* that they like *most*, and that *most* that they like *least*. But nothing strange has happened to me in the said exultation over my words by the secessionist newspapers in Great Britain or elsewhere. The common example of those who do not go at all, playing off those who go farthest against those who go, but do not go fast and far enough, is but repeated in this exultation; and if I mistake not, in other days, there were often utterances of the *Liberator* itself, both on the eve and in the middle of Presidential campaigns, which caused even greater exultation among the known enemies of liberty against timid, short-sighted and trimming anti-slavery men in the high places of the country, than anything I ever wrote concerning Mr. Lincoln and his Administration could produce.

"Address of the Colored National Convention to the People of the United States," October 4, 1864[60] (excerpts)

***Proceedings of the National Convention of Colored Men, Held in the City of Syracuse, N.Y., October 4, 5, 6, and 7, 1864* (Boston: J. S. Rock and Geo. L. Ruffin, 1864)**

Again: had, for instance, the present Administration, at the beginning of the war, boldly planted itself upon the doctrine of human equality as taught in the Declaration of Independence; proclaimed liberty to all the slaves in all the Slave States; armed every colored man, previously a slave or a freeman, who would or could fight under the loyal flag; recognized black men as soldiers of the Republic; avenged the first act of violence upon colored prisoners, in contravention of the laws of war; sided with the radical emancipation party in Maryland and Missouri; stood by its antislavery generals, instead of casting them aside,—history would never have had to record the scandalous platform adopted at Chicago, nor the immeasurable horrors of Fort Pillow.[61] The weakness and hesitation of our friends, where promptness and vigor were required, have invited the contempt and rigor of our enemies. Seeing that, while perilling every thing for the protection and security of our country, our country did not think itself bound to protect and secure us, the rebels felt a license to treat us as outlaws. Seeing that our Government did not treat us as men, they did not feel bound to treat us as soldiers. It is, therefore, not the malignity of enemies alone we have to fear, but the deflection from the straight line of principle by those who are known throughout the world as our special friends. We may survive the arrows of the known negro-haters of our country; but woe to the colored race when their champions fail to demand, from any reason, equal liberty in every respect! . . .

[Douglass proceeded to criticize the Democratic Party for fighting to perpetuate slavery, and the Republican Party for supporting prejudice on account of color—especially for denying equal rights to black soldiers.]

Even in the matter of the abolition of slavery,—to which, by its platform, the Republican party is strongly committed, as well by President Lincoln's celebrated Proclamation of the first of January, 1863, and by his recent letter "To whom it may concern,"—there is still room for painful doubt and apprehension.[62] It is very evident, that the Republican party, though a party composed of the best men of the country, is not prepared to make the abolition of slavery, in all the Rebel States, a consideration precedent to the re-establishment of the Union. However antislavery in sentiment the President may be, and however disposed he may be to continue the war till slavery is abolished, it is plain that in this he would not be sustained by his party. A single reverse to our arms, in such a war, would raise the hands of the party in opposition to their chief. The hope of the speedy and complete abolition of slavery, hangs, therefore, not upon the disposition of the Republican party, not upon the disposition of President Lincoln; but upon the slender thread of Rebel power, pride, and persistence. In returning to the Union, slavery has a fair chance to live; out of the Union, it has a still better chance to live: but, fighting against the Union, it has no chance for any thing but destruction. Thus the freedom of our race and the welfare of our country tremble together in the balance of events.

This somewhat gloomy view of the condition of affairs—which to the enthusiastic, who have already convinced themselves that slavery is dead, may not only seem gloomy, but untruthful—is nevertheless amply supported, not only by the well-known sentiment of the country, the controlling pressure of which is seriously felt by the Administration; but it is sustained by the many attempts lately made by the Republican press to explain away the natural import of the President's recent address "To whom it may concern," in which he makes the abolition of Slavery a primary condition to the restoration of the Union; and especially is this gloomy view supported by the remarkable speech delivered only a few weeks ago at Auburn, by Hon. William H. Seward . . . [Douglass quoted Seward saying that when the war ended, all "war measures . . . will cease also" and "political questions," including those involving slavery, would "pass over" to the courts and Congress.]

These, fellow-citizens, are studied words, full of solemn and fearful import. They mean that our Republican Administration is not only ready to make peace with the Rebels, but to make peace with slavery also; that all executive and legislative action launched against the slave-system, whether of proclamation or confiscation, will cease the instant the Rebels shall disband their armies, and lay down their arms. The hope that the war will put an end to slavery, has, according to this exposition, only one foundation; and that is, that the courts and Congress will so decree. But what ground have we here? Congress has already spoken, and has refused to alter the Constitution so as to abolish Slavery.[63] The Supreme Court has yet to speak; but what it will say, if this question shall come before it, is very easily divined. We will not assert positively what it will say; but indications of its judgment are clearly against us. What then have we? Only this, as our surest and best ground of hope; namely, that the Rebels, in their madness, will continue to make war upon the Government, until they shall not only become destitute of men, money, and the munitions of war, but utterly divested of their slaves also.

Letter to Theodore Tilton,[64] dated Rochester, New York, October 15, 1864 (excerpts)
James Fraser Gluck Collection, Buffalo and Erie County Public Library

I am obliged by your favor containing a copy of your recent [October 7] speech in Latimer hall. I had read that speech in the Tribune several days ago, and in my heart thanked you for daring thus to break the spell of enchantment which slavery, though wounded[,] dying and despised, is still able to bind the tongues of our republican orators. It was a timely word wisely and well spoken, the best and most luminous spark struck from the flint and steel of this canvass. To all appearance we have been more ashamed of the negro during this canvass than those of 56 and 60. The President's "To whom it may concern," frightened his party and his party in return frightened the President. I found him in this alarmed condition when I called upon him *six weeks ago*—and it is well to note the time. The country was struck with one [of] those bewilderments which dethrone reason for the moment. Every body was thinking and dreaming of peace—and the impression had gone abroad that the Presidents antislavery policy was about the only thing which prevented a peaceful settlement with the Rebels. McClellan was nominated—and at that time his prospects were bright as Mr Lincolns were gloomy. You must therefore, judge the President's words in the light of the circumstances in which he spoke. Atlanta had not fallen;

Sheridan had not swept the Shenandoah—and men were ready for peace almost at any price. The President was pressed on every hand to modify his letter *"To whom it may concern"*—How to meet this pressure he did me the honor to ask my opinion. He showed me a letter written with a view to meet the peace clamour raised against him.[65] The first point made in it was the important fact that no man or set of men authorized to speak for the Confederate Government had ever submitted a proposition for peace to him. Hence the charge that he had in some way stood in the way of peace fell to the ground. He had always stood ready to listen to any such propositions.

The next point referred to was the charge that he had in his Niagara letter[66] committed himself and the country to an abolition war rather than a war for the union, so that even if the latter could be attained by negotiation, the war would go on for Abolition.

The President did not propose to take back what he had said in his Niagara letter but wished to releave the fears of his peace friends, by making it appear that the thing which they feared could not happen, and was wholly beyond his power. Even if I would, I could not carry on the war for the abolition of slavery. The country would not sustain such a war—and I could do nothing without the support of Congress. I could not make the abolition of slavery an absolute, prior condition to the reestablishment of the union. All that the President said on this point was to make manifest his want of power to do the thing which his enemies and pretended friends professed to be afraid he would do. Now the question he put to me was—shall I send forth this letter? To which I answered—certainly not—It would be given a broader meaning than you intend to convey—it would be taken as a complete surrender of your antislavery policy—and do you serious damage. In answer to your Copperhead accusers—your friends can make this argument of your want of power—but you cannot wisely say a word on that point. I have looked and feared that Mr Lincoln would say something of the sort, but he has been perfectly silent on that point—and I think will remain so.

But the thing which alarmed me most—was this: The President said he wanted some plan devised by which we could get more of the slaves within our lines—He thought that now was there [their] time—and *that such only of them as succeeded in getting within our lines would be free after the war is over.* This shows that the President only has faith in his proclamations of freedom—during the war—and that he believes their operation will cease with the war. We were long together and there was much said—but this is enough—

I gave my address—to the People of the U.S.[67] to the Committee appointed to publish the Minutes of the Convention. It is too lengthy for a newspaper article—though of course I should be very glad to see it noticed in the Independent. . . .

I am not doing much in this Presidential Canvass—for the reason—that Republican Committees do not wish to expose themselves to the charge of being the "Niggar" party. The negro is the deformed child, which is put out of the room when company comes. I hope to speak some after the Election—though not much before—and I am inclined to think I shall be able to speak all the more usefully because I have had so little to say during the present canvass. I now look upon the Election of Mr Lincoln [as] settled. When there was any shadow of a hope that a man of more decided antislavery convictions and policy could be elected—I was not for Mr Lincoln—but as soon as the Chicago convention—my mind was made up—and it is made up still. All dates changed with the nomination of McClellan.

I hope, that in listening to Mr Stanton's version of my visit to the President you kept in mind something of Mr Stanton's own state of mind concerning public affairs. I found him in a very gloomy state of mind—much less hopeful than myself—and yet more cheerful than I expected to find him. I judge from your note that he must have imparted somewhat of the hue of his own mind to my statements. He thinks far less of the President's honesty than I do—and far less of his antislavery than I do. I have not yet come to think that honesty and politics are incompatible.

Letter Written in December 1864 and Read at an Anniversary Celebration of the Emancipation Proclamation at National Hall, Philadelphia, January 2, 1865 (excerpts)

The Liberator, January 20, 1865

The work of an age has been suddenly compressed into a single day. Events have succeeded each other so rapidly, overlapping and overstepping each other so thickly, each rising higher than the other, that we are puzzled to separate and estimate at its value any one of all of them. Their variety, velocity, and proximity dazzle us and cause us to lose our reckoning. Only aftercoming generations of men, far remote from this stormy and bewildering hour, will be able to describe with accuracy these great events, and give to each its true grandeur and importance. There is one, however, which towers aloft above all the rest, like the mountain rock amid the dashing waves of a troubled ocean—solid, calm, unshaken, and immoveable—and that is the Emancipation Proclamation of President Lincoln, whose second anniversary you are about to commemorate. Hayti and Liberia recognized; the colored man received at the capital of the United States; slavery abolished in the District of Columbia; slavery prohibited in all the Territories of the country;[68] slavery recognized as the cause of the war, and its abolition decreed as the only wise remedy; Virginia half free; Missouri soon to follow; Tennessee not far behind; Kentucky trembling; "Maryland, My Maryland," unfettered, her chains broken, and her limbs all free; Judge Taney dead;[69] Judge Chase alive; McClellan defeated; Abraham Lincoln elected; slaveholding abolished; and brave black men, side by side with loyal white soldiers, winning laurels for their race upon every battlefield where they are permitted to confront the foe—constitute a few of the points of progress which rivet the attention, command our gratitude, and waken high hopes for the future of our race upon this our native soil. . . .

Until the colored man can handle the ballot as well as the musket—until he can vote in the country, as well as fight under its flag—until he shall be as welcome as a citizen as he now is as a soldier, he will be a despised and persecuted man, floundering in the depths of social degradation, a tempting target for all that is mean and malicious in the American mind and heart—having no rights which a white man is bound to respect.[70] Let no man say within himself that this is untimely. The iron is hot, and now is the time to strike. The nation is looking about for safe anchoring ground for the ship of state, and you and I know where the safe ground is. Then let us firmly point out that ground. Our own cause, and the cause of the country, alike demand this at our hands.

Letter to Julia Griffiths Crofts, dated Rochester, New York, January 4, 1865[71] (excerpt)

Leeds Mercury, February 2, 1865

I long to be able to report all chains broken, and the slaves free; the end, however, is not yet, though I believe the long prayed-for event is at hand, and that I shall live to see it, and to tell you that the work is done. The dreadful war in our country is drawing to a close; the rebellion will be suppressed, and I now have high hopes that slavery will go down with it. My reasons are, first, the re-election of Mr. Lincoln, who was mainly opposed on the ground of his alleged abolition designs; secondly, the elevation of your old friend and correspondent, Salmon P. Chase, to the Chief-Justiceship of the Republic, in place of Judge Taney, deceased; thirdly, the general tone of public opinion, demanding the entire abolition of slavery and the unification of the nation on the basis of universal freedom. Any other end of the war must brand it as murderous and useless, for the country can never be united while slavery exists. The signs of the times are nearly all indicative of abolition. The Constitution will be changed, if not by this congress, certainly by the next, so that no slave State can ever be a member of the Union.

Address on the Fall of Richmond, Delivered at Faneuil Hall, Boston, April 4, 1865 (excerpts)

The Liberator, April 7, 1865

I, for the first time in my life, have the assurance, not only of a country redeemed, of a country regenerated, but of my race free and having a future in this land. [Douglass described the accomplishments of black men in putting down the rebellion, as well as other subjects.] . . . And remember that hereafter, at the South, the negro will be looked upon with a fiercer and intenser hate than ever before. Every one of those who have been interested in the rebellion will look upon the negro as one of the causes of the failure of that rebellion.

I tell you, the negro is coming up—he is rising—rising. (Laughter and applause.) Why, only a little while ago we were the Lazaruses of the South; the Dives of the South was the slaveholder; and how singular it is that we have here another illustration of that Scripture![72] Once there was a certain rich man who fared sumptuously every day, and was arrayed in purple and fine linen. He came North, clothed in silk and in satin, and shining with gold, and his breast sparkling with diamonds—his table loaded with the good things of this world. And a certain Lazarus sat at his gate, desiring the crumbs that fell from his table. Such was the record. But now a change has taken place. That rich man is lifting up his eyes in torments *down there*, (tremendous applause), and seeing Lazarus afar off in Abraham's bosom, (tumultuous laughter and applause,) is all the time calling on Father Abraham to send Lazarus back. But Father Abraham says, "If they hear not Grant nor Sherman, neither will they be persuaded though I send Lazarus unto them." (Prolonged and vociferous applause.) I say we are way up yonder now, no mistake. (This was said with an expressive gesture, that called forth another outburst of applause.)

My friends, I will not inflict a speech upon you. (Loud cries of "Go on.") O, no; I am afraid I shall spoil it. (Great merriment.)

Part 4
Eulogies

In the wake of Lincoln's assassination, Americans looked to their religious, political, and community leaders for words of consolation, hope, and meaning. When the citizens of Rochester gathered on April 15 to express their grief, they called upon Frederick Douglass to address them. Speaking extemporaneously, Douglass expressed the optimism of many African Americans at the end of the Civil War: "that though Abraham Lincoln dies, the republic lives" and "the nation is saved and liberty established forever." Still, he cautioned that the crimes of the Confederacy ought not to be forgotten and insisted that black men be granted the vote. "Let us not be in too much haste in the work of restoration," he warned. "Let us not be in a hurry to clasp to our bosom that spirit which gave birth to Booth."[1]

Three days later Douglass addressed another Rochester audience (in a speech that has never before been anthologized), this time focusing on his personal interactions with Lincoln—a theme that he would return to time and again for the remainder of his life. When they met, Douglass found Lincoln "utterly free" of prejudice, and judged that he "had done his work, and done it well."[2]

When Lincoln's funeral procession passed through New York City on April 25, the city council tried to prevent black residents from participating—an insult that did not bode well for their future. A few weeks later, on June 1, Douglass delivered a eulogy at the

Cooper Union in which he reminded Americans of the connection between slavery and assassination, and the need to finish the work that Lincoln had begun. To Douglass, Lincoln was "unsurpassed in his devotion, to the welfare of the white race." And yet, unlike all previous presidents, he was "emphatically the black mans President: the first to show any respect for their rights as men."[3] Despite Douglass's frustrations with Lincoln as a wartime leader, Lincoln was a man ahead of his time who should be emulated. This nuanced assessment foreshadowed Douglass's more famous 1876 oration dedicating a statue of Lincoln in Washington, DC.

Douglass developed the main themes of his Cooper Union address further in a December speech in Portland, Maine. As would be the case for the rest of his life, when Douglass pointed to Lincoln, he did so to advance the cause of equal rights.

Remarks at City Hall in Rochester, New York, April 15, 1865
Rochester Daily Union and Advertiser, April 17, 1865

Mayor Moore and Fellow Citizens:

This call to address you on this occasion was quite unexpected to me, and one to which I find it almost impossible to respond. If you have deep grief in the death of Abraham Lincoln, and feel in it a severe stab at Republican institutions, I feel it on all these accounts and more. I feel it as a personal as well as national calamity; on account of the race to which I belong, and the deep interest which that good man ever took in its elevation. This is not an occasion for speech making, but for silence. I have scarcely been able to say a word to any of those friends who have taken my hand and looked sadly in my eyes to-day. A dreadful disaster has befallen the nation. It is a day for silence and meditation; for grief and tears. Yet I feel that though Abraham Lincoln dies, the republic lives, (cheers); though that great and good man, one of the noblest men that trod God's earth, (applause,) is struck down by the hand of the assassin, yet I know that the nation is saved and liberty established forever. (Loud applause.) The human mind naturally turns from a calamity like this, and endeavors, through its tears and anguish, to catch some gleam of hope—some good that may be born of the tremendous evil. And I think it is not inconsistent with this tearful occasion to discover through the blinding mists that rise from this yawning gulf, the beautiful bow of promise spanning the gloom and giving hope to all. (Applause.)

Only the other day, it seemed as if this nation were in danger of losing a just appreciation of the awful crimes of this rebellion. We were manifesting almost as much gratitude to Gen. Lee for surrendering as to Gen. Grant for compelling him to surrender! (Cheers.) It seemed to me that Gen. Lee was about the most popular man in America. (Applause and laughter.) The crimes of treason and slavery were being rapidly forgotten, and we talked of amnesty and oblivion in behalf of men whose hands are red with the best blood of the land. (Loud cheers.) Republics have proverbially short memories. I was afraid the American people were growing weak. It may be in the inscrutable wisdom of Him who controls the destinies of Nations, that this drawing of the Nation's most precious heart's blood was necessary to bring us back to that equilibrium which we must maintain if the Republic was to be permanently redeemed. (Applause.)

How I have to-day mourned for our noble President, I dare not attempt to tell. It was only a few weeks ago that I shook his brave, honest hand, and looked into his gentle eye and heard his kindly voice uttering those memorable words—words which will live immortal in history, and be read with increasing admiration from age to age:

Fondly do we hope, fervently do we pray that this mighty scourge of war may speedily pass away. Yet if God will[s] that it continue until all the wealth piled by the bondman's two hundred and fifty years of unrequited toil shall be sunk, and until every drop of blood drawn by the lash shall be paid by another, drawn with the sword, as was said three thousand years ago, so still must it be said, that the judgments of the Lord are righteous altogether. (Loud continued applause.)

Brave, good words are those; and I think, with Dr. Robinson,[4] that if treason expects to gain anything by this hell-black assassination, it will be awfully disappointed. To-day, to-day as never before this North is a unit! (Great applause.) To-day, to-day as never before, the American people, although they know they cannot have indemnity for the past—for the countless treasure and the precious blood—yet they resolve to-day that they will exact ample security for the future! (Cheers.) And if it teaches us this lesson, it may be that the blood of our beloved martyred President will be the salvation of our country. Good man we call him; good man he was. If "an honest man is the noblest work of God,"[5] we need have no fears[6] for the soul of Abraham Lincoln. (Applause.)

This new demonstration of the guilt of slavery teaches another lesson. Hereafter we must not despise any hand or any arm that has been uplifted in defence of the Nation's life. Let us not be in too much haste in the work of restoration. Let us not be in a hurry to clasp to our bosom that spirit which gave birth to Booth. When we take to our arms again, as brethren, our Southern foes, let us see to it that we take also our Southern friends. (Cheers.) Let us not forget that justice to the negro is safety to the Nation. When the tall heads of this Rebellion are swept off (as they will be,) (applause,) in their tracks will spring up another race, their luckless sons, to whom the wretched traitors will bequeath some infernal passions like that which has caused our great bereavement. By their hand other officers of the government will be stricken down. Where is our remedy? It is here: know no man hereafter in all these States by his complexion, but know every man by his loyalty, (cheers) and wherever there is a patriot in the North or South, white or black, helping on the good cause, hail him as a citizen, a kinsman, a clansman, a brother beloved! (Great applause.) Let us not remember our enemies and forget our friends. Let us not enfranchise our enemies and disfranchise our friends. The black man will not only run everywhere to bring us information and to warn us of dangerous plots, through marsh and fen and forest, will not only bear exposure and privation, and lead and feed our fugitive prisoners, and bind up their wounded feet—sheltering them by day and piloting them in the darkness—will not only build for you ramparts of earth and solid stone, but they offer you ramparts of flesh, and fight the battles of the nation amid contumely and persecution. (Cheers.) For the safety of all, let justice be done to each. I thank you, gentlemen, for the privilege of mingling my sorrows and hopes with yours on this memorable occasion.

Speech at Rochester, New York, April 18, 1865
Washington Daily Morning Chronicle, April 27, 1865

It was my fortune to be made acquainted with Mr. Lincoln two years ago, and since then I have had repeated interviews with him; and sensitive as I am, and quick to see and resent any prejudice against the colored man, either by want of cordiality or by a patronizing tone, yet I could not detect the slightest feeling of this. I found Mr. Lincoln an Israelite indeed, utterly free from a feeling which in some form is all but universal. When I went to the White House I found the keepers of the doors, the same servants who had held positions under former Presidents, and who had inherited all the feelings about the approach of the colored man which then prevailed, and thus educated they showed a disposition to turn me away. How were they astonished when they saw Mr. Lincoln meet me at the door with all the warmth and cordiality with which one meets an old and familiar friend after long parting. The effect was good; and as I turned to go in I saw the servants turn one to another with a look which said: "Well, times have changed, and it is all right after all." Among the last words Mr. Lincoln said to me in our last interview were: "Douglass, I hate slavery as much as you do, and I want to see it abolished altogether."[7]

It is not for me, I do not think that it is for any man, to attempt to measure the character of Mr. Lincoln. I feel his loss too deeply as a personal bereavement to do this, but I may, I will say, that I think in large measures Abraham Lincoln had done his work, and done it well.

Manuscript of Eulogy Delivered at the Cooper Union, New York City, June 1, 1865
Frederick Douglass Papers, Manuscript Division, Library of Congress

I come before you this Evening with much diffedence: The rarest gifts, the best eloquence, the highest order of genius to which the nation has given birth, might well be employed here and now, and yet fail of justice to the dignity and solemnity of this occasion.

The character of the illustrious deceased, the position he occupied at the head of our Government, the extraordinary manner of his death, with all the attendant circumstances of the country, are fruitful themes, of the most interesting nature;—themes which must depend upon the historian, rather than upon the orator, for elaborate and appropriate celebration.

Had Abraham Lincoln died, from any of the numerous ills to which flesh is heir, and by which men are removed from the scenes of life; Had he reached that good old age, of which his vigorous constitution, and his temperate habits gave promise: Had he seen the end of the great work which it was his good[8] fortune to inaugurate; Had the curtain of death been but gradually drawn around him;—our task this evening, though sad, and painful would be very simple.

But dying as he did die, by the red hand of violence; snatched suddenly away from his work without warning;—killed, murdered, assassinated, not because of personal hate, for no man who knew Abraham Lincoln, could hate him; but solely because he was the President, the faithful, loyal President of the United States—true to his country, and true to the cause of human freedom, taking care that the Constitution and the laws were obeyed; for this reason he was slain, murdered, assasinated, and for this all commanding reason—he to day commands our homage and the homage of good men everywhere as a glorious martyr—one who must be viewed[,] if viewed rightly, in connection with his country and with all that pertains to his country.

Very evidently here is a large field opened, but the most any man can do, with a subject like this, and at a time like this, when every faculty of thought and feeling, is intensely active, when the press, the pulpit and the platform, when poetry and art in all her departments—has been occupied with this one great event for weeks: I say, the most I can do, the most any man can do, is in some humble measure, to give back to the country, the thoughts and feelings which are derived from the country:—The speaker upon occasions like this, is but as the wave to the ocean; he borrows all his weight and volume, from the sea out of which he rises.

To day all over this country—men have been thinking of Abraham Lincoln: Our statesmen[,] scholars and poets—have been celebrating as never before the memory of our martyred President. It is well. He is worthy of it all—and it is becoming in all—to join however humbly in these tokens of respect and veneration.

One thing will be at once conceded by all generous minds; No people or class of people in this country, have a better reason for lamenting the death of Abraham Lincoln, and for desiring to honor and perpetuate his memory, than have the colored people; and yet we are about the only people who have been in any case forbiden to exhibit our sorrow, or to show our respect for the deceased president publicly.[9] The attempt to exclude colored people from his funeral procession in New York—was one of the most disgraceful, and sickening manifestations of moral emptiness, ever exhibited by any nation or people professing to be civilized: But what was A. Lincoln to the colored people or they to him? As compared with the long line of his predecessors, many of whom were merely the facile and servile instruments of the slave power; Abraham Lincoln, while unsurpassed in his devotion, to the welfare of the white race, was also in a sense hitherto without example, emphatically the black mans President: the first to show any respect for their rights as men.[10]

To our white fellow countrymen therefore we say, follow your martyred president to his grave, lay the foundation of his monument broad and strong—let its capstone rise towards the sky—do homage to his character, forever perpetuate his memory; but as you respect genuine sorrow, unfeigned grief, and sincere bereavement, let the colored people of this country—for whom he did so much, have space at least, for one stone in that monument—one which shall tell to aftercoming generations the story of their love and gratitude to Abraham Lincoln.

Those love most to whom most is forgiven.[11] One of the most touching scenes connected with the funeral of our lamented President, occurred at the gate of the Presidential mansion: A colored woman standing at the gate weeping, was asked the cause of her tears; Oh! sir she said we have lost our Moses: But said the gentleman, the Lord will send you another: That may be said the weeping woman—but Ah! we had him. To her mind one as good; or better might come in his stead—but no such possibility to her was equal to—to the reality, actual possession in the person of Abraham Lincoln.

The colored people, from first to last, and through all, whether through good or through evil report, fully believed in Abraham Lincoln. Even though he sometimes smote them, and wounded them severely, yet they firmly trusted in him:[12] This was however, no blind trust unsupported by reason: They early caught a glimpse of the man, and from the evidence of their senses, they believed in him: They viewed him not in the light of seperate individual facts—but in the light of his mission—in his manifest relation to events—and in the philosophy of his statesmanship—Viewing him thus they trusted him—as men are seldom trusted. They did not care what forms of expression the President adopted, whether it were justice, expediency, or military necessity so that they saw slavery abolished—and Liberty was established in the country.

Under Abraham Lincolns beneficent rule, they saw themselves being gradually lifted to the broad plain of equal manhood: Under his rule, and by measures approved by him, they saw gradually fading the hand writing of ages which was against them: Under his rule, they saw millions of their bretheren proclaimed free and invested with the right to defend their freedom: Under his rule, they saw the

Confederate states—that boldest of all conspiracies against the just rights of human nature, broken to pieces, overpowered[,] conquered, shattered to fragments—ground to powder and swept from the face of existence: Under his rule, they saw the Independence of Hayti and Liberia recognized—and the whole colored race steadily rising into the friendly consideration of the American people: In their broad practical common sense, they took no captious exceptions to the unpleasant incidents of their transition from slavery to freedom. All they wanted to know was that those incidents were only transitional not permanent.

But we speak here to night not merely as colored men, but as men among men, and as American citizens—having the same interest in the welfare[,] permanence and prosperity, of the country—that any other class of citizens may be supposed to have. We survey the facts of the hour with reference to this relation to our fellow citizens:—From this outlook we find the prospect bright & glorious.

The greatness and grandeur of the American republic never appeared more conspicuosly than in connection with the death of Abraham Lincoln: Though always great and always powerful, we have seemed to need the presence of some great, and widespread calamity, some overwhelming sorrow, to reveal to ourselves and the world, in glorified forms, all the elements of our national strength and greatness. While it cannot be affirmed, that our long torn and distracted country, has already reached the desired condition of peace, it may be said, and said in the face of all prophecies of failure—freely indulged in at one time at home as well as abroad that we have survived the terrible agonies of a fierce and sanguinary rebellion, and have before us a fair prospect of a just and lasting peace,[13] a peace which if *we are wise*, and just, can never be disturbed or broken by the remains of still insolent and designing slave oligarchy.

Already a strong hand is felt upon the helm of state;[14] Already the key note of justice has been sounded; Already the majesty of the Law and the power of the Government are bringing order out of confusion, by making the Law a terror to evil doers, as well as a praise to those who do well: The word has gone forth that traitors and assassins whither of low or of high degree, whether male or female,[15] are to be punished: That loyal and true men are to be rewarded and protected: That slavery[,] the haggard and damning offense of many generations, is to be entirely and forever abolished: that the Emancipated negro, so long outraged and degraded[,] is to be enfranchised and clothed with the dignity of American citizenship: That the poor white man of the south—scornfully denominated by the rich slaveholders, as the poor white trash, so long deceived, misled and plundered by the slaveholding arristocracy—are to be delivered from their political and social debasement: That the loyal and patriot dead, whether dying of wounds on the field or of starvation in Rebel prisons, whether falling in open combat or by the stealthy dagger of the assassin—are to be gratefully remembered and honored forever. That the toil worn, scarred, ma[i]med and battered veterans, of all nationalities and of all colors, now returning home from the scenes of strife, are to be welcomed home, and taught by the respect and gratitude they receive from their country—that they have been fighting for *their* country—and not merely for the empty and delusive hope of a country.

Henceforth we have a new date, a new Era for our great Republic: Henceforth a new account is opened, between the government and the people of the United States: Henceforth their [there] is to be no north[,] no south in American politics, but a common country of all for all: Henceforth the nation assumes a new position and a new relation to the nations of the Earth: Henceforth an American citizen may defend his country at the tribunal of the world's judgement, without defending—a glaring inconsistency and a scandalous crime: Henceforth there is an end to that compromising statesmanship—which has so deeply demoralized both the government and the people: Henceforth we shall stand an acknowledged power among the great powers of Europe and exert a beneficent influence in the destiny of nations. Out of the vast and dreadful concatenation of evils which have environed us, brought upon us during these four years of treason[,] rebellion and assassination, we shall yet be the recipients of immeasurable and priceless blessings: It is something that the crash has come, and that the worst is known—that the storm cloud has burst, and sent down its bolt, and has left the blue sky above, calm and bright as when the morning stars sang together for joy!

Spanning the horrible gulf, the fearful chasm—made by the sad, the mournful, and tragic death of our greatly loved, greatly honored[,] greatly trusted and greatly lamented President, we behold from side to side, a perfect bow of promise[16] with all its beautiful beams undimmed, dispelling fear, and kindling hope anew for the future of the republic.

This occassion therefore, though sad and solemn when we contemplate our martyred president, is not one of gloom, when we consider the future of the country. There is here joy as well as sorrow, gratulation as well as grief, great gain as well as great loss. This last drop in our cup of bitterness[17] was perhaps needed: No nation ever passed an ordeal better fitted to try its strength, or to test the value of its institutions. Know theyself[18] is a wise admonition to nations as well as to individuals, Such national self knowledge has been imparted by the war and by this last act of the war. It had long been the settled opinion of European statesmen and philosophers, that our ship of state was too weak for stormy weather. They predicted that though beautiful to the eye, strong to the touch and swift upon the wave, our gallant bark would go down in the first great storm. They had little faith in the wisdom or virtue of the people, and as little in the form and substance of popular government. I have no reproaches for these foreigners of little faith, for it cannot be denied that many thoughtful and patriotic men at home, have doubted and trembled while contemplating the possibility of just such a conflict as that through which we have no[w] so nearly and happily passed.

The cost of the experiment in blood and treasure has been vast, but the results attained and made attainable by it will fully compensate for all loss: Already we are realizing its blessings: At this moment as never before in our history we are enjoying not, I trust, a haughty but a healthy consciousness of our strength: Already there is a feeling of national repose, an assured faith in the ability of the people, and in the stability of Republican Government—such as never before existed.

Happily too: this confidence is not limited to our own country—It is defusing itself through all countries—and over all continents. Writhing under the heel of an imported despotism, the worst of all the despotisms of Europe—Mexico to day, lifts up her dejected and woe smitten head, with revived and reinvigorated hope,[19] and the friends of free Institutions throughout the world, will recognize in our great national triumph over rebellion and slavery, a powerful gaurantee, of the ultimate universal establishment of free Institutions.

But I will not stop here to argue the value of the results thus far of our conflict. When measured by the hardships endured, and the fearful loss of human life involved, such arguments[,] however just, may savour too much of indifference to human suffering.

A more tranquilizing thought comes to us on this occasion. That thought is the inevitability of the conflict. It was beyond the power of human will or wisdom—to have prevented just what has happened. We should never forget that this dreadful war with all its incidents, was a part of—and sprung out of the fundamental elements of our national structure—and was in the nature of things unavoidable. We have but reaped where we had sown. Its hour had come, and there was nothing left but to make room for it, to accept it, and derive from it, whatever advantage it brought. We could no more evade it, than we could unmake our antecedents.

When slavery was first planted in the national soil, treason, rebellion and assassination were planted with it and their bloody fruit was bequeathed to the present generation—and if in the coming reconstruction, we shall incorporate any of the seeds of injustice, any of the remains of slavery, we shall repeat the mistake of our fathers, with the certainty that our children after us will reap a similar harvest of blood to that we have just experienced.

All the great nations of the Earth, no matter how isolated their location; no matter how iron like their rule, no matter how conservative their statesmen, no matter how carefully they exclude the light of new ideas—are fated to pass through what may be termed their historical periods—certain grand epochs, made up by the irrepressible tendencies of their inherent social forces, coming upon them whither they will or not.

Their political astrologers and wisemen, look upward and read as they think the signs of the times: they see the crises coming just as they see the storm gathering in the sky. They may utter their warning, but can neither avert nor hinder the event[.] There is however nothing aimless[,] capricious[,] arbitrary or blind in the oncoming of such periods. They are prepared for, provided for, by violation of law[;] they come when they are ready and they depart when their work is done. Such epochs[,] occuring at different points of time and in different nations, are the great teachers of mankind, they disclose in striking forms and colors, the active elements of the national life[,] good and bad, of each individual nation, making each better acquainted with itself and better known to all other nation[s].

As a people though less disturbed and more fortunate than most other nations we are no exception to the general rule applying to all. One such period as this happened to us, four score and nine years ago.[20] It was when our delegates sat in solemn assembly in Philadelphia and openly declared our independence of Great Britain—and when the American people, with a courage that never quailed—and a faith that knew no doubt[,] marched through bloody fields during all the length of seven years to make that declaration a solid reality.

Another and mightier than that, is the one compressed within the narrow limits of the last four years. There is not one jot of all this space from the first of june sixty one, to the first of june sixty five, which is not studded with stupendous events destined to engage the thoughts, and thrill the hearts of mankind away into the depths of coming ages. I repeat nothing strange has happened unto us. We have been simply playing our appointed part in the subtle machinery of human advancement and civilization. We had within our midst a gigantic system of injustice, and barbarism, a shocking offense against the enlightened judgement of mankind—a system which the world had outgrown, one which we were required by the necessity of our existence and our relations to mankind to put away: Peacibly if we could, forcibly if we must.[21]

In doing this great work for ourselves, we have done other, if not greater service.

To the grand sum of human knowledge, as to what men have done, will do; as to what great nations and states have done and will do, when vital interests are involved and powerful human passions are stirred, we have during these four years—added our special and peculiar contribution, such an one as no other nation of modern times could add.

Our experience has been full of instruction and our example brilliant and striking beyond a parralell: The very ends of the earth may look and learn. During this tremendous struggle for national [missing word], so fierce, bitter and sanguinary, so long protracted and so desperate, we have illustrated both extremes of human possibilities. As a nation we have exemplified the best and noblest qualities—which distinguish human nature, as well as those which most blot and disgrace it.

The history of this war for the union and for Free Institutions, will possess many thrilling chapters full of moving incidents, full battles, sieges, hair breadths escape, of gallant achievements upon flood and field, but it will have none, which will so interest, so *astound* and amaze mankind as that which shall contain a faithful record of the events and scenes which have transpired in our country during the last seven weeks.

We have here, the concentrated *virus*[,] the moral poison, accumulated by more than two centuries of human slavery, pouring itself out upon the nation as a vial of wrath—in one dreadful and shocking crime[,] the first of its kind in the annals of the country.

The accursed thing, so long defended in the name of the Bible and religion—defended thus while known to live upon blood and tears—the hateful crime, so long defended in the name of law and order, properly celebrates its own death by a crime that sends a shudder around the world.

England, France, Germany[,] all European nations have been literally struck dumb, by this appropriate exhibition of slaveholding hate. It is well that slavery, should give this mean and bloody sign at its death, cradled in theft, and living by robbery, it is meet that it should go to its grave under a storm of execration from every quarter of the globe.

Hereafter when men think of slavery, they will think of murder, Hereafter when men think of slaveholders, they will think of assassins: Hereafter when men think of southern chivalry they will think of our starving prisoners at Andersonville, Hereafter when men think of southern honor, they will think of the assassination of Abraham Lincoln.

Deny it who will, Doubt it who may—that hell black deed sprung from the very heart of the aristocratic class of the south.

I know that some of the leaders of the rebellion have affected to deplore it, Some have even ventured to plead their honorable character as proof [of] their innocence of that foul and ghastly crime. But such pleas cannot be received. They are utterly vain and worthless—These slaveholders know, we know, and the world knows where the responsibility for this crime belongs.

The assassin not less than any member of the late Confederate Government, represented a cause, and was the very image and superscription of that cause. Those who have by fraud, treachery[,] robbery[,] broken oaths and piracy, carried on a war during four years to break up this union, with no better, or other motive than to make human bondage perpetual, will have to bring better evidence than their own word of honor, to remove from their shoulders this heavy responsibility.

Booth the assassin is of the south[.] His affiliations such as they were, are of the south. He fired his deadly shot in the interest of the south, His motto of defense after committing the atrocious crime, was copied from the south;[22] From the first of the war he took sides with the south. His first thought, upon the commission of the crime, was escape to the south. There is nothing in his morals or manners, or in the crime itself to seperate him from the south—or that should make the south disown him. As types, and representative men of southern civilization—Booth and Brooks stand well together. Brooks, attempted to assassinate Mr Sumner of Massachusetts—a noble representative of New England culture—and statesmanship—and was applauded, publicly applauded all over the south. And I undertake to say, knowing the south as I do—that the same south, or what is left of it, which applauded the assassination of Hon: Charles Sumner—in its inmost heart will applaud the assassination of Abraham Lincoln.

Let us not, mistake public opinion either at the north or the south. This mistake is the danger, the imminent danger of the hour. We have done too much of this in other days.

Public journals, there are all over the north—which have sympathised from the first with the rebels and traitors—just so far as they could do so with safety—are endeavoring to serve their old friends and allies to day by persuading their readers—that the south disowns Booth—and laments as sincerely as we do the death of Abraham Lincoln. To this there is just one word to be said—It comes entirely too late, and is utterly inconsistent with the past. Take the federal soldiers from the so called Confederate states—and tomorrow the very elite of the south will drink to the memory of Booth the assassin.

Besides, the crime accords well, with the several attempts to burn up sleeping women and innocent children in hotels:[23] It accords well with the attempt to through [throw] crowded Railway trains from the tracks; It accords well with the torpedo and infernal machine mode of warfare, so universally adopted by the chivalry of the south: It accords well with the horrid profanation of the graves of our brave soldiers, and making ornaments of their bones: It accords well with the massacre at Fort Pillow—It accords well with the system of starvation adopted by the Confederate government in its treatment of our prisoners. And it accords generally with the cowardly ferocity—with which the system of slavery naturally inspires her worshippers:

Men who whip women with their hands tied, and burn their names into their flesh with hot irons—cannot be allowed any especial abhorrence of assassination—or for any other crime it may seem for their interest to commit.

Another strong argument in favor of this theory of southern responsibility for the assassination, is found in the fact, that that crime was freely talked of at the south, and the time and the place, were specified previously to Mr Lincolns first inauguration: His journey to Washington was the time and Baltimore was the appointed place for the tragedy. Even men here at the North, by winks and nods, and other intimations, which would not now be tolerated, gave us to understand then, that though elected—Mr Lincoln could never be inaugurated:

That their evil prophecies were not fulfilled, we all know was owing to his travelling by an irregular train and arriving in Baltimore at an unexpected time.

Booth the miserable assassin only did at the last what was meditated[,] threatened, and expected at the very outset of the rebellion.

Great as was his crime, he is at this moment not one whit guiltier, than is General Lee and other Leaders of the rebellion.

The beginning of the rebellion is assassination, the end of the rebellion is assassination—It is consistent throughout. It ends as it began, not a line of analogy is missing. Booth and Beauregard,[24] Payne[25] and President Davis[,] Adzerot[26] and Breckenridge, were servants of a common cause, and will go down in history as clansmen and kinsmen—and brothers beloved in a common conspiracy and a common crime.

It has been sometimes regretted that Booth was not captured alive, that he might have been regularily tried, condemned, sentenced and executed.

I shall waste no unavailing regrets upon this point. The ends of justice in his case have been satisfied. His punishment has been indeed swift and terrible.

Men at the north where they have dared do so, have been heard to extol the bravery of Booth.

That he had more courage than his captain may be freely admitted. Yet in no honorable or desireable sense was Booth a brave man. His courage was the courage of the thief—the burglar, the highway robber, who murder at midnight and escape in the darkness—by plans and appliances arranged weeks in advance.

His courage was no bar to his suffering: In his ten days wanderings after committing his crime he must have suffered more than a hundred deaths[.]

I can conceive of no torture more exquisite and extreme than his. Reckless of life as he affected to be, when captured no criminal ever made a more desperate effort to save his life than he did, while their [there] seemed the least chance of saving it.

To imagine the intense anguish he suffered those ten days we need not track him in his perilous flight, with a broken leg at the start, inflamed by liquour and swelling with pain; we need not follow him as he hobbled along—on either side of the Potomac in the darkness seeking safety and finding none. We need not go with him into that dismal swamp wherein he whirled about upon his crutch, startled by every sound like a hunted wolf in an iron trap—hemmed in all sides, all chance of escape cut off, with sleep murdered[,] appetite gone, his broken limb all the while getting worse[,] no friend daring to approach him with succor, the lines of his pursuers steadily drawing more closely around him: as certain for days of final capture, as though the iron hand of the Law had already fallen heavily upon him. I say we need not follow him through these scenes to imagine his terrible suffering, nor even to that last scene of all, wherein he pitiously begs the by standers to kill him—to put an end to his pains, and remove him from the horrible thing he was—to his own sight.

The simple fact that he had shed innocent blood, and that a whole nation was roused for his capture—and that no assylum awaited him—in any country except the south—and that the south was now utterly impossible to him, will give a destressing idea enough—of the living death through which he dragged himself during those ten terrible days.

No: assassination finds no encouragement in the fate of Booth—as treason finds no countenence in the capture of Davis.

But let us turn away from the hateful assassin, and think of the loved and honored martyr who fell by the hand of the assassin.

The world is old, an[d] its experience vast, but was there ever such an hour, caused by the announcement of the death of any monarch, as was caused by the news of the death of Abraham Lincoln? Was ever any people so instantly and so universally overwhelmed with grief? Did ever a great and victorious nation so suddenly pass from triumph to tears—from exaltation and joy to the very dust and ashes of mourning[?] I know of none and the world knows of none[.]

The monstrous blow came when, as at no time before during all the war, we were rejoicing in great and decisive victories. The rebel capital had fallen, General Lee had surrendered: Mobile was in our hands; the rebel army was scattered, blown away like the fine dust, before the strong north wind: the press, the Loyal press, had put off the wrinckled front of war[27]—and was appealing for clemency in behalf of the defeated rebels. The feeling of resentment and wrath was everywhere giving way to a spirit of forgiveness and oblivion; the whole national horizon seemed fringed with the golden dawn of peace; when all at once, we were startled, amazed, struck down,[28] overwhelmed, by this most foul and dreadful murder. The gentle, the amiable, character of the man—the man, with malice towards none, but charity towards—all[29]—the last man in the world—one would think to tempt the assassins dagger—The thought was full of astonishment as well as horror. The event itself, was so sudden, so tragic, and so out of joint with all seeming probability, so in contradiction to all our feelings that few could at the first believe the dreadful news[.]

You remember all the circumstances, and yet it seems fit in an address like this that we reiterate their leading features. The story is soon told: While seated with his wife, in a private box at Ford's theatre, set apart by its proprietor, for the President and his family;—while putting off the burdens of state for the moment, observing the play entitled Our American Cousin, which he had been specially invited to witness—all unconscious of danger to himself or to the state: Abraham Lincoln was shot down by an assassin who stood behind him—and died from the wound the ensuing morning: Such was the shocking news flashed from Washington on the Fifteenth [of] April—Along with it also came the stunning announcement that Hon: William H. Seward—Secretary of State had been assassinated in his chamber, upon a bed where some thought he had days before laid down to die: and that both himself and his son, the assistant Secretary of State must die from the terrible wounds inflicted by the assassin.

Further on still, their [there] came the intimation hardly needed, that these assassinations were not the self moved, individual outbreaks of the malign passions of miscreants: That they were representative men. They were but as the hands of the clock, in front and in sight, but the cunning machinery that moved them was behind and out of sight. It was seen at the moment that the assassins had only accomplished a part of the bloody work, marked out for their hands. Murder was to have had a more extended circle. All the heads of the State—and the head of the Army, were to have fallen: Men everywhere recognized in it the hand and heart of the rebellion: The life taken was not the life the murderer sought. It was not the President but, but the country—they would strike down through him.

But what a day! What a day to the American people was that fourteenth of April. For the moment we seemed suspended over the howling abyss of Anarchy and social chaos: At that moment a breath or an atom might have detached us from the moorings [of] civil order—and plunged us into national ruin.

One feature of the moment was the feeling of astonishment: In the condition of the country—and the threats so frequently made, the event ought to have been looked for. Men are men, here as elsewhere. History is but repeating itself—said Mr Seward—as soon as able to speak—The remark is strictly philosophical. We ought to have expected it—Yet it caught us all unprepared.

Had the solid earth opened and swallowed up one of our chief cities, had the tombs, burst beneath our feet, and the sheeted dead[30] walked forth from the dust of ages, the sensation of astonishment and horror could not have been more profound and all pervading.

A hush, a solemn stillness went out over the land, as though each man had heard a voice from heaven, an uninterpreted sound from the sky, and had tremblingly paused to learn its meaning.

Men spoke to each other with bated breath, with voices—broken and scarcely audable. The heads of the people were bowed—like the waves of the sea when first swept by the tempest, only to rise higher later in the storm.

I shall not undertake to describe the grand tumult of emotions that throbbed in all loyal hearts that day. A thought of the assassin caused a shudder, as if one had in the darkness of a lonely way come upon the fierce glaring eyes of a ferocious beast—or trodden upon a poisonous reptile. We were smitten with a feeling of shame for the fiendish possibilities of human nature.

For a moment there stole through men's hearts a strange distrust of each other.

They looked at their fellow citizens with a searching glance, which said not so much who are you but what are you and how do you feel at this mournful hour? for none could tell how far the dark spirit of assassination had travelled north nor where the blow would next fall.

Still as I look back to that day, and analize the emotions every where excited, I must say, the one sentiment, the one feeling,—vastly more intense, more prominent and all pervading, than all others; the one that stirred deepest, the hearts of men, and caused their eyes to alternate between—tears at one moment, and sparks of fire at another, was a feeling of sorrow—a sense of personal bereavement—in the death of Abraham Lincoln. This one great feeling—overlapped and interlaced all others—and colored every object to the eye and spirit.

What was the real cause of this deep sorrow? Who can explain whence the hold this man had upon the American people? His high official character, no doubt had something to do with it—but very evidently this was not all. Other Presidents have died, though none have been assassinated before President Lincoln—yet none were ever so mourned.

So far as the contingency of the loss[31] of the president was concerned, it was already provided for. It is one of the marvels to the outside world that the confidence of the country—was so easily and promptly transferred from the President dead to the President Living. The death of a monarch is looked to—as an event of great political changes if not of revolution—but we have shown that even in times of great troubles and calamities—our country can pass from the hands of one ruler to those a [of] another without noise or detriment of any sort: In this fact we have a renewed garantee of the perpetuity of Republican Institutions.

What then was the cause of our grief? Whence our bereavement: I affirm that it was not because the country had lost a president, but because the world had lost a man—one whose like we may not see again.

The fact is the people in the very depths of their souls loved Abraham Lincoln. They knew him, and knew him as one brother knows another, and they loved him as one brother loves another. He was not only the President of the country, but a member of each loyal family—in the country. The very picture of his plain American face, was loved—as the picture of a dear relation.

Abraham Lincoln was no exotic,—no imported growth of king craft or of Priest craft. He was no imitator of foreign customs or copiest of foreign manners, but thoroughly American in all that distinguished his character—There was not a fibre in his whole composition—that did not identify him with his country to the fullest extent. He was a self made man, the architect of his own fortune. And the American people—indebted to themselves for themselves, saw in him, a full length portrait of themselves. In him they saw their better qualities represented—incarnated, and glorified—and as such they loved him.

Other men have, perhaps, been as much honored, but no American has been so much loved—by the American people.

But we stand even yet, too near the newly made grave of Abraham Lincoln, either for a just analysis of his character—or for a dispassionate review of his official life. The wound caused by his death is yet too deep—too fresh, the sorrow too lasting, and the mind too excited with the scenes of sorrow for just criticism or unbiased Eulogy.

The sad and solemn pageantry of his funeral has not yet faded from our vision: The long and imposing procession winding its way through distant states, towards the setting sun is still in sight. The sable drapery of mourning has scarcely ceased to sadden on dwellings or streets. The booming of distant cannon proclaiming a nation's grief, has hardly ceased to reverberate. Muffled drums are still beating funeral marches to his grave, the national flag still waves sadly at half mast against the hollow sky, while the image of him who has gone, lingers in our hearts, like the last smile of a loving mother—just quitting the shores of time.

It was my privilege to know Abraham Lincoln and to know him well. I saw and conversed with him at different times during his administration, and upon two occasions at least, by his special invitation. He was the first American President, who thus rose above the prejudices of his times, and country.

I mention it as a proof of his independence. He knew that he could do nothing which would call down upon him more fiercely the ribaldry of the vulgar—than by showing any respect to a colored man.

I found him as you all know him to have been a plain man. There was neither paint nor varnish about him. His manners were simple, unaffected[,] unstudied. His language was like himself—plain[,] strong, sinewy—and earnest. He stated his views with great clearness and strength. Few men could state a case so strongly and convincingly. His utterances were always to the point and without ornament.

Though a western man—he was entirely free from extravagance or exaggeration in thought or speech: He was conscious of the vast responsibilities resting upon him, but bore himself—as one able to bear them successfully. His dignity as the President, never stood in the way of his ami[a]bility as a man. He was like his pictures, the same man from whichever side you viewed him. He neither awed by his silence nor silenced by the volubility or authority of his speech. While willing to give, he was equally willing to receive: and so far from feeling restrained, in his presence, he acted upon me as all truly great men act upon their fellow men, as a Liberator,—He set me at perfect Liberty—to state where I differed from him as freely, as where I agreed with him. From the first five minutes I seemed to myself, to have been acquainted with [him] during all my life. He was one of the most solid men I ever met, and one of the most transparent.

What Mr Lincoln was among white men; How he bore himself towards them, I do not know, but this much I am bound to say, that he was one of the very few white Americans who could converse with a negro without anything like condecension, and without in anywise reminding him of the unpopularity of his color.

If you will pardon the seeming egotism I will mention a fact or two in further illustration of the character of President Lincoln and of his kindly disposition towards colored people. He seemed to want to know them thor[o]ughly. Born in Kentucky—living in Illinois—accustomed to seeing the colored man in most unfavorable conditions[,] it was natural to expect from him at the first—as those made to the colored people he called about him during the first years of the war.[32] But Mr Lincoln soon outgrew his colonization ideas and schemes—and came to look upon the Blackman as an American citizen.

On one occasion while conversing with him, his messenger twice announced that Governor Buckenham[33] of Connecticut was in an adjoining room, and was very desirous of seeing him. Tell the Governor to wait—said Mr Lincoln—I want to have a long talk with my friend Douglass. I remained a full hour after this with the President, while Governor Buckenham waited patiently in an adjoining room the Presidents pleasure to see.

This was probably the first time in the history of the country when the Governor of a state, was required to wait for an interview, because the President of the United States, was engaged in conversation with a negro.

"Assassination of President Lincoln," Manuscript of Address Delivered at City Hall, Portland, Maine, December 8, 1865[34] Frederick Douglass Papers, Manuscript Division, Library of Congress

The present year will long be remembered for two very important and instructive events in American history: one of which brought unspeakable joy and hope to the national heart, for it was the sudden collapse—and downfall—of a stubborn, protracted, fierce and sanguinary rebellion, undertaken and prosecuted, for no other earthly object, than *to perpetuate a privileged class* in the southern states and to make slavery perpetual on this continent. The other event to which I refer, and which will mainly occupy our attention this Evening, filled the national heart with the bitterest anguish it ever knew, for it was, the assassas[ination] of Abraham Lincoln, one of the best men that ever presided over the destinies of this or any other country. This eventful year is now drawing to a close, but a few days of it remain to us—for good or for evil: Yet judging from the ominous clouds that hang on the political sky, this same year of ours which has borne so many marked features, is fated to bear still another—one which shall be more striking, and revolting than either rebellion or assassination. [Here Douglass crossed out a sentence about Andrew Johnson's reconstruction policy, calling it "the crime of crimes," which he said he would come back to later in the speech.]

The American people have experienced many shocks during the last four years: some of these have been heavy and terrible in the extreme causing the very pillars of the state to tremble and the boldest to quail in view of the possible fate of the Republic: but the shock caused by the ass[ass]ination of Abraham Lincoln was the heaviest of all—and should never be forgotten.

It was as if some grand convulsion in nature had occurred; for had the solid Earth opened and swallowed up one [of] our chief towns or cities—had the tombs burst beneath our feet and the sheeted dead risen from the dust of ages and stalked through our streets in open day the sensation of horror, could not have been more profound—than when this terrible crime was first announced: A hush fell upon the land as though each man in it heard a voice from Heaven, an uninterpreted sound from the sky and had paused to learn its meaning.

The calamity was so sudden, so out of joint with the prevailing sense of security, involved such a transition from one extreme of feeling to another, now the wildest joy and exultation of victory to the very dust and ashes of sorrow and mourning—that few could at first believe it.

As at no time before during all the war, the Loyal people were rejoicing in great and decisive victories. The rebel capital so long besieged and so desperately defended had fallen. General Lee with his boasted invincible army—composed of the elite of Virginia—had surrendered to General Grant. Mobile and Wilmington had capitulated. Loyal Black troops were timing their high footsteps to the tune of Old John Brown in the City of Charleston, the very nest of the rebellion. The rebel army was every where beaten in the field—scattered like the dust before the north wind, and the end of the rebellion seemed at the door:

The great North was even then beginning to soften down its justly kindled wrath, and to exhibit unexampled magnanimity—in its clemency and forgiveness towards the rebels. The tone of our public journals was rapidly assuming that sickly sentimental character which so disgusted earnest men during the first two years of the war.

Southern Generals were becoming decidedly popular at the North. Lee was spoken of with only a little less respect than General Grant. Men seemed as thankful to General Lee for surrendering as to General Grant for making him surrender. The south was no longer our deadly foe but our erring Brother.

It was at such a time as this when the nation was weary of war—sick of blood, gladly laying off its armour, meditating mercy—it was when the whole southern horizon so long dark and grim with clouds of war, was fringed with the golden dawn of peace, that slavery dealt us its heaviest blow—and committed its most stupendous crime—

I do not intend to treat you to a lecture entirely devoted to the life and character of Abraham Lincoln. That is already a well trodden field. It has been gleaned from centre to circumference. The press[,] the pulpit, the platform, poetry and song, art and skill in all their departments have been busily employed in illustrating his character—and commending his many virtues. All, therefore, that I can do in what I have to say of him, will be to give back in some humble measure to my audience their own thoughts and feelings.

The function of the orator is high, but it is seldom higher or nobler than this. When most successful, he resembles his audience as the wave the ocean. His weight and volume[,] his strength and beauty[,] are borrowed from the sea out of which he rises.

There is a charm about the life and character of the illustrious deceased which will never lose its power.

A thousand years hence, when even the solid marble that shades his honored dust shall have crumbled, when the great names of military heroes which are now every where greeted with a shout shall cease to dazzle and shall be forgotten by the masses, when even the harrowing details of the late rebellion shall have faded from the page of history, and when the tremendous war which filled the eye of the civilized world during four years, shall seem but as a speck upon the immense distance of time, the name of Abraham Lincoln like that of Dear Old John Brown, will still hold its place in the memories of men, and find eloquent tongues to discourse of his virtues and hold up his character for admiration and imitation.

For wherever men love good Government and abhor treason; Wherever simple manhood commands respect, and kindness of heart awakens love; Wherever freedom has an advocate, the oppressed a friend and the tyrant a foe, the name of Abraham Lincoln, will be honored, venerated, loved.

His life requires a book rather than a lecture. More history that will *live* has been made in connection with his name, than with that of any other American, not excepting Washington. The position he occupied at the head of the American Government, the grandest of the continent and which may even yet be the grandest of the globe; the social depression from which [he] rose to eminence and greatness illustrating in his character the best peculiarities of his country, and the benignant tendencies of free Institutions; the mighty perils through which he successfully conducted the country; the singular purity of his life, and the tragic manner of his death, afford matter for volumes.

One great charm of his life is that he was indebted to himself for himself. He was the architect of his own fortune, a self made man, a flat boat captain, a splitter of Rails; a man of toil—one who travelled far but made the road on which he travelled—one who ascended high, but with hard hands and honest work built the ladder on which he climbed. Flung upon the sea of life in the midnight storm, without oars or life preservers he bravely buffetted the billows—and with sinewy arms swam in safety, where other men despair and sink.

You all know his life by heart: All know of his excellent temper which no insolence could disturb[.] His good natured anecdotes—so humble and yet so wise; all know of his caution, his vigilence, his firmness, his industry, and his honest devotion to his duties as the chief magistrate of the Republic, and are familiar with the leading qualities of the man.

Why then do I make him the subject of discourse on this occasion? The answer is ready—The assassassination of Abraham Lincoln, is an instructive and convenient meadium through which we may survey to some extent the dangers, and learn the solemn duties of this hour.

We are indebted to our enemies here as elsewhere. They have given us in this, as in many other instances during the last thirty years the events which have been most efficient in the overthrow of slavery and the slave power.

They annexed Texas twenty years ago and swelled the vote for freedom—from seven thousand to seventy;[35] They repealed the

Missouri Compromise,[36] and thereby unmasked their revolting designs to nationalize slavery; They thronged the virgin soil of Kansas with border ruffians and thereby roused the loyal North to make Kansas a free state; they enacted a fugitive slave Bill, and each slave caught made a thousand abolitionists. They hanged John Brown, and thereby kindled the wrath of the civilized world against slavery—and placed his name with those of saints and heroes.

Had Abraham Lincoln died from any of the numerous ills, that flesh is heir to, and by which men are ordinarily removed from the busy scenes of life; had he reached that good old age of which his excellent constitution and his equally excellent temperate habits gave promise, the curtain of death falling gradually around him, we should have followed him sadly enough to his honored grave: placing him side by side with our most honored dead,—but without any special distinction, and without the manifestation of those unusual signs of national bereavement—for which his funeral will be ever memorable.

But dying as he did die, for a Cause that takes hold of human nature; Dying as he did die, by the red hand of violence; Dying as he did die at a moment when evincing his greatest trust in the people,—going among them freely like a common man without a guard when he was Commander in Chief of a million of armed men—snatched suddenly away from his work without warning—killed, murdered, assassinated not because of any personal hate which any malice in him provoked, for no man who knew Abraham Lincoln could hate him.

No man ever defined his character better, than himself, when he said—as in his last inaugural—he had malice towards none but charity towards all; but he died as I have said for a cause. He died for the country—for loyalty as against treason, for—Republican Government baised upon Liberty and Equal rights—as against a proud and selfish class Government based upon the enslavement of millions of their fellow men.

Dying thus, his name becomes a text from which to preach that Liberty, and that human Equality, to strike down which he was ruthlessly murdered.

The name of Abraham Lincoln pleads to day with all the eloquence of myrterdom, for the utter extinction, of every root, and fibre, not merely of slavery, but of the insolent, aggressive, and malignant oligarchy—or privileged class founded upon it.

Since his death, every man who gives his voice or his vote, in a way to uphold this privileged class at the south stamps upon the grave of Abraham Lincoln, insults his memory, and wounds the Martyr afresh. [A page appears to be missing here.]

He will shrink from all those manly enterprizes which require strength and develope energy. The same is true of a nation.

The weak man depends upon cunning. He conceals his opinion if he dares to have one, for fear of inability to defend it: He is ever ready for a compromise when resisted. He does not dare to espouse the cause of the weak against the strong—but folds his hands and talks about the wisdom of minding his own business—and leaving other people to manage their own affairs. The courageous, the noble and heroic, do not exist for him. Self preservation becomes his constant and all controlling thought.

Now it cannot be denied that our Nationality under the name of the Union has leaned very much towards the ignoble attitude of the weak man. Under the predecessor of our Martyred President [James Buchanan] the union was too weak to defend itself from treason. The preservation of the Union was with all parties a few years ago—as the very end of the Law for Righteousness. The dear old union was always sick just before an Election—and the leaders of the people insisted that if certain things were done, or certain things were left undone the union would dissolve. We were kept constantly in a state of alarm. The general aim was not to *do*—but to be.

The opinion formed of our National Government by European statesmen and Political Philosophers was not calculated to increase our faith in Free Institutions. They warned us that though well enough in a calm—the ship of state was too weak for stormy weather—that though beautiful to the eye, strong to the touch and swift upon the waves—when the skies were bright and the wind fair—she would go down in the first great storm.

With them there was nothing stable but thrones, nothing powerful but standing armies—nothing author[it]ative, unsupported by the pretention of Divine right. It is not strange that men educated in distrust of the wisdom and virtue of the people should entertain such opinions. We should waste no indignation on those foreigners of little faith. It was natural for them to see, as they did see, at the beginning of the slaveholders rebellion the certain downfall of the American Republic.

The same thing was felt at home, and if thus in the *Green tree*, of vigourous democratic institutions, what else could have been expected in the dried up, mummyfied, king craft and priest craft Governments of the old world!

Nor was doubt of free popular Government confined to unfriendly thinkers at home or abroad. Many of the most patriotic men of this country shared in that doubt. Thomas Jefferson saw the conflict coming and trembled for his country.[37] Many of the Fathers of the Republic argued in favor of a strong [missing word] and against the union on the ground of its weakness.

Well, the trial has come. The experiment has been tried. The strength of the Republic has been tested—tried by treason, by rebellion and by the assassination of its Chief; tried as few forms of Government were ever tried before.

What is the result? This it is, the Country was never stronger than to day. Certainty has taken the place of doubt. Strength has taken the place of weakness—and men now talk of principles where they once dreamed only of compromise. A solid nation takes the place of a deceptive union—and the national *will* dictates the Law instead of an insolent oligarchy composed of the traffickers in human flesh. We no longer tremble for the safety of the ship of state. There is a feeling of security and repose among all on board, except those of the crew who attempted to convert our gallant bark into a pirate.

Happily too, this general confidence is not confined to the limits of our own country. Over the seas, and distant continents it has gone: [A page may be missing here.]

He never awed by his silence, nor silenced by the volubility or authority of his speech: Willing always to give, he was ever, equally willing to receive. He managed to leave his visitor not only free to utter his opinions, but by a wise reserve in the manner of insisting upon his own, he got even a little more from his visitor than his visitor got from him.

From the first moment of my interview with him I seemed to myself to have been acquainted with him for years—for while he was among the most solid men I ever met he was among the most transparent.

What Mr Lincoln was when in company with white men, of course I cannot tell. I saw him mostly alone; but this much I can say of him; he was one of the very few Americans who could entertain a negro and converse with him without in anywise reminding him of the unpopularity of his color.

If you will pardon the egotism, I will mention a fact or two in further illustration of his friendly feeling for the colored race. On one occasion, I remember while conversing with him, his messenger twice announced as in an adjoining room and as wishing to see him Governor Buckingham of Connecticut. Tell the Governor to wait, said President Lincoln—I wish to have a long talk with my friend Douglass. I remained a full hour after this, while the Governor of Connecticut waited without for an interview.

The last days of Mr Lincoln were his best days. If he did not control events he had the wisdom to be instructed by them.[38] When he could no longer withstand the current he swam with it. What he said on the steps of the Capital four years ago did not determine what the same lips should utter four years afterward. No two papers are in stronger contrast than his first and his last Inaugural addresses. The first was intended to reconcile the rebels to the Government by argument and persuasion, the second was a recognition of the operation [of] inevitable and universal Laws. In this he was willing to let justice have its course. You all remember with what solemn emphasis he expressed this on the fourth of March—six weeks before his assassination:

"Fondly do we hope, fervently do we pray that this mighty scourge of war shall soon pass away. Yet if God wills it continue till all the treasure piled by two hundred and fifty years of the bondman's unrequited toil shall have been wasted, and [every] drop of blood drawn by the lash shall have been paid for by one drawn by the sword, we must still say, as was said three thousand years ago—the judgements of the Lord are true and rightious altogether."

Had Mr Lincoln lived, we might have looked for still greater progress. Learning wisdom by war, he would have learned more from Peace. Already he had expressed himself in favor of extending the right of suffrage to two classes [of] colored men, first to the brave colored soldiers who had fought under our flag—and second to the very intelligent part of the colored population [of the] south. This declaration on his part though it seemed to mean but little meant a great deal. It was like Abraham Lincoln. He never shocked prejudices unnecessarily. Having learned statesmanship while splitting rails, he always used the thin edge of the wedge first—and the fact that he used this at all meant that he would if need be, use the thick as well as the thin. He saw the absurdity of asking men to fight for a Government which should degrade them—and the meanness of enfranchising enemies and disfranchising friends. He was a progressive man, a humane man, an honorable man, and at heart an antislavery man. He had exhausted the resources of conciliation upon rebels and slaveholders and now looked to the principles of Liberty and Justice, for the peace, security[,] happiness and prosperity of his country. I assume therefore, had Abraham Lincoln been spared to see this day, the negro of the south would have more than a hope of enfranchisement and no rebels would hold the reins of Government in any one of the late rebellious states. Whosoever else, have cause to mourn the loss of Abraham Lincoln, to the colored people of the country—his death is an unspeakable calamity.[39]

Frederick Douglass in Chicago, late February 1864. Collection of Lucas E. Morel

Part 5
Postwar Correspondence

Within days of Lincoln's assassination, Douglass sent two letters to British abolitionists that offered candid views of his most pressing concerns as the Civil War came to a close. While in mourning for the president he considered a friend, Douglass feared that Reconstruction would find ex-rebels back in power and black Americans without the political means of defending themselves. Douglass naively expected Andrew Johnson to protect black Americans better than Lincoln would have. He likely drew these high hopes from remarks Johnson made before a black crowd in Nashville on October 24, 1864—the day he issued his own emancipation proclamation to Tennessee slaves. (Lincoln excluded Tennessee from the Emancipation Proclamation since the state, with Johnson as military governor, was under Union control.) When the crowd shouted, "We want no Moses but you," Johnson replied that "if no other better shall be found, I will indeed be your Moses." He then added that "I speak now as one who feels the world his country, and all who love equal rights his friends." Speaking of Tennessee's postwar future, Johnson added, "Loyal men, whether white or black, shall alone control her destinies," and "we shall have a better state of things" where "every man has a fair chance in the race of life."[1]

Douglass also engaged in national conversations over how black Americans should commemorate Lincoln's legacy. In a pointed letter to William J. Wilson, a black educator in Washington, DC, Douglass opposed the establishment of a segregated educational institution in Lincoln's honor. He also did not want black people to raise money for the college by exploiting the nation's sorrow over Lincoln's death.

Finally, Douglass showed heartfelt concern for Lincoln's widow and was grateful to her for giving him her husband's favorite cane. As Mary Lincoln had fallen on hard times, he and other black leaders agreed to deliver lectures to raise funds for her. The letters reproduced here—written to Mary's seamstress and confidante, Elizabeth Keckley—omit several passages about the planning of these events. Douglass did not know when he wrote these letters that Mary had declined this aid.

Letter to Russell or Mary Carpenter, dated Rochester, New York, April 18, 1865 (excerpt)
London *Inquirer*, May 13, 1865

After expressing the horror and sadness with which the first news of the assassination of the President had filled his mind, Mr. Douglass says:—

While I mourn the death of Mr. Lincoln as of a personal friend—for he was to me a personal friend—while I remember the good acts of his life towards my enslaved people, I still think that the man who succeeds him will answer better the stern requirements of the hour than even Mr. Lincoln. He was too much under the dominion of his amiable qualities. He thought the rebels should not be punished but petted, not conquered but conciliated. The recent victories of the Union armies relaxed all his sterner qualities, and he thought to win back his enemies by his kindness, rather than compel their respect and obedience by his power. He forgave without repentance, and, while murder and assassination were darkly sheltered in rebel hearts and homes, he took the sullen submission of treason as evidence of loyalty, and was willing to concede them everything but their slavery, and allow them still to be the dominant and ruling class at the South. Owning the land as they do, and organised as they are, with their negroes disfranchised, and the poor whites ignorant, the Government of the South in their hands, they could easily find a substitute for slavery, and lord it over both white and black as they pleased. Andrew Johnson, the man now at the head of the Government, understands this better than Mr. Lincoln, and I hope more of him than I dared to hope from Mr. Lincoln. As a man he is not equal to Mr. Lincoln, but as a ruler I think he will prove superior. Perhaps in Mr. Lincoln's place, during the past four years, he would have done no better; he might have done worse; but that first work is done, and we need men of a different mould for what remains.

Nothing short of equality before the laws can give the black man any security in this country, and for nothing less than that do I ask the American people and Government. If I had a thousand constitutional guarantees of freedom, they would be a mockery without the ability of the black man to sue and testify in the Courts, and vote for the men who are to make the laws. In a country where the great mass of the people are disfranchised, it is comparatively easy to be one of that mass. Masses of men can take care of themselves anywhere, but to be deprived of a privilege enjoyed by everybody is a hardship and blight upon the proscribed race. I think Mr. Johnson is in favour of enfranchising the negro. Give the negro this one right, and I ask nothing more for him. Whatever else he may lack after that will come finally, without special effort.

Letter to Julia Griffiths Crofts, dated Rochester, New York, April 20, 1865 (excerpt)
Leeds Mercury, May 12, 1865

I write with a sad heart to-day. The very powers of darkness seem to be let loose among us—slavery, war, rebellion, murder, assassination, are the bitter ingredients of our national cup. You will get the news ere this reaches you that our President Lincoln, kind, amiable man, is dead, and that your old friend and correspondent, Governor Seward,

Secretary of State, and his son, are nearly dead, and all by the hand of conspirators and assassins. Mr. Seward was stabbed three times on his sick bed, where he already lay doubtful of recovery. The assassination is a part of the slaveholding rebellion. Beaten on the battle field, they seek to do by assassination what they have failed to do by open war. It is evident that the murder of the President and Mr. Seward was only a part of the work of blood. They intended to strike down at one blow the heads of all the departments of Government, and by killing the whole Cabinet, introduce anarchy and social chaos.

Oh! the terrible blackness and horror of this deed. The deepest gloom hangs over this whole land. The slaughter of thousands on the field of battle is nothing to this. In the murder of Mr. Lincoln the rebels have slain the man of all others in the Government who stood between them and the loyal wrath their crimes have provoked. He was for moderation, for conciliation, and for restoration. He would give them their houses, their lands, their cattle, and restore them to their forfeited citizenship, only stipulating for the abolition of slavery. I now think that even this dreadful crime, though intended to strike down both the Government and the cause of the slave, will tend to the advantage of both. It will unite the North in the prosecution of the war, and prevent that hasty reunion of the South with the North which boded no good to the coloured race. I think the first great work of Mr. Lincoln was done. By his excellent qualities, his wonderful moderation, his remarkable caution, and his extreme amiability, he held the country together, in the presence of this tremendous rebellion, better than any other man perhaps could have done. The very villany of the rebellion was unable to move him to rigorous hostility to slavery. He struck "more in sorrow than in anger,"[2] and then only from military necessity. For one, I have always looked with apprehension to the day of settlement. A reconstruction was, and still is, the great danger to the coloured race. Once let the South ask for terms as a condition of the return to the Union, then will be the real trial of Northern virtue. Mr. Lincoln did well while the rebels were in arms, but his very amiability might have led him wrong when confronted by apparent repentance.

It is not for me to discourse of the plans and purposes of Divine Providence. Some talk as if the murder had been planned in heaven. I hope to steer clear of this profanity. Looking at the matter only with human understanding, I think I see that good will be brought out of this terrible evil, as out of many others; and that slavery has now been killed by its friends, beyond the hope of recovery. I think, too, that Mr. Johnson is, in many respects, better qualified for the work to come than was Mr. Lincoln. Like Mr. Lincoln, he is a self-made man. Like Mr. Lincoln, he was born in a slave State; but, unlike Mr. Lincoln, he has lived all his life in a slave State, and better understands than Mr. Lincoln did the necessity of putting down not only slavery but the slave power. This power, owning the land of the South, possessing the influence which education gives, and which it has so long wielded as an aristocracy in favour of slavery, would be dangerous to liberty even after the fall of slavery. This Mr. Johnson, the present President, well understands. I hope much of him. I hope he will see to it that the negro is made every way equal before the laws of the South. Without the ballot, freedom for the negro in the slave States will be but little better than a name.

You speak of efforts in behalf of the freedmen. My opinion is that all such efforts would be rendered unnecessary in two years after the war if the American people would give the negro the elective franchise. The great evil is that the American people desire to make their pity a substitute for justice. I want you, and other good friends of my race in England, to be on the lookout for those who come to ask alms of you in the name of my race, to tell them, from me, that they would do a far better work for the negro by staying home and exerting their influence in favour of giving the negro the means of protecting himself, by giving him the ballot-box. We have been greatly wronged as slaves. We are now likely to be equally wronged by persons, in the garb of friendship, representing us as a helpless race.

Letter to William J. Wilson, August 8, 1865
***The Liberator*, September 29, 1865**

ROCHESTER, N.Y. Aug. 8th, 1865.

W. J. WILSON, ESQ.—*My Dear Sir:* In answer to your note requesting me to allow my name to stand as one of the officers of the "Educational Monument Association," I beg to state that I cannot allow my name as you request, nor can I, with my present views, favor the plan adopted by the Association. On many accounts, I wish I could unite with you in this enterprise, and not the least among them is the pleasure I experience in finding myself coöperating with yourself, and other gentlemen connected with this Educational Monument Association, for the common elevation and improvement of our condition as a people. But I must be true to my conviction of fitness.

When I go for anything, I like to go strong, and when I cannot go thus, I had better not go at all. You cannot want a man among you who cannot bring his whole heart to the work. I can't do this, and hence will not fill the place, which, if filled at all, should be filled more worthily.

You will, my old friend, naturally inquire why I cannot do this? Here there is no difficulty but the time required to answer. There is much I could say, but I must be brief. First of all, then, I must say, this whole monument business, in its present shape, strikes me as an offence against good taste, and as calculated to place the colored people in an undesirable and discreditable position before the country. Such, I say, is my present conviction. Do not consider me hostile to monuments nor to colleges; I am not to either. Things good in standing alone are not always good when *mixed.*

Now, a monument by the colored people, erected at the expense of the colored people, in honor of the memory of Abraham Lincoln, expressive of their gratitude and affection for their friend and great benefactor, however humble and inexpensive the marble, I could understand and appreciate, and the world would understand and appreciate the effort. A monument like this would express one of the holiest sentiments of the human heart. It would be, as all such offerings should be, free from all taint of self-love or self-interest on our part, as a class. It would be our own act and deed, and would show the aftercoming generations, in some degree, the sentiments awakened among the oppressed by the death of Mr. Lincoln. A monument of this kind, erected by the colored people—that is, by the voluntary offerings of the colored people—is a very different thing from a monument built by money contributed by white men to enable colored people to build a monument. We should bury our own dead and build our own monuments, and all monuments which we would build to the memory of our friends, if we would not invite the continued contempt of the white race upon our heads. Now, whenever a movement shall be made for such a monument, I am with it, heart and soul, and will do my best to make it a success. So much for the monument part of your plan.

Now a word of the college. I am heartily in favor of all needful educational institutions for the present education of colored people, even though they be separate institutions. Present circumstances are the only apology for such institutions. When a colored lad or girl can go to school or college with the white people of the country, it is best for all that they should do so. Hence, I am not for building up permanent separate institutions for colored people of any kind. Even in the matter of the college, therefore, in so far as the idea of permanent isolation is contemplated, I am opposed to your plan. The lesson now flashed upon the attention of the American people, the lesson which they must learn, or neglect to do so at their peril, is that "equal manhood means equal rights," and further, that the American people must stand each for all and all for each, without respect to color or race. The spirit of the age is against all institutions based upon prejudice, or providing for prejudice of race. I, therefore, am opposed to doing anything looking to the perpetuity of prejudice. I expect to see the colored people of this country enjoying the same freedom, voting at the same ballot-box, using the same cartridge box,[3] going to the same schools, attending the same churches, travelling in the same street-cars, in the same railroad-cars, on the same steamboats, proud of the same country, fighting the same foe, and enjoying the same peace and all its advantages. This is no new position with me. Having held it when the prospect was dark, I shall not relinquish it now when the clouds are disappearing and the heavens are bright.

But, supposing the college a desirable thing, I am opposed to obtaining it in the way proposed. As I understand the matter, you propose to establish a general collecting agency, persons to travel and solicit *five hundred thousand dollars* from the public, white as well as colored, to enable you to build a monument to the memory of your departed friend and benefactor, which monument you propose shall be in the form of a college, for the exclusive use of colored people. If I am right in this statement, I beg you to hear me a moment further.

A college is a college, and has its own peculiar claims, and ought to stand upon its own merits. A monument is a monument, and has its own peculiar claims and merits. The two things spring from different motives, and are suggestive of different ideas and sentiments. For a monument, by itself, and upon its own merits, I say good. For a college, by itself, (with the limitations already suggested,) and upon its own merits, I say *good.* But for a college-monument, or for a monument-college, I do not say good; for the things, however good separately, are incongruous and offensive when connected as now proposed. The whole scheme is derogatory to the character of the colored people of the United States. It carries on its front a distasteful implication. *It looks to me like an attempt to wash the black man's face in the nation's tears for Abraham Lincoln!* It places the paddle-wheels of the colored man's boat in the tide of the popular grief, with a view to his special advantage. I am for washing the black man's face, (that is, educating his mind,) for that is a good thing to be done, and I appreciate the nation's tears for Abraham Lincoln; but I am not so enterprising as to think of turning the nation's veneration for our martyred President into a means of advantage to the colored people, and of sending around the hat to a mourning public.

When the colored people want a college, let them beg for a college on its own merits, and in the name of the living, and I am with them. When they want a monument to perpetuate the memory of a good man, I am with them. But when they want to raise a college for themselves out of the general affection of the American people for the dead, I am not with them, and frankness requires me to say so in all earnestness. If these views are ill-founded, and you can show them to be so, I shall only be too happy to abandon them.

With best wishes and great respect for you, personally, I am, dear sir, very truly yours,

FREDERICK DOUGLASS.[4]

Letter to Mary Lincoln, August 17, 1865
Gilder Lehrman Collection

Rochester. N.Y. August 17. 1865.

Mrs Abraham Lincoln:

Dear Madam: Allow me to thank you, as I certainly do thank you most sincerely for your thoughtful kindness in making me the owner of a cane—which was formerly the property and the favorite walking staff of your late lamented husband, the honored and venerated President of the United States.

I assure you, that this inestimable memmento of his Excellency will be retained in my possession while I live—an object of sacred interest—a token not merely of the kind consideration in which I have reason to know that the President was pleased to hold me personally, but as an indication of his humane interest [in the] welfare of my whole race.

With every proper sentiment of Respect and Esteem

I am, Dear Madam, Your Obdt Srvt.

Frederick Douglass

Letters to Elizabeth Keckley, October and November 1867 (excerpts)
Elizabeth Keckley, *Behind the Scenes; Or, Thirty Years a Slave, and Four Years in the White House* (New York: G. W. Carleton, 1868)

ROCHESTER, Oct. 18, 1867.

MY DEAR MRS. KECKLEY:—You judge me rightly—I am willing to do what I can to place the widow of our martyr President in the affluent position which her relation to that good man and to the country entitles her to. But I doubt the wisdom of getting up a series of lectures for that purpose; that is just the last thing that should be done. Still, if the thing is done, it should be done on a grand scale. The best speakers in the country should be secured for the purpose. You should not place me at the head nor at the foot of the list, but sandwich me between, for thus out of the way, it would not give *color* to the idea. I am to speak in Newark on Wednesday evening next, and will endeavor to see you on the subject. Of course, if it would not be too much to ask, I would gladly see Mrs. Lincoln, if this could be done in a quiet way without the reporters getting hold of it, and using it in some way to the prejudice of that already much abused lady.

Elizabeth Keckley. Frontispiece of *Behind the Scenes* (1868). Courtesy of the National Portrait Gallery, Smithsonian Institution

POTTSVILLE, Oct. 29, 1867.

MY DEAR MRS. KECKLEY:—You know the drift of my views concerning the subscription for Mrs. Lincoln. Yet I wish to place them more distinctly before you, so that, if you have occasion to refer to me in connection with the matter, you can do so with accuracy and certainty.

It is due Mrs. Lincoln that she should be indemnified, as far as money can do so, for the loss of her beloved husband. Honor, gratitude, and a manly sympathy, all say yes to this. I am willing to go farther than this, and say that Mrs. Lincoln herself should be the judge of the amount which shall be deemed sufficient, believing that she would not transcend reasonable limits. The obligation resting on the nation at large is great and increasing, but especially does it become colored men to recognize that obligation. It was the hand of Abraham Lincoln that broke the fetters of our enslaved people, and let them out of the house of bondage. When he was slain, our great benefactor fell, and left his wife and children to the care of those for whom he gave up all. Shame on the man or woman who, under such circumstances, would grudge a few paltry dollars, to smooth the pathway of such a widow! All this, and more, I feel and believe. But such is the condition of this question, owing to party feeling, and personal animosities now mixed up with it, that we are compelled to consider these in the effort we are making to obtain subscriptions. . . .

[Douglass here discussed ways to promote a lecture at the Cooper Union so that "the people, without regard to party, come up to the discharge of this national duty." He added that "the cause" should not "be made ridiculous by failure at the outset."]

ROCHESTER, Nov. 10, 1867.

MY DEAR MRS. KECKLEY: . . .

I thank you sincerely for the note containing a published letter of dear Mrs. Lincoln; both letters do credit to the excellent lady. I prize her beautiful letter to me very highly. It is the letter of a refined and spirited lady, let the world say what it will of her. I would write her a word of acknowledgment but for fear to burden her with correspondence. . . .

[Douglass here discussed logistics for putting on an event to raise money for Mrs. Lincoln.] This testimonial must be more than a negro testimonial. It is a great national duty. Mr. Lincoln did everything for the black man, but he did it not for the black man's sake, but for the nation's sake. His life was given for the nation; but for being President, Mr. Lincoln would have been alive, and Mrs. Lincoln would have been a wife, and not a widow as now. Do all you can, dear Mrs. Keckley—nobody can do more than you in removing the mountains of prejudice towards that good lady, and opening the way of success in the plan.

I am, dear madam, very truly yours,

FREDERICK DOUGLASS.

Part 6
Autobiography

The following excerpts include the most substantive commentary on Lincoln from Douglass's third autobiography, *Life and Times of Frederick Douglass.* Originally published in 1881, these excerpts are drawn from the revised 1892 edition because Douglass cleaned up infelicities in his prose. In recounting his experiences, Douglass downplayed or omitted many of his earlier criticisms of Lincoln.

"Increasing Demands of the Slave Power" (excerpt from part 2, chapter 9)

As a measure of agitation, the repeal of the Missouri Compromise alluded to was perhaps the most effective. It was that which brought Abraham Lincoln into prominence, and into conflict with Stephen A. Douglas (who was the author of that measure) and compelled the Western States to take a deeper interest than they ever had done before in the whole question. Pregnant words were now spoken on the side of freedom, words which went straight to the heart of the nation. It was Mr. Lincoln who told the American people at this crisis that the "Union could not long endure half slave and half free; that they must be all one or the other, and that the public mind could find no resting place but in the belief in the ultimate extinction of slavery."[1] These were not the words of an abolitionist—branded a fanatic, and carried away by an enthusiastic devotion to the Negro—but the calm, cool, deliberate utterance of a statesman, comprehensive enough to take in the welfare of the whole country. No wonder that the friends of freedom saw in this plain man of Illinois the proper standard-bearer of all the moral and political forces which could be united and wielded against the slave power. In a few simple words he had embodied the thought of the loyal nation, and indicated the character fit to lead and guide the country amid perils present and to come.

The South was not far behind the North in recognizing Abraham Lincoln as the natural leader of the rising political sentiment of the country against slavery, and it was equally quick in its efforts to counteract and destroy his influence. Its papers teemed with the bitterest invectives against the "backwoodsman of Illinois," the "flat-boatman," the "rail-splitter," the "third-rate lawyer," and much else and worse.

"The Beginning of the End" (excerpts from part 2, chapter 10)

Though disappointed in my tour on the Continent, and called home by one of the saddest events that can afflict the domestic circle,[2] my presence here was fortunate, since it enabled me to participate in the most important and memorable presidential canvass ever witnessed in the United States, and to labor for the election of a man who in the order of events was destined to do a greater service to his country and to mankind than any man who had gone before him in the presidential office. It is something to couple one's name with great occasions, and it was a great thing to me to be permitted to bear some humble part in this, the greatest that had thus far come to the American people. It was a great thing to achieve American independence when we numbered three millions, but it was a greater thing to save this country from dismemberment and ruin when it numbered thirty millions. He alone of all our Presidents was to have the opportunity to destroy slavery, and to lift into manhood millions of his countrymen hitherto held as chattels and numbered with the beasts of the field.

The presidential canvass of 1860 was three-sided, and each side had its distinctive doctrine as to the question of slavery and slavery extension. We had three candidates in the field. Stephen A. Douglas was the standard-bearer of what may be called the western faction of the old divided democratic party, and John C. Breckenridge was the standard-bearer of the southern or slaveholding faction of that party. Abraham Lincoln represented the then young, growing, and united republican party. The lines between these parties and candidates were about as distinctly and clearly drawn as political lines are capable of being drawn. The name of Douglas stood for territorial sovereignty, or, in other words, for the right of the people of a territory to admit or exclude, to establish or abolish, slavery, as to them might seem best. The doctrine of Breckenridge was that slaveholders were entitled to carry their slaves into any territory of the United States and to hold them there, with or without the consent of the people of the territory; that the Constitution of its own force carried slavery into any territory open for settlement in the United States, and protected it there. To both these parties, factions, and doctrines, Abraham Lincoln and the republican party stood opposed. They held that the Federal Government had the right and the power to exclude slavery from the territories of the United States, and that that right and power ought to be exercised to the extent of confining slavery inside the slave States, with a view to its ultimate extinction. . . .

Against both Douglas and Breckenridge Abraham Lincoln proposed his grand historic doctrine of the power and duty of the National Government to prevent the spread and perpetuity of slavery.

Into this contest I threw myself, with firmer faith and more ardent hope than ever before, and what I could do by pen or voice was done with a will. The most remarkable and memorable feature of this canvass was, that it was prosecuted under the portentous shadow of a threat: leading public men of the South had, with the vehemence of fiery purpose, given it out in advance that in case of their failure to elect their candidate (Mr. John C. Breckenridge) they would proceed to take the slaveholding States out of the Union, and that, in no event whatever, would they submit to the rule of Abraham Lincoln. To many of the peace-loving friends of the Union, this was a fearful announcement, and it doubtless cost the Republican candidates many votes. To many others, however, it was deemed a mere bravado—sound and fury signifying nothing.[3] With a third class its effect was very different. They were tired of the rule-or-ruin intimidation adopted by the South, and felt then, if never before, that they had quailed before it too often and too long. It came as an insult and a challenge in one, and imperatively called upon them for independence, self-assertion, and resentment. Had southern men puzzled their brains to find the most effective means to array against slavery and slaveholding manners the solid opposition of the North, they could not have hit upon any expedient better suited to that end than was this threat. It was not only unfair, but insolent, and more like an address to cowardly slaves than one to independent freemen. It had in it the meanness of the horse-jockey who, on entering a race, proposes, if beaten, to run off with the stakes. In all my speeches made during this canvass, I did not fail to take advantage of this southern bluster and bullying.

As I have said, this southern threat lost many votes, but it gained more than would cover the lost. It frightened the timid, but stimulated the brave; and the result was—the triumphant election of Abraham Lincoln. . . .

The reaction from the glorious assertion of freedom and independence on the part of the North in the triumphant election of Abraham Lincoln, was a painful and humiliating development of its weakness. It seemed as if all that had been gained in the canvass was about to be surrendered to the vanquished, and that the South, though beaten at the polls, was to be victorious and have everything its own way in the final result. During all the intervening months, from November to the ensuing March, the drift of Northern sentiment was towards compromise. To smooth the way for this, most of the Northern legislatures repealed their personal liberty bills, as they were supposed to embarrass the surrender of fugitive slaves to their claimants. The feeling everywhere seemed to be that something must be done to convince the South that the election of Mr. Lincoln meant no harm to slavery or the slave power, and that the North was sound on the question of the right of the master to hold and hunt his slave as long as he pleased, and that even the right to hold slaves in the Territories should be submitted to the supreme court, which would probably decide in favor of the most extravagant demands of the slave States.

"Secession and War" (excerpt from part 2, chapter 11)

THE BLACK MAN AT THE WHITE HOUSE.

My efforts to secure just and fair treatment for the colored soldiers did not stop at letters and speeches. At the suggestion of my friend, Major Stearns, to whom the foregoing letter was addressed,[4] I was induced to go to Washington and lay the complaints of my people before President Lincoln and the Secretary of War and to urge upon them such action as should secure to the colored troops then fighting for the country a reasonable degree of fair play. I need not say that at the time I undertook this mission it required much more nerve than a similar one would require now. The distance then between the black man and the white American citizen was immeasurable. I was an ex-slave, identified with a despised race, and yet I was to meet the most exalted person in this great republic. It was altogether an unwelcome duty, and one from which I would gladly have been excused. I could not know what kind of a reception would be accorded me. I might be told to go home and mind my business, and leave such questions as I had come to discuss to be managed by the men wisely chosen by the American people to deal with them. Or I might be refused an interview altogether. Nevertheless, I felt bound to go, and my acquaintance with Senators Charles Sumner, Henry Wilson, Samuel Pomeroy, Secretary Salmon P. Chase, Secretary William H. Seward, and Assistant Secretary of War Charles A. Dana encouraged me to hope at least for a civil reception.

My confidence was fully justified in the result. I shall never forget my first interview with this great man. I was accompanied to the executive mansion and introduced to President Lincoln by Senator Pomeroy. The room in which he received visitors was the one now used by the President's secretaries. I entered it with a moderate estimate of my own consequence, and yet there I was to talk with, and even to advise, the head man of a great nation. Happily for me, there was no vain pomp and ceremony about him. I was never more quickly or more completely put at ease in the presence of a great man than in that of Abraham Lincoln. He was seated, when I entered, in a low armchair with his feet extended on the floor, surrounded by a large number of documents and several busy secretaries. The room bore the marks of business, and the persons in it, the President included, appeared to be much over-worked and tired. Long lines of care were already deeply written on Mr. Lincoln's brow, and his strong face, full of earnestness, lighted up as soon as my name was mentioned.

As I approached and was introduced to him he arose and extended his hand, and bade me welcome. I at once felt myself in the presence of an honest man—one whom I could love, honor, and trust without reserve or doubt. Proceeding to tell him who I was and what I was doing, he promptly, but kindly, stopped me, saying: "I know who you are, Mr. Douglass; Mr. Seward has told me all about you. Sit down. I am glad to see you." I then told him the object of my visit: that I was assisting to raise colored troops; that several months before I had been very successful in getting men to enlist, but that now it was not easy to induce the colored men to enter the service, because there was a feeling among them that the government did not, in several respects, deal fairly with them. Mr. Lincoln asked me to state particulars. I replied that there were three particulars which I wished to bring to his attention. First, that colored soldiers ought to receive the same wages as those paid to white soldiers. Second, that colored soldiers ought to receive the same protection when taken prisoners, and be exchanged as readily and on the same terms as any other prisoners, and if Jefferson Davis should shoot or hang colored soldiers in cold blood the United States government should, without delay, retaliate in kind and degree upon Confederate prisoners in its hands. Third, when colored soldiers, seeking "the bubble reputation at the cannon's mouth,"[5] performed great and uncommon service on the battle-field, they should be rewarded by distinction and promotion precisely as white soldiers are rewarded for like services.

Mr. Lincoln listened with patience and silence to all I had to say. He was serious and even troubled by what I had said and by what he himself had evidently before thought upon the same points. He, by his silent listening not less than by his earnest reply to my words, impressed me with the solid gravity of his character.

He began by saying that the employment of colored troops at all was a great gain to the colored people; that the measure could not have been successfully adopted at the beginning of the war; that the wisdom of making colored men soldiers was still doubted; that their enlistment was a serious offense to popular prejudice; that they had larger motives for being soldiers than white men; that they ought to be willing to enter the service upon any condition; that the fact that they were not to receive the same pay as white soldiers seemed a necessary concession to smooth the way to their employment at all as soldiers, but that ultimately they would receive the same. On the second point, in respect to equal protection, he said the case was more difficult. Retaliation was a terrible remedy, and one which it was very difficult to apply; that, if once begun, there was no telling where it would end; that if he could get hold of the Confederate soldiers who had been guilty of treating colored soldiers as felons he could easily retaliate, but the thought of hanging men for a crime perpetrated by others was revolting to his feelings. He thought that the rebels themselves would stop such barbarous warfare; that less evil would be done if retaliation were not resorted to and that he had already received information that colored soldiers were being treated as prisoners of war. In all this I saw the tender heart of the man rather than the stern warrior and commander-in-chief of the American army and navy, and, while I could not agree with him, I could but respect his humane spirit.

On the third point he appeared to have less difficulty, though he did not absolutely commit himself. He simply said that he would sign any commission to colored soldiers whom his Secretary of War should commend to him. Though I was not entirely satisfied with his views, I was so well satisfied with the man and with the educating tendency of the conflict that I determined to go on with the recruiting.

"Hope for the Nation" (excerpts from part 2, chapter 12)

The first of January, 1863, was a memorable day in the progress of American liberty and civilization. It was the turning-point in the conflict between freedom and slavery. . . . This proclamation changed everything. It gave a new direction to the councils of the Cabinet, and to the conduct of the national arms. I shall leave to the statesman, the philosopher and the historian, the more comprehensive discussion of this document, and only tell how it touched me, and those in like condition with me at the time. . . . [Douglass described being at Tremont Temple in Boston awaiting word that Lincoln signed the proclamation.] Although the conditions on which Mr. Lincoln had promised to withhold it had not been complied with,[6] yet, from many considerations, there was room to doubt and fear. Mr. Lincoln was known to be a man of tender heart, and boundless patience: no man could tell to what length he might go, or might refrain from going, in the direction of peace and reconciliation. Hitherto, he had not shown himself a man of heroic measures, and, properly enough, this step belonged to that class. It must be the end of all compromises with slavery—a declaration that thereafter the war was to be conducted on a new principle, with a new aim. It would be a full and fair assertion that the government would neither trifle, or be trifled with, any longer. But would it come? On the side of doubt, it was said that Mr. Lincoln's kindly nature might cause him to relent at the last moment; that Mrs. Lincoln, coming from an old slaveholding family, would influence him to delay, and to give the slaveholders one other chance. . . . [Douglass then described the "wild and grand" scene when word finally arrived.]

The proclamation itself was throughout like Mr. Lincoln. It was framed with a view to the least harm and the most good possible in the circumstances, and with especial consideration of the latter. It was thoughtful, cautious, and well guarded at all points. While he hated slavery, and really desired its destruction, he always proceeded against it in a manner the least likely to shock or drive from him any who were truly in sympathy with the preservation of the Union, but who were not friendly to emancipation. For this he kept up the distinction between loyal and disloyal slaveholders, and discriminated in favor of the one, as against the other. In a word, in all that he did, or attempted, he made it manifest that the one great and all-commanding object with him was the peace and preservation of the Union, and that this was the motive and main-spring of all his measures. His wisdom and moderation at this point were for a season useful to the loyal cause in the border States, but it may be fairly questioned whether it did not chill the union ardor of the loyal people of the North in some degree, and diminish rather than increase the sum of our power against the rebellion; for moderate, cautious, and guarded as was this proclamation, it created a howl of indignation and wrath amongst the rebels and their allies. The old cry was raised by the copperhead organs of "an abolition war," and a pretext was thus found for an excuse for refusing to enlist, and for marshaling all the negro prejudice of the North on the rebel side. Men could say they were willing to fight for the Union, but that they were not willing to fight for the freedom of the negroes; and thus it was made difficult to procure enlistments or to enforce the draft. . . .

My interviews with President Lincoln and his able Secretary [Stanton], before narrated, greatly increased my confidence in the anti-slavery integrity of the government, although I confess I was greatly disappointed at my failure to receive the commission promised me by Secretary Stanton. I, however, faithfully believed, and loudly proclaimed my belief, that the rebellion would be suppressed, the Union preserved, the slaves emancipated and that the colored soldiers would in the end have justice done them. This confidence was immeasurably strengthened when I saw Gen. George B. McClellan relieved from the command of the army of the Potomac and Gen. U.S. Grant placed at its head, and in command of all the armies of the United States. . . .[7]

It was when General Grant was fighting his way through the Wilderness[8] to Richmond, on the "line" he meant to pursue "if it took all summer," and every reverse to his arms was made the occasion for a fresh demand for peace without emancipation, that President Lincoln did me the honor to invite me to the Executive Mansion for a conference on the situation. I need not say I went most gladly. The main subject on which he wished to confer with me was as to the means most desirable to be employed outside the army to induce the slaves in the rebel States to come within the Federal lines. The increasing opposition to the war, in the North, and the mad cry against it, because it was being made an abolition war, alarmed Mr. Lincoln, and made him apprehensive that a peace might be forced upon him which would leave still in slavery all who had not come within our lines. What he wanted was to make his proclamation as effective as possible in the event of such a peace. He said, in a regretful tone, "The slaves are not coming so rapidly and so numerously to us as I had hoped." I replied that the slaveholders knew how to keep such things from their slaves, and probably very few knew of his proclamation. "Well," he said, "I want you to set about devising some means of making them acquainted with it, and for bringing them into our lines." He spoke with great earnestness and much solicitude, and seemed troubled by the attitude of Mr. Greeley and by the growing impatience at the war that was being manifested throughout the North. He said he was being accused of protracting the war beyond its legitimate object and of failing to make peace when he might have done so to advantage. He was afraid of what might come of all these complaints, but was persuaded that no solid and lasting peace could come short of absolute submission on the part of the rebels, and he was not for giving them rest by futile conferences with unauthorized persons, at Niagara Falls, or elsewhere. He saw the danger of premature peace, and, like a thoughtful and sagacious man as he was, wished to provide means of rendering such consummation as harmless as possible.

I was the more impressed by this benevolent consideration because he before said, in answer to the peace clamor, that his object was to *save the Union*, and to do so with or without slavery.[9] What he said on this day showed a deeper moral conviction against slavery than I had ever seen before in anything spoken or written by him. I listened with the deepest interest and profoundest satisfaction, and, at his suggestion, agreed to undertake the organizing a band of scouts, composed of colored men, whose business should be somewhat after the original plan of John Brown, to go into the rebel States, beyond the lines of our armies, and carry the news of emancipation, and urge the slaves to come within our boundaries.[10]

This plan, however, was very soon rendered unnecessary, by the success of the war in the Wilderness[11] and elsewhere, and by its termination in the complete abolition of slavery.

I refer to this conversation because I think that, on Mr. Lincoln's part, it is evidence conclusive that the proclamation, so far at least as he was concerned, was not effected merely as a "necessity."

An incident occurred during this interview which illustrates the character of this great man, though the mention of it may savor a little of vanity on my part. While in conversation with him his Secretary twice announced "Governor Buckingham of Connecticut," one of the noblest and most patriotic of the loyal governors. Mr. Lincoln said, "Tell Governor Buckingham to wait, for I want to have a long talk with my friend Frederick Douglass." I interposed, and begged him to see the Governor at once, as I could wait; but no, he persisted that he wanted to talk with me and that Governor Buckingham could wait. This was probably the first time in the history of this Republic when its chief magistrate had found an occasion or shown a disposition to exercise such an act of impartiality between persons so widely different in their positions and supposed claims upon his attention. From the manner of the Governor, when he was finally admitted, I inferred that he was as well satisfied with what Mr. Lincoln had done, or had omitted to do, as I was.

I have often said elsewhere what I wish to repeat here, that Mr. Lincoln was not only a great President, but a GREAT MAN—too great to be small in anything. In his company I was never in any way reminded of my humble origin, or of my unpopular color. While I am, as it may seem, boasting of the kind consideration which I have reason to believe that Mr. Lincoln entertained towards me, I may mention one thing more. At the door of my friend John A. Gray, where I was stopping in Washington, I found one afternoon the carriage of Secretary Dole,[12] and a messenger from President Lincoln with an invitation for me to take tea with him at the Soldiers'

Home, where he then passed his nights, riding out after the business of the day was over at the Executive Mansion. Unfortunately, I had an engagement to speak that evening, and having made it one of the rules of my conduct in life never to break an engagement if possible to keep it, I felt obliged to decline the honor. I have often regretted that I did not make this an exception to my general rule. Could I have known that no such opportunity could come to me again, I should have justified myself in disappointing a large audience for the sake of such a visit with Abraham Lincoln.

It is due perhaps to myself to say here that I did not take Mr. Lincoln's attentions as due to my merits or personal qualities. While I have no doubt that Messrs. Seward and Chase had spoken well of me to him, and that the fact of my having been a slave and gained my freedom and of having picked up some sort of an education, and being in some sense a "self-made man,"[13] and having made myself useful as an advocate of the claims of my people, gave me favor in his eyes; yet I am quite sure that the main thing which gave me consideration with him was my well-known relation to the colored people of the Republic, and especially the help which that relation enabled me to give to the work of suppressing the rebellion and of placing the Union on a firmer basis than it ever had or could have sustained in the days of slavery. . . .

The . . . Emancipation proclamation by Abraham Lincoln, had given slavery many and deadly wounds, yet it was in fact only wounded and crippled, not disabled and killed. With this condition of national affairs came the summer of 1864, and with it the revived Democratic party with the story in its mouth that the war was a failure, and with Gen. George B. McClellan, the greatest failure of the war, as its candidate for the presidency. It is needless to say that the success of such a party, on such a platform, with such a candidate, at such a time, would have been a fatal calamity. All that had been done toward suppressing the rebellion and abolishing slavery would have proved of no avail, . . .

When we were thus asked to exchange Abraham Lincoln for George B. McClellan—a successful Union President for an unsuccessful Union general—a party earnestly endeavoring to save the Union, torn and rent by a gigantic rebellion, I thought with Mr. Lincoln that it was not wise to "swap horses while crossing a stream."[14] Regarding, as I did, the continuance of the war to the complete suppression of the rebellion and the retention in office of President Lincoln as essential to the total destruction of slavery, I certainly exerted myself to the uttermost in my small way to secure his reëlection. This most important object was not attained, however, by speeches, letters, or other electioneering appliances. The staggering blows dealt upon the rebellion that year by the armies under Grant and Sherman, and his own great character, ground all opposition to dust and made his election sure even before the question reached the polls. Since William the Silent, who was the soul of the mighty war for religious liberty against Spain and the Spanish inquisition, no leader of men has been loved and trusted in such generous measures as was Abraham Lincoln. His election silenced in a good degree the discontent felt at the length of the war and the complaints of its being an abolition war. Every victory of our arms on flood and field was a rebuke to McClellan and the Democratic party, and an indorsement of Abraham Lincoln for President and of his new policy.

It was my good fortune to be present at his inauguration in March, and to hear on that occasion his remarkable inaugural address. On the night previous I took tea with Chief Justice Chase and assisted his beloved daughter, Mrs. [Kate] Sprague, in placing over her honored father's shoulders the new robe then being made, in which he was to administer the oath of office to the reëlected President. There was a dignity and grandeur about the Chief Justice which marked him as one born great. He had known me in early anti-slavery days and had welcomed me to his home and his table when to do so was a strange thing in Washington, and the fact was by no means an insignificant one.

The inauguration, like the election, was a most important event. Four years before, after Mr. Lincoln's first election, the pro-slavery spirit determined against his inauguration, and it no doubt would have accomplished its purpose had he attempted to pass openly and recognized through Baltimore. There was murder in the air then, and there was murder in the air now. His first inauguration arrested the fall of the Republic, and the second was to restore it to enduring foundations. At the time of the second inauguration the rebellion was apparently vigorous, defiant, and formidable, but in reality, weak, dejected, and desperate. It had reached that verge of madness when it had called upon the negro for help to fight against the freedom which he so longed to find, for the bondage he would escape—against Lincoln the emancipator for Davis the enslaver.[15] But desperation discards logic as well as law, and the South was desperate. Sherman was marching to the sea, and Virginia with its rebel capital was in the firm grasp of Ulysses S. Grant. To those who knew the situation it was evident that unless some startling change was made the Confederacy had but a short time to live, and that time full of misery.

This condition of things made the air at Washington dark and lowering. The friends of the Confederate cause here were neither few nor insignificant. They were among the rich and influential. A wink or a nod from such men might unchain the hand of violence and set order and law at defiance. To those who saw beneath the surface it was clearly perceived that there was danger abroad, and as the procession passed down Pennsylvania avenue I for one felt an instinctive apprehension that at any moment a shot from some assassin in the crowd might end the glittering pageant and throw the country into the depths of anarchy. I did not then know, what has since become history, that the plot was already formed and its execution which, though several weeks delayed, at last accomplished its deadly work was contemplated for that very day.

Reaching the Capitol, I took my place in the crowd where I could see the presidential procession as it came upon the east portico, and where I could hear and see all that took place. There was no such throng as that which celebrated the inauguration of President Garfield nor that of President Rutherford B. Hayes. The whole proceeding was wonderfully quiet, earnest, and solemn. From the oath as administered by Chief Justice Chase, to the brief but weighty address delivered by Mr. Lincoln, there was a leaden stillness about the crowd. The address sounded more like a sermon than like a state paper. In the fewest words possible he referred to the condition of the country four years before on his first accession to the presidency, to the causes of the war, and the reasons on both sides for which it had been waged. "Neither party," he said, "expected for the war the magnitude or the duration which it had already attained. Neither anticipated that the cause of the conflict might cease with or even before the conflict itself should cease. Each looked for an easier triumph and a result less fundamental and astounding." Then in a few short sentences admitting the conviction that slavery had been the "offense which in the providence of God must needs come, and the war as the woe due to those by whom the offense came," he asks if there can be "discerned in this any departure from those Divine attributes which the believers in a loving God always ascribe to him? Fondly do we hope," he continued, "fervently do we pray, that this mighty scourge of war may speedily pass away. Yet if God wills that it continue until all the wealth piled by the bondman's two hundred and fifty years of unrequited toil shall be sunk, and until every drop of blood drawn with the lash shall be paid for by another drawn with the sword, as was said three thousand years ago, so still it must be said, 'The judgments of the Lord are true and righteous altogether.'

"With malice toward none, with charity for all, with firmness in the right as God gives us to see the right, let us strive to finish the work we are in, to bind up the nation's wounds, to care for him who shall have borne the battle, and for his widow and his orphans, to do all which may achieve and cherish a just and lasting peace among ourselves and with all nations."

I know not how many times and before how many people I have quoted these solemn words of our martyred President. They struck me at the time, and have seemed to me ever since to contain more vital substance than I have ever seen compressed in a space so narrow; yet on this memorable occasion, when I clapped my hands in gladness and thanksgiving at their utterance, I saw in the faces of many about me expressions of widely different emotion.

On this inauguration day, while waiting for the opening of the ceremonies, I made a discovery in regard to the Vice President, Andrew Johnson. There are moments in the lives of most men when the doors of their souls are open, and, unconsciously to themselves, their true characters may be read by the observant eye. It was at such an instant that I caught a glimpse of the real nature of this man, which all subsequent developments proved true. I was standing in the crowd by the side of Mrs. Thomas J. Dorsey, when Mr. Lincoln touched Mr. Johnson and pointed me out to him. The first expression which came to his face, and which I think was the true index of his heart, was one of bitter contempt and aversion. Seeing that I observed him, he tried to assume a more friendly appearance, but it was too late; it is useless to close the door when all within has been seen. His first glance was the frown of the man; the second was the bland and sickly smile of the demagogue. I turned to Mrs. Dorsey and said, "Whatever Andrew Johnson may be, he certainly is no friend of our race."[16]

No stronger contrast between two men could well be presented than the one exhibited on this day between President Lincoln and Vice-President Johnson. Mr. Lincoln was like one who was treading the hard and thorny path of duty and self-denial; Mr. Johnson was like one just from a drunken debauch. The face of the one was full of manly humility, although at the topmost height of power and pride; that of the other was full of pomp and swaggering vanity. The fact was, though it was yet early in the day, Mr. Johnson was drunk.

In the evening of the day of the inauguration, another new experience awaited me. The usual reception was given at the executive mansion, and though no colored persons had ever ventured to present themselves on such occasions, it seemed, now that freedom had become the law of the republic, and colored men were on the battle-field mingling their blood with that of white men in one common effort to save the country, that it was not too great an assumption for a colored man to offer his congratulations to the President with those of other citizens. I decided to go, and sought in vain for some one of my own color to accompany me. It is never an agreeable experience to go where there can be any doubt of welcome, and my colored friends had too often realized discomfiture from this cause to be willing to subject themselves to such unhappiness; they wished me to go, as my New England colored friends in the long-ago liked very well to have me take passage on the first-class cars, and be hauled out and pounded by rough-handed brakemen, to make way for them. It was plain, then, that some one must lead the way, and that if the colored man would have his rights, he must take them; and now, though it was plainly quite the thing for me to attend President Lincoln's reception, "they all with one accord began to make excuse."[17]

It was finally arranged that Mrs. Dorsey should bear me company, so together we joined in the grand procession of citizens from all parts of the country, and moved slowly towards the executive mansion. I had for some time looked upon myself as a man, but now in this multitude of the élite of the land, I felt myself a man among men. I regret to be obliged to say, however, that this comfortable assurance was not of long duration, for on reaching the door, two policemen stationed there took me rudely by the arm and ordered me to stand back, for their directions were to admit no persons of my color. The reader need not be told that this was a disagreeable set-back. But once in the battle, I did not think it well to submit to repulse. I told the officers I was quite sure there must be some mistake, for no such order could have emanated from President Lincoln; and that if he knew I was at the door he would desire my admission. They then, to put an end to the parley, as I suppose, for we were obstructing the doorway, and were not easily pushed aside, assumed an air of politeness, and offered to conduct me in. We followed their lead, and soon found ourselves walking some planks out of a window, which had been arranged as a temporary passage for the exit of visitors. We halted so soon as we saw the trick, and I said to the officers: "You have deceived me. I shall not go out of this building till I see President Lincoln." At this moment a gentleman who was passing in recognized me, and I said to him: "Be so kind as to say to Mr. Lincoln that Frederick Douglass is detained by officers at the door."

It was not long before Mrs. Dorsey and I walked into the spacious East Room, amid a scene of elegance such as in this country I had never before witnessed. Like a mountain pine high above all others, Mr. Lincoln stood, in his grand simplicity, and *home-like beauty*. Recognizing me, even before I reached him, he exclaimed, so that all around could hear him, "Here comes my friend Douglass." Taking me by the hand, he said, "I am glad to see you. I saw you in the crowd to-day, listening to my inaugural address; how did you like it?" I said, "Mr. Lincoln, I must not detain you with my poor opinion, when there are thousands waiting to shake hands with you." "No, no," he said, "you must stop a little, Douglass; there is no man in the country whose opinion I value more than yours. I want to know what you think of it?" I replied, "Mr. Lincoln, that was a sacred effort." "I am glad you liked it!" he said; and I passed on, feeling that any man, however distinguished, might well regard himself honored by such expressions, from such a man.

It came out that the officers at the White House had received no orders from Mr. Lincoln, or from any one else. They were simply complying with an old custom, the outgrowth of slavery, as dogs will sometimes rub their necks, long after their collars are removed, thinking they are still there. My colored friends were well pleased with what had seemed to them a doubtful experiment, and I believe were encouraged by its success to follow my example. I have found in my experience that the way to break down an unreasonable custom, is to contradict it in practice. To be sure in pursuing this course I have had to contend not merely with the white race, but with the black. The one has condemned me for my presumption in daring to associate with it, and the other for pushing myself where it takes it for granted I am not wanted. I am pained to think that the latter objection springs largely from a consciousness of inferiority, for as colors alone can have nothing against each other, and the conditions of human association are founded upon character rather than color, and character depends upon mind and morals, there can be nothing blameworthy in people thus equal meeting each other on the plane of civil or social rights. . . .

After the fall of Richmond the collapse of the rebellion was not long delayed, though it did not perish without adding to its long list of atrocities one which sent a thrill of horror throughout the civilized world, in the assassination of Abraham Lincoln; a man so amiable, so kind, humane, and honest, that one is at a loss to know how he could have had an enemy on earth. . . .

Mr. Lincoln had reason to look forward to a peaceful and happy term of office. To all appearance, we were on the eve of a restoration of the union and of a solid and lasting peace. He had served one term as President of the Disunited States, he was now for the first time to be President of the United States. Heavy had been his burden, hard had been his toil, bitter had been his trials, and terrible had been his anxiety; but the future seemed now bright and full of hope. Richmond had fallen, Grant had General Lee and the army of Virginia firmly in his clutch; Sherman had fought and found his way from the banks of the great river to the shores of the sea, leaving the two ends of the rebellion squirming and twisting in agony, like the severed parts of a serpent, doomed to inevitable death; and now there was but a little time longer for the good President to bear his burden, and be the target of reproach. His accusers, in whose opinion he was always too fast or too slow, too weak or too strong, too conciliatory or too aggressive, would soon become his admirers; it was soon to be seen that he had conducted the affairs of the nation with singular wisdom, and with absolute fidelity to the great trust confided in him. A country redeemed and regenerated from the foulest crime against human nature that ever saw the sun! What a bright vision of peace, prosperity, and happiness must have come to that tired and over-worked brain, and weary spirit.

Men used to talk of his jokes, and he no doubt indulged in them; but I seemed never to have the faculty of calling them to the surface. I saw him oftener than many who have reported him, but I never saw any levity in him. He always impressed me as a strong, earnest man, having no time or disposition to trifle; grappling with all his might the work he had in hand. The expression of his face was a blending of suffering with patience and fortitude. Men called him homely, and homely he was; but it was manifestly a human homeliness, for there was nothing of the tiger or other wild animal about him. His eyes had in them the tenderness of motherhood, and his mouth and other features the highest perfection of a genuine manhood. His picture, by [William] Marshall, now before me in my study, corresponds well with the impression I have of him. But, alas! what are all good and great qualities; what are human hopes and human happiness to the revengeful hand of an assassin? What are sweet dreams of peace; what are visions of the future? A simple leaden bullet and a few grains of powder are sufficient in the shortest limit of time to blast and ruin all that is precious in human existence, not alone of the murdered, but of the murderer. I write this in the deep gloom flung over my spirit by the cruel, wanton, and cold-blooded attempted assassination of Abraham Garfield,[18] as well as that of Abraham Lincoln.

I was in Rochester, N.Y., where I then resided, when news of the death of Mr. Lincoln was received. Our citizens, not knowing what else to do in the agony of the hour, betook themselves to the city hall. Though all hearts ached for utterance, few felt like speaking. We were stunned and overwhelmed by a crime and calamity hitherto unknown to our country and our government. The hour was hardly one for speech, for no speech could rise to the level of feeling. Doctor [Ezekiel] Robinson, then of Rochester University, but now of Brown University, Providence, R.I., was prevailed upon to take the stand, and made one of the most touching and eloquent speeches I ever heard. At the close of his address, I was called upon, and spoke out of the fullness of my heart, and, happily, gave expression to so much of the soul of the people present that my voice was several times utterly silenced by the sympathetic tumult of the great audience. I had resided long in Rochester, and had made many speeches there which had more or less touched the hearts of my hearers, but never till this day was I brought into such close accord with them.[19] We shared in common a terrible calamity, and this "touch of nature made us" more than countrymen, it made us "kin."[20]

Part 7
Remembrances

Between 1866 and 1894, Douglass gave more than a dozen speeches and interviews that mentioned Lincoln in a significant way. Some occurred on Lincoln's birthday or on the anniversary of emancipation in Washington, DC. (Douglass lived in the nation's capital from 1872 until his death in 1895.) He frequently recounted his two private meetings at the White House, as well as his attendance at Lincoln's second inauguration and the reception that followed. Rare were the reflections that did not have some political purpose in mind, especially as the gains of Reconstruction succumbed to ex-Confederate control of southern state governments.

While Douglass had expected Lincoln's successor to be a champion for black rights,[1] by late summer 1865, Andrew Johnson was acting more like a friend to ex-rebels than ex-slaves by pardoning hundreds of former Confederates and preparing the speedy readmission of the southern states. In late September, Douglass concluded that "the persistent determination of the present Executive of the Nation . . . to hold and treat us in a degraded relation" would require black solidarity "for the present" as a means of political survival.[2]

An interview with Johnson at the White House in February 1866 dashed any hopes Douglass had for the new president. At the meeting, Douglass cited Lincoln's employment of black soldiers as a model for Johnson to support black suffrage. Just as black men with the rifle had helped to save the Union, giving them the ballot would help them save themselves from ex-Confederates. Johnson rudely rebuffed the idea, and after Douglass and his companions departed, Johnson called them "those d—d sons of b—s," adding that Douglass was "just like any nigger" and "would sooner cut a white man's throat than not."[3] With this experience fresh in his mind, a week later, Douglass reminisced about the kindness Lincoln had shown him at the White House.

Within a decade of the war's conclusion, white southerners were using both law and violence to reassert control over the black population in the South. This was the context for Douglass's most astute assessment of Lincoln as president: his "Oration in Memory of Abraham Lincoln," delivered on April 14, 1876, in Washington, DC. Douglass was the keynote speaker at the dedication of the "Freedmen's Memorial," a statue of Lincoln extending a hand of benediction over a crouching, newly freed slave. He took the occasion of the unveiling of a statue paid for by black veterans and former slaves to share how black Americans—ever vigilant, forbearing, and hopeful—had viewed Lincoln's presidency. With President Ulysses S. Grant and his cabinet, the Supreme Court, and members of Congress in attendance, Douglass gave a surprisingly frank and somewhat critical assessment of Lincoln. Calling him "pre-eminently the white man's President, entirely devoted to the welfare of white men," Douglass identified Lincoln with the loyal white majority of Americans to emphasize his reputation as the savior of the Union—a hero for white America—and not simply as the Great Emancipator—a hero for black America.[4]

The climax of the speech found Douglass as candid about the limits of his own abolitionism as he was about Lincoln's racial prejudices. He admitted that prematurely turning a war for Union into a war for abolition would have undermined both objectives. Lincoln needed the support of loyal white Americans to preserve the Union as well as free the slaves. Douglass intoned, "Viewed from the genuine abolition ground, Mr. Lincoln seemed tardy, cold, dull, and indifferent; but measuring him by the sentiment of his country, a sentiment he was bound as a statesman to consult, he was swift, zealous, radical, and determined."[5] With Reconstruction crumbling, the national leaders in his audience needed to finish the work Lincoln had begun by securing equal rights to the formerly enslaved.

In the final decade of his life, Douglass would offer assessments that were far less critical than his 1876 oration. Celebrating Lincoln's birthday in 1893, for example, he opined that Lincoln "was far above the prevailing prejudices of his countrymen."[6] As circumstances deteriorated for black Americans in the late 19th century—with the Supreme Court gutting the meaning of the Civil War amendments, Jim Crow laws segregating the races, organized violence stripping black voting rights, and lynching becoming a national scourge—Douglass pointed to Lincoln as an aspirational model for all Americans to follow.

Douglass would share his observations about Lincoln as late as 1894, just a year before he died on February 20, 1895, at the age of 77. His comments about Lincoln continued to matter because Lincoln mattered to most of the country well beyond the Reconstruction era. Both men saw the United States as "worthy of the saving"[7] if it stayed true to "the principles of liberty and humanity expressed in the Declaration of Independence and the Constitution of the United States."[8]

Interview with Andrew Johnson at the White House, February 7, 1866 (excerpt)
Washington, DC, *National Republican*, February 8, 1866, second edition

Mr. President, we are not here to enlighten you as to your duties as the Chief Magistrate of this Republic, but to show our respect and present the claims of our race.[9] In the order of Divine Providence you were placed in the position to save or destroy, bless or blast us.[10] Your noble and humane predecessor placed in our hands the sword to assist in saving the nation, and we do hope that you, as his successor,[11] will place in our hands the ballot, that we may save ourselves. We are subject to taxes, and have to bear the burdens of the State, and we think it not improper[12] to have the privileges of State.

"Assassination and Its Lessons," Report of an Address Delivered at the First Presbyterian Church in Washington, DC, on February 13, 1866[13] (excerpts)

Washington, DC, *Daily Morning Chronicle*, February 14, 1866

Mankind were indebted for the progress they have made in civilization to two kinds of teachers—great men and great events. There were some minds able to discover in the most occult beginning[s] a grand result, but most men were taught by events. From them are learned those principles without which no nation can be permanently prosperous or great. . . .

The past year has witnessed two great events. The first was the downfall of the rebellion. . . . The other event was something unprecedented in our history; it was the inauguration of a new crime—a stranger to our latitude. We had heard of it among the monarchs of Europe, where men were goaded to desperation by tyranny, but had never dreamed that in this land of free ballots, a crime so monstrous as the assassination of our Chief Magistrate could be possible. But we were mistaken. We had a fiend among us whose presence had not been taken into account.

A new year had lately dawned upon us. We had hoped much upon it, but there was reason for grave apprehension. There was reason to fear that it might witness something worse than even assassination, and this crime which we had cause to dread was nothing less than the abandonment of all the advantages won by the war—the freeing of the American bondman. Oh! when will the American people learn rightly the lessons of their own history? Many shocks have fallen upon them, chief among which was the assassination. Had the question of settling the status of the negro been submitted to them on the morning after that event, there is no doubt as to what they would have done. They would have put away from among them every vestige of slavery.

It was not necessary that he should call attention to the effect of that atrocious crime; the recollection of it was fresh in every mind. It was as if some strong convulsion of nature had occurred. Had a city been swallowed up by an earthquake, had the graves opened and the sheeted dead walked forth in our streets,[14] it could not have produced a more profound sensation than did this startling event. The calamity was so sudden, and so out of joint with the sense of security prevailing among us, that few of us could believe the dreadful news to be true. As at no time before, the loyal people were rejoicing in victory: Richmond had fallen; Lee, the patrician, commanding an army composed of the *elite* of the South, had surrendered to Grant, the plebeian; Wilmington and Mobile were in our hands; South Carolina had received from Sherman the chastisement she merited, and in Charleston, the cradle of secession, loyal black troops had marched through the streets to the tune of "Old John Brown."

The people were already beginning to manifest a desire to conciliate, and that maudlin magnanimity that is now our greatest danger. It was becoming fashionable to speak of rebel generals in terms of the highest respect, and men were almost as thankful to Lee for surrender as to Grant for making him surrender. But what did this leniency avail? Was the iron heart of slavery softened by it? No; nor ever will be. Nothing will ever soften it save the military power of the United States. For it seized that moment when there was nothing to be gained, and when we of the North were meditating mercy, to deal upon the nation's head its heaviest blow, by murdering a man the most beloved the nation has ever known.

He was not here to deliver a lecture on the character of Mr. Lincoln. On this there is little left to be said, especially after the brilliant oration of yesterday;[15] and yet there is a charm in it which makes it always an interesting subject to an American audience. When our great military chieftains are forgotten, and the war itself shall seem a mere speck in the distance, Abraham Lincoln, like dear old John Brown, will still find eloquent tongues to speak of his name. The difficulties that he met on the threshold of his power, the conscientious earnestness and energy with which he grappled them, the singular purity of his life, and the tragic manner of his death will ever be fertile themes for the historian. One peculiarity endeared him, and ever must endear him to all who have struggled up from a low to a high position. He was a self-made man, a rail-splitter, the captain of a flatboat; he took hold of life in the rough of it. He travelled far, but he made the road in which he advanced; he climbed high, but he made the ladder on which he ascended. This will ever make the name of Abraham Lincoln dear to all the toilers of our land. All know him well—know of his independence, his amiable temper, his devotion to his country, his temperance, his vigilance, his ability to bring together extremes and opposites in the cause of the nation.

But why take this theme now, it may be asked. Because he would underscore the assassination, and warn the American people to have a care that, in the process of reconstruction, they do not leave in the soil some root or fibre out of which may spring other rebellions and other assassinations.

The speaker said he was indebted to our enemies for his text, as the friends of freedom had been indebted to them for many steps in our progress. The annexation of Texas and the fugitive slave law had added to the ranks of the abolitionists. The repeal of the Missouri Compromise and the invasion of Kansas by border ruffians only roused in the loyal masses the determination to make Kansas a free State. And had Abraham Lincoln lived to the old age which his strong constitution and his temperate habits promised him, we should have followed him to his grave with nothing like the emotion we felt at his death. Dying as he did, his name becomes a text from which to show that the tree on which grew such fruit must not merely be cut down, but taken up by the roots, and that no vestige of the slave code must be left.

It was the speaker's exceeding great privilege to know Abraham Lincoln; to get near to him; and from his conversations with him, he believed that had Mr. Lincoln been living to-day, he would have stood with those who stand foremost, and gone with those who go farthest, in the cause of equal and universal suffrage.

Perhaps, said the speaker, you would like to know how I came to visit Mr. Lincoln. He invited me. It was a significant fact both for the men and the times. First, it showed that he had moral courage; that he remembered he was a man as well as a President; and if there is one thing to-night that impresses me more than another, it is that we have presiding over this meeting one [Chief Justice Salmon P. Chase] who remembers that he is a man and a Christian, notwithstanding the ermine.[16] It required moral courage to open this church to-night for a meeting of this character. But let me say that I remember a time when abolitionism could ride in an omnibus. He said he had known it in its infancy and in its childhood, and to-day he saw it a giant, and woe betide those who stand in its pathway, for they must fall. Some men had physical courage, and would look down the throat of a cannon, but could not encounter a prejudice that required moral courage. This courage Mr. Lincoln had; and not only did he invite a black man to his house, but also invited him to the Soldiers' Home to take tea with him.

The speaker had observed, in his intercourse with men, that the higher the sphere in which he moved, the less prejudice did he find. Prejudice flourished most vigorously among those who had the least to boast of in the form of intellectual acquirements. He here related an incident that occurred to him in a train between Baltimore and Washington. He was requested to leave the car in which he had taken a seat, and at the same moment he saw a lady enter with a dog in her arms. He looked forward to a time when a black man might go where a dog could be permitted.

But this invitation implied more than moral courage and freedom from prejudice. It showed that Mr. Lincoln comprehended the situation, and saw what was coming. He was a tall man, morally as well as physically, and great moral truths shed their lustre on his brow long before they reached the dwellers in valleys or delvers in copper mines. He had before said that had Mr. Lincoln been living to-day, he would have stood with those who stood foremost, and gone with those who went farthest. He said this because he knew him to be a progressive man—one who did not begin as a Moses and end as a Pharaoh.[17] He learned wisdom from war, and he would have learned it from peace. He had during his life expressed the opinion that two classes of colored men should be enfranchised—those who had fought in our armies, and those who were educated; and at the same time he desired to see the means provided whereby all could receive the education necessary to fit them for this privilege.[18]

Certain curious questions arise in connection with his death. Why should one so amiable be stricken with death? It may be that it required this sacrifice to bring us to a knowledge of the truth. We can see good arising out of this terrible calamity. We were on the eve of clasping hands with those men who had been in rebellion against the Government, without demanding the securities that were essential. We needed this event to enable us to know ourselves, and to know the spirit of our enemies. It was well, perhaps, that the rebellion should end as it did, for it was certain that there was nothing in all the battles of the war which impressed mankind as did this crime. Besides, it was well that slavery should expire by a crime that sent a shudder around the world. Hereafter, when men think of slavery, they will think of murder. Not because slaveholders are worse than other men by nature. He knew by his own observations that this was not the case; that the spirit of slavery is assassination.

He had said this event was necessary, and he charged it home on slavery. It was true that it had been disclaimed on the part of the South. Mason, the rebel emissary in England, had hastened to tell us that she was not responsible;[19] yet the shadow does not cling closer to the object by which it is cast than does this crime to slavery. For thirty years the language of slavery has been death to any one who ventured to oppose it; besides, this crime accords with the whole catalogue of the barbarities of the war, which extended even to the going down into their bloody graves of sons and brothers, to steal their skulls for drinking cups and their bones for trinkets. Where will you find anything like it? It accords well with the throwing off the railroad track of trains bearing women and children and other non-combatants, the firing of hotels in the hearts of populous cities, the poisoning of springs, the attempt to spread

Frederick Douglass in Philadelphia, April 26, 1870. Prints and Photographs Division, Library of Congress

infection, the starving of our prisoners, and the infamous crime of poisoning them by vaccination. It also raises the suspicion that Abraham Lincoln was not the first victim. [President William Henry] Harrison, after serving one month, died, and was succeeded by a man devoted to the interest of slavery. [President Zachary] Taylor had but just announced himself in favor of the admission of California as a free State when he passed away, and gave place to a Northern sycophant [Millard Fillmore], whose name is found at the bottom of the fugitive slave law. Even James Buchanan was poisoned at the National Hotel, and had he died, would have been succeeded by [John] Breckinridge.

The slave power is like the robber who stops you on your way and demands your money or your life. The slaveholder says to the slave, your labor or your life.

He here proceeded to show that Booth drew his inspiration directly from the South; that he had been in communication with officials in the South; that the words he repeated after committing the crime were the motto of a Southern State; that his first thought of escape was turned southward, and, had he reached the South, and had the South achieved its independence, he would have been hailed as a hero, and the women who presented canes to [Preston] Brooks, of South Carolina, in compliment to his attempt to assassinate Senator [Charles] Sumner, would have showered similar testimonials upon Booth.

"Sources of Danger to the Republic," speech at National Hall, Philadelphia, January 3, 1867 (excerpts)

Philadelphia Daily Evening Telegraph, January 4, 1867[20]

Another secret of our success was this:—We happened, for it was only a happening, to have in the Presidential chair an honest man.

(Cheers.) It was our exceedingly good fortune that Abraham Lincoln, and not William H. Seward received the nomination in 1860. Had William H. Seward, had Millard Fillmore, had John Tyler, or had the vilest embodiment of ingratitude and baseness, who shall be nameless now (laughter and cheers), occupied the Presidential chair, the Government of which we are so proud to-day, might have been only a matter of history. . . .

[After reviewing the failures of James Buchanan, Douglass continued:] we saw no help for the Republic until the honest man, Abraham Lincoln, came to the rescue. (Cheers.)

But it is sad to think that half the glory, honor, and moral advantage to this nation of the great beneficent measures already adopted were lost—lost in the meanness of their performance. Even for the abolition of slavery we have no one to thank; we have not the nation to thank for that by any means. What was done in that direction was done reluctantly. We are about as justly required to thank the American people for emancipating the slaves as Pharaoh of old was entitled to the thanks of the Israelites for releasing them from bondage. (Cheers.) For it was not until judgment, wide spreading, far reaching, and overwhelming, overtook us—it was not until we saw the Southern horizon studded all around with military disasters, that we consented to part with our reverence for slavery, and to arm the black man in defense of the flag. (Cheers.)

Oh that we could have done this from a holy, sacred choice of right for right's sake, for the truth's sake, for man's sake! Oh that it could have been done from a high and holy motive of disinterested benevolence! As it was, it has gone into history as simply a piece of military strategy or necessity. Justice had but little to do with it.

"An Appeal to Colored Voters,"[21] Washington, DC, August 9, 1872 (excerpt)

New York Times, August 12, 1872

We in the South have been liberated from slavery by the direct agency of the Republican Party. Had Greeley been President instead of Lincoln, we would today have been in a worse bondage under the Slave Republic of the Southern Confederate States than ever before. Greeley advocated this policy and did his best to establish the Republic of which slavery was to be the chief corner-stone.[22]

"Oration in Memory of Abraham Lincoln," April 14, 1876

Oration by Frederick Douglass Delivered on the Occasion of the Unveiling of the Freedmen's Monument in Memory of Abraham Lincoln, in Lincoln Park, Washington, D.C., April 14th, 1876.
(Washington, DC: Gibson Brothers, 1876)

Friends and Fellow-Citizens:

I warmly congratulate you upon the highly interesting object which has caused you to assemble in such numbers and spirit as you have to-day. This occasion is in some respects remarkable. Wise and thoughtful men of our race, who shall come after us, and study the lesson of our history in the United States; who shall survey the long and dreary spaces over which we have travelled; who shall count the links in the great chain of events by which we have reached our present position, will make a note of this occasion; they will think of it and speak of it with a sense of manly pride and complacency.

I congratulate you, also, upon the very favorable circumstances in which we meet to-day. They are high, inspiring, and uncommon. They lend grace, glory, and significance to the object for which we have met. Nowhere else in this great country, with its uncounted towns and cities, unlimited wealth, and immeasurable territory extending from sea to sea, could conditions be found more favorable to the success of this occasion than here.

We stand to-day at the national centre to perform something like a national act—an act which is to go into history; and we are here where every pulsation of the national heart can be heard, felt, and reciprocated. A thousand wires, fed with thought and winged with lightning, put us in instantaneous communication with the loyal and true men all over the country.

Few facts could better illustrate the vast and wonderful change which has taken place in our condition as a people than the fact of our assembling here for the purpose we have to-day. Harmless, beautiful, proper, and praiseworthy as this demonstration is, I cannot forget that no such demonstration would have been tolerated here twenty years ago. The spirit of slavery and barbarism, which still lingers to blight and destroy in some dark and distant parts of our country, would have made our assembling here the signal and excuse for opening upon us all the flood-gates of wrath and violence. That we are here in peace to-day is a compliment and a credit to American civilization, and a prophecy of still greater national enlightenment and progress in the future. I refer to the past not in malice, for this is no day for malice; but simply to place more distinctly in front the gratifying and glorious change which has come both to our white fellow-citizens and ourselves, and to congratulate all upon the contrast between now and then; the new dispensation of freedom with its thousand blessings to both races, and the old dispensation of slavery with its ten thousand evils to both races—white and black. In view, then, of the past, the present, and the future, with the long and dark history of our bondage behind us, and with liberty, progress, and enlightenment before us, I again congratulate you upon this auspicious day and hour.

Friends and fellow-citizens, the story of our presence here is soon and easily told. We are here in the District of Columbia, here in the city of Washington, the most luminous point of American territory; a city recently transformed and made beautiful in its body and in its spirit; we are here in the place where the ablest and best men of the country are sent to devise the policy, enact the laws, and shape the destiny of the Republic; we are here, with the stately pillars and majestic dome of the Capitol of the nation looking down upon us; we are here, with the broad earth freshly adorned with the foliage and flowers of spring for our church, and all races, colors, and conditions of men for our congregation—in a word, we are here to express, as best we may, by appropriate forms and ceremonies, our grateful sense of the vast, high, and pre-eminent services rendered to ourselves, to our race, to our country, and to the whole world by Abraham Lincoln.

The sentiment that brings us here to-day is one of the noblest that can stir and thrill the human heart. It has crowned and made glorious the high places of all civilized nations with the grandest and most enduring works of art, designed to illustrate the characters and perpetuate the memories of great public men. It is the sentiment which from year to year adorns with fragrant and beautiful flowers the graves of our loyal, brave, and patriotic soldiers who fell in defence of the Union and liberty. It is the sentiment of gratitude and appreciation, which often, in [the] presence of many who hear me, has filled yonder heights of Arlington with the eloquence of eulogy and the sublime enthusiasm of poetry and song; a sentiment which can never die while the Republic lives.

For the first time in the history of our people, and in the history of the whole American people, we join in this high worship, and march conspicuously in the line of this time-honored custom. First things are always interesting, and this is one of our first things. It is the first time that, in this form and manner, we have sought to do honor to an American great man, however deserving and illustrious.[23] I commend the fact to notice; let it be told in every part of the Republic; let men of all parties and opinions hear it; let those who despise us, not less than those who respect us, know that now and here, in the spirit of liberty, loyalty, and gratitude, let it be known everywhere, and by everybody who takes an interest in human progress and in the amelioration of the condition of mankind, that, in the presence and with the approval of the members of the American House of Representatives, reflecting the general sentiment of the country; that in the presence of that august body, the American Senate, representing the highest intelligence and the calmest judgment of the country; in [the] presence of the Supreme Court and Chief-Justice of the United States, to whose decisions we all patriotically bow; in the presence and under the steady eye of the honored and trusted President of the United States, with the members of his wise and patriotic Cabinet, we, the colored people, newly emancipated and rejoicing in our blood-bought freedom, near the close of the first century in the life of this Republic, have now and here unveiled, set apart, and dedicated a monument of enduring granite and bronze, in every line, feature, and figure of which the men of this generation may read, and those of after-coming generations may read, something of the exalted character and great works of Abraham Lincoln, the first martyr President of the United States.

Fellow-citizens, in what we have said and done to-day, and in what we may say and do hereafter, we disclaim everything like arrogance and assumption. We claim for ourselves no superior devotion to the character, history, and memory of the illustrious name whose monument we have here dedicated to-day. We fully comprehend the relation of Abraham Lincoln both to ourselves and to the white people of the United States. Truth is proper and beautiful at all times and in all places, and it is never more proper and beautiful in any case than when speaking of a great public man whose example is likely to be commended for honor and imitation long after his departure to the solemn shades, the silent continents of eternity. It must be admitted, truth compels me to admit, even here in the presence of the monument we have erected to his memory, Abraham Lincoln was not, in the fullest sense of the word, either our man or our model. In his interests, in his associations, in his habits of thought, and in his prejudices, he was a white man.

Charlotte Scott, a former slave from Virginia, donated $5 toward a monument for Lincoln, which eventually resulted in the statue in Lincoln Park in Washington, DC. Prints and Photographs Division, Library of Congress

He was pre-eminently the white man's President, entirely devoted to the welfare of white men. He was ready and willing at any time during the first years of his administration to deny, postpone, and sacrifice the rights of humanity in the colored people to promote the welfare of the white people of this country. In all his education and feeling he was an American of the Americans. He came into the Presidential chair upon one principle alone, namely, opposition to the extension of slavery. His arguments in furtherance of this policy had their motive and mainspring in his patriotic devotion to the interests of his own race. To protect, defend, and perpetuate slavery in the States where it existed Abraham Lincoln was not less ready than any other President to draw the sword of the nation. He was ready to execute all the supposed constitutional guarantees of the United States Constitution in favor of the slave system anywhere inside the slave States. He was willing to pursue, recapture, and send back the fugitive slave to his master, and to suppress a slave rising for liberty, though his guilty master were already in arms against the Government. The race to which we belong were not the special objects of his consideration. Knowing this, I concede to you, my white fellow-citizens, a pre-eminence in this worship at once full and supreme. First, midst, and last, you and yours were the objects of his deepest affection and his most earnest solicitude. You are the children of Abraham Lincoln. We are at best only his step-children; children by adoption, children by force of circumstances and necessity. To you it especially belongs to sound his praises, to preserve and perpetuate his memory, to multiply his statues, to hang his pictures high upon your walls, and commend his example, for to you he was a great and glorious friend and benefactor. Instead of supplanting you at his altar, we would exhort you to build high his monuments; let them be of the most costly material, of the most cunning workmanship; let their forms be symmetrical, beautiful, and perfect; let their bases be upon solid rocks, and their summits lean against the unchanging blue, overhanging sky, and let them endure forever! But while in the abundance of your wealth, and in the fulness of your just and patriotic devotion, you do all this, we entreat you to despise not the humble offering we this day unveil to view; for while Abraham Lincoln saved for you a country, he delivered us from a bondage, according to Jefferson, one hour of which was worse than ages of the oppression your fathers rose in rebellion to oppose.[24]

Fellow-citizens, ours is no new-born zeal and devotion—merely a thing of this moment. The name of Abraham Lincoln was near and dear to our hearts in the darkest and most perilous hours of the Republic. We were no more ashamed of him when shrouded in clouds of darkness, of doubt, and defeat than when we saw him crowned with victory, honor, and glory. Our faith in him was often taxed and strained to the uttermost, but it never failed. When he tarried long in the mountain; when he strangely told us that we were the cause of the war;[25] when he still more strangely told us to leave the land in which we were born; when he refused to employ our arms in defence of the Union; when, after accepting our services as colored soldiers, he refused to retaliate our murder and torture as colored prisoners; when he told us he would save the Union if he could with slavery;[26] when he revoked the Proclamation of Emancipation of General Frémont; when he refused to remove the popular commander of the Army of the Potomac [George B. McClellan], in the days of its inaction and defeat, who was more zealous in his efforts to protect slavery than to suppress rebellion; when we saw all this, and more, we were at times grieved, stunned, and greatly bewildered; but our hearts believed while they ached and bled. Nor was this, even at that time, a blind and unreasoning superstition. Despite the mist and haze that surrounded him; despite the tumult, the hurry, and confusion of the hour, we were able to take a comprehensive view of Abraham Lincoln, and to make reasonable allowance for the circumstances of his position. We saw him, measured him, and estimated him; not by stray utterances to injudicious and tedious delegations, who often tried his patience; not by isolated facts torn from their connection; not by any partial and imperfect glimpses, caught at inopportune moments; but by a broad survey, in the light of the stern logic of great events, and in view of that divinity which shapes our ends, rough hew them how we will,[27] we came to the conclusion that the hour and the man of our redemption had somehow met in the person of Abraham Lincoln. It mattered little to us what language he might employ on special occasions; it mattered little to us, when we fully knew him, whether he was swift or slow in his movements; it was enough for us that Abraham Lincoln was at the head of a great movement, and was in living and earnest sympathy with that movement, which, in the nature of things, must go on until slavery should be utterly and forever abolished in the United States.

When, therefore, it shall be asked what we have to do with the memory of Abraham Lincoln, or what Abraham Lincoln had to do with us, the answer is ready, full, and complete. Though he loved Caesar less than Rome,[28] though the Union was more to him than our freedom or our future, under his wise and beneficent rule we saw ourselves gradually lifted from the depths of slavery to the heights of liberty and manhood; under his wise and beneficent rule, and by measures approved and vigorously pressed by him, we saw that the handwriting of ages, in the form of prejudice and proscription, was rapidly fading away from the face of our whole country; under his rule, and in due time, about as soon after all as the country could tolerate the strange spectacle, we saw our brave sons and brothers laying off the rags of bondage, and being clothed all over in the blue uniforms of the soldiers of the United States; under his rule we saw two hundred thousand of our dark and dusky people responding to the call of Abraham Lincoln, and with muskets on their shoulders, and eagles on their buttons, timing their high footsteps to liberty and union under the national flag; under his rule we saw the independence of the black republic of Hayti, the special object of slaveholding aversion and horror, fully recognized, and her minister, a colored gentleman, duly received here in the city of Washington; under his rule we saw the internal slave-trade, which so long disgraced the nation, abolished, and slavery abolished in the District of Columbia; under his rule we saw for the first time the law enforced against the foreign slave-trade, and the first slave-trader hanged like any other pirate or murderer;[29] under his rule, assisted by the greatest captain of our age, and his inspiration, we saw the Confederate States, based upon the idea that our race must be slaves,[30] and slaves forever, battered to pieces and scattered to the four winds; under his rule, and in the fullness of time, we saw Abraham Lincoln, after giving the slaveholders three months' grace in which to save their hateful slave system, penning the immortal paper, which, though special in its language, was general in its principles and effect, making slavery forever impossible in the United States. Though we waited long, we saw all this and more.

Can any colored man, or any white man friendly to the freedom of all men, ever forget the night which followed the first day of January, 1863, when the world was to see if Abraham Lincoln would prove to be as good as his word? I shall never forget that memorable night, when in a distant city I waited and watched at a public meeting, with three thousand others not less anxious than myself, for the word of deliverance which we have heard read to-day. Nor shall I ever forget the outburst of joy and thanksgiving that rent the air when the lightning brought to us the emancipation proclamation. In that happy hour we forgot all delay, and forgot all tardiness, forgot that the President had bribed the rebels to lay down their arms by a promise to withhold the bolt which would smite the slave-system with destruction; and we were thenceforward willing to allow the President all the latitude of time, phraseology, and every honorable device that statesmanship might require for the achievement of a great and beneficent measure of liberty and progress.

Fellow-citizens, there is little necessity on this occasion to speak at length and critically of this great and good man, and of his high mission in the world. That ground has been fully occupied and completely covered both here and elsewhere. The whole field of fact and fancy has been gleaned and garnered. Any man can say things that are true of Abraham Lincoln, but no man can say anything that is new of Abraham Lincoln. His personal traits and public acts are better known to the American people than are those of any other man of his age. He was a mystery to no man who saw him and heard him. Though high in position, the humblest could approach him and feel at home in his presence. Though deep, he was transparent; though strong, he was gentle; though decided and pronounced in his convictions, he was tolerant towards those who differed from him, and patient under reproaches. Even those who only knew him through his public utterances obtained a tolerably clear idea of his character and personality. The image of the man went out with his words, and those who read them, knew him.

I have said that President Lincoln was a white man, and shared the prejudices common to his countrymen towards the colored race. Looking back to his times and to the condition of his country, we are compelled to admit that this unfriendly feeling on his part may be safely set down as one element of his wonderful success in organizing the loyal American people for the tremendous conflict before them, and bringing them safely through that conflict. His great mission was to accomplish two things: first, to save his country from dismemberment and ruin; and second, to free his country from the great crime of slavery. To do one or the other, or both, he must have the earnest sympathy and the powerful co-operation of his loyal fellow-countrymen. Without this primary and essential condition to success his efforts must have been vain and utterly fruitless. Had he put the abolition of slavery before the salvation of the Union, he would have inevitably driven from him a powerful class of the American people and rendered resistance to rebellion impossible. Viewed from the genuine abolition ground, Mr. Lincoln seemed tardy, cold, dull, and indifferent; but measuring him by the sentiment of his country, a sentiment he was bound as a statesman to consult, he was swift, zealous, radical, and determined.

Though Mr. Lincoln shared the prejudices of his white fellow-countrymen against the negro, it is hardly necessary to say that in his heart of hearts he loathed and hated slavery.[31] The man who could say, "Fondly do we hope, fervently do we pray, that this mighty scourge of war shall soon pass away, yet if God wills it continue till all the wealth piled by two hundred years of bondage shall have been wasted, and each drop of blood drawn by the lash shall have been paid for by one drawn by the sword, the judgments of the Lord are true and righteous altogether,"[32] gives all needed proof of his feeling on the subject of slavery. He was willing, while the South was loyal, that it should have its pound of flesh,[33] because he thought that it was so nominated in the bond; but farther than this no earthly power could make him go.

Fellow-citizens, whatever else in this world may be partial, unjust, and uncertain, time, time! is impartial, just, and certain in its action. In the realm of mind, as well as in the realm of matter, it is a great worker, and often works wonders. The honest and comprehensive statesman, clearly discerning the needs of his country, and earnestly endeavoring to do his whole duty, though covered and blistered with reproaches, may safely leave his course to the silent judgment of time. Few great public men have ever been the victims of fiercer denunciation than Abraham Lincoln was during his administration. He was often wounded in the house of his friends.[34] Reproaches came thick and fast upon him from within and from without, and from opposite quarters. He was assailed by Abolitionists; he was assailed by slaveholders; he was assailed by the men who were for peace at any price; he was assailed by those who were for a more vigorous prosecution of the war; he was assailed for not making the war an abolition war; and he was most bitterly assailed for making the war an abolition war.

But now behold the change: the judgment of the present hour is, that taking him for all in all, measuring the tremendous magnitude of the work before him, considering the necessary means to ends, and surveying the end from the beginning, infinite wisdom has seldom sent any man into the world better fitted for his mission than Abraham Lincoln. His birth, his training, and his natural endowments, both mental and physical, were strongly in his favor. Born and reared among the lowly, a stranger to wealth and luxury, compelled to grapple single-handed with the flintiest hardships of life, from tender youth to sturdy manhood, he grew strong in the manly and heroic qualities demanded by the great mission to which he was called by the votes of his countrymen. The hard condition of his early life, which would have depressed and broken down weaker men, only gave greater life, vigor, and buoyancy to the heroic spirit of Abraham Lincoln. He was ready for any kind and any quality of work. What other young men dreaded in the shape of toil, he took hold of with the utmost cheerfulness.

A spade, a rake, a hoe,
A pick-axe, or a bill;
A hook to reap, a scythe to mow,
A flail, or what you will.[35]

All day long he could split heavy rails in the woods, and half the night long he could study his English Grammar by the uncertain flare and glare of the light made by a pine-knot. He was at home on the land with his axe, with his maul, with gluts, and his wedges; and he was equally at home on water, with his oars, with his poles, with his planks, and with his boat-hooks. And whether in his flat-boat on the Mississippi river, or at the fireside of his frontier cabin, he was a man of work. A son of toil himself, he was linked in brotherly sympathy with the sons of toil in every loyal part of the Republic. This very fact gave him tremendous power with the American people, and materially contributed not only to selecting him to the Presidency, but in sustaining his administration of the Government.

Upon his inauguration as President of the United States, an office, even when[36] assumed under the most favorable conditions, fitted to tax and strain the largest abilities, Abraham Lincoln was met by a tremendous crisis. He was called upon not merely to administer the Government, but to decide, in the face of terrible odds, the fate of the Republic.

A formidable rebellion rose in his path before him; the Union was already practically dissolved; his country was torn and rent asunder at the centre. Hostile armies were already organized against the Republic, armed with the munitions of war which the Republic had provided for its own defence. The tremendous question for him to decide was whether his country should survive the crisis and flourish, or be dismembered and perish. His predecessor in office had already decided the question in favor of national dismemberment, by denying to it the right of self-defence and self-preservation—a right which belongs to the meanest insect.

Happily for the country, happily for you and for me, the judgment of James Buchanan, the patrician, was not the judgment of Abraham Lincoln, the plebeian. He brought his strong common sense, sharpened in the school of adversity, to bear upon the question. He did not hesitate, he did not doubt, he did not falter; but at once resolved that at whatever peril, at whatever cost, the union of the States should be preserved. A patriot himself, his faith was strong and unwavering in the patriotism of his countrymen. Timid men said before Mr. Lincoln's inauguration, that we had seen the last President of the United States. A voice in influential quarters said, "Let the Union slide."[37] Some said that a Union maintained by the sword was worthless. Others said a rebellion of 8,000,000 cannot be suppressed; but in the midst of all this tumult and timidity, and against all this, Abraham Lincoln was clear in his duty, and had an oath in heaven. He calmly and bravely heard the voice of doubt and fear all around him; but he had an oath in heaven, and there was not power enough on earth to make this honest boatman, back-woodsman, and broad-handed splitter of rails evade or violate that sacred oath. He had not been schooled in the ethics of slavery; his plain life had favored his love of truth. He had not been taught that treason and perjury were the proof of honor and honesty. His moral training was against his saying one thing when he meant another. The trust that Abraham Lincoln had in himself and in the people was surprising and grand, but it was also enlightened and well founded. He knew the American people better than they knew themselves, and his truth was based upon this knowledge.

Fellow-citizens, the fourteenth day of April, 1865, of which this is the eleventh anniversary, is now and will ever remain a memorable day in the annals of this Republic. It was on the evening of this day, while a fierce and sanguinary rebellion was in the last stages of its desolating power; while its armies were broken and scattered before the invincible armies of Grant and Sherman; while a great nation, torn and rent by war, was already beginning to raise to the skies loud anthems of joy at the dawn of peace, it was startled, amazed, and overwhelmed by the crowning crime of slavery—the assassination of Abraham Lincoln. It was a new crime, a pure act of malice. No purpose of the rebellion was to be served by it. It was the simple gratification of a hell-black spirit of revenge. But it has done good after all. It has filled the country with a deeper abhorrence of slavery and a deeper love for the great liberator.

Had Abraham Lincoln died from any of the numerous ills to which flesh is heir; had he reached that good old age of which his vigorous constitution and his temperate habits gave promise; had he been permitted to see the end of his great work; had the solemn curtain of death come down but gradually—we should still have been smitten with a heavy grief, and treasured his name lovingly. But dying as he did die, by the red hand of violence, killed, assassinated, taken off without warning, not because of personal hate—for no man who knew Abraham Lincoln could hate him—but because of his fidelity to union and liberty, he is doubly dear to us, and his memory will be precious forever.

Fellow-citizens, I end, as I began, with congratulations. We have done a good work for our race to-day. In doing honor to the memory of our friend and liberator, we have been doing highest honors to ourselves and those who come after us; we have been fastening ourselves to a name and fame imperishable and immortal; we have also been defending ourselves from a blighting scandal. When now it shall be said that the colored man is soulless, that he has no appreciation of benefits or benefactors; when the foul reproach of ingratitude is hurled at us, and it is attempted to scourge us beyond the range of

Frederick Douglass delivered the dedication speech at the unveiling of Thomas Ball's "Freedmen's Memorial" in Lincoln Park, Washington, DC. Prints and Photographs Division, Library of Congress

human brotherhood, we may calmly point to the monument we have this day erected to the memory of Abraham Lincoln.

"A Suggestion," Letter to the Editor of the *National Republican*, April 19, 1876
Washington, DC, *National Republican*, April 19, 1876

To the Editor of the National Republican:

SIR: Admirable as is the monument by Mr. Ball in Lincoln park,[38] it does not, as it seems to me, tell the whole truth, and perhaps no one monument could be made to tell the whole truth of any subject which it might be designed to illustrate. The mere act of breaking the negro's chains was the act of Abraham Lincoln, and is beautifully expressed in this monument. But the act by which the negro was made a citizen of the United States and invested with the elective franchise was pre-eminently the act of President U.S. Grant, and this is nowhere seen in the Lincoln monument. The negro here, though rising, is still on his knees and nude. What I want to see before I die is a monument representing the negro, not couchant on his knees like a four-footed animal, but erect on his feet like a man. There is room in Lincoln park for another monument, and I throw out this suggestion to the end that it may be taken up and acted upon.

FREDERICK DOUGLASS.

Comment on Lincoln and Grant, April 19, 1876
Washington, DC, *National Republican*, April 19, 1876

An emancipated people cannot pay too great a tribute to the memory of a man from whose lips came the words that released them from the misery and darkness of slavery. Whatever the motives may have been that induced the great leader to free the slaves in the South, whether it was the prime object of his political life or not, it still remains that the act emanated from a strong conviction of right.

Abraham Lincoln freed the slave, but it remained for President Grant to raise the negro people, who were a humiliated race in this country, to the independence of citizenship. As chief of the military power, General Grant enforced with great vigor the mandate of freedom. As President of the United States, U.S. Grant finished the great work begun by Abraham Lincoln, and granted to the colored man complete citizenship.

Memorial Day Oration Delivered at Union Square, New York City, May 30, 1878 (excerpts)
New York Times, May 31, 1878

FRIENDS AND FELLOW-CITIZENS: In this place, hallowed and made glorious by a statue of the best man, truest patriot, and wisest statesman of his time and country,[39] I have been invited—I might say ordered—by Lincoln Post of the Grand Army of the Republic,[40] to say a few words to you in appropriate celebration of this annual national memorial day. Deeply sensible of the honor thus conferred, and properly impressed with the dignity of this occasion, I accept the invitation cheerfully and gratefully; but not so much as an honor to myself, as a generous recognition of that class of our fellow-citizens to which I belong; a class hitherto excluded by popular prejudice from prominent participation in the memorial glories of our common country. Lincoln Post—most worthily named—will pardon me if I stop right here to commend it for this innovation upon an old custom; for its moral courage and soldierly independence. Abraham Lincoln was the first President of the United States brave enough to invite a colored gentleman to sit at table with him, and the post that bears his honored name is the first in this great City to invite any colored man to deliver an address on national memorial day. . . .

Fellow-citizens, I am not here to fan the flame of sectional animosity, to revive old issues, or to stir up strife between races; but no candid man, looking at the political situation of the hour, can fail to see that we are still afflicted by the painful [con]sequences both of slavery and of the late rebellion. In the spirit of the noble man whose image now looks down upon us we should have "charity toward all, and malice toward none." In the language of our greatest soldier, twice honored with the Presidency of the nation, "Let us have peace."[41] Yes, let us have peace, but let us have liberty, law, and justice first. Let us have the Constitution, with its thirteenth, fourteenth, and fifteenth amendments, fairly interpreted,[42] faithfully executed, and cheerfully obeyed in the fullness of their spirit and the completeness of their letter.

Tribute to Abraham Lincoln, 1880
Gilder Lehrman Collection[43]

A great man: Tender of heart, strong of nerve, of boundless patience and broadest sympathies, with no motive apart from his country. He could receive counsel from a child and give counsel to a sage. The simple approached him with ease—and the learned approached him with deference. Take him for all in all[,] Abraham Lincoln was one of the noblest[,] wisest and best men I ever knew.

Fredk. Douglass
1880

"The Color Line" (excerpt)
North American Review, June 1881

The writer has met and mingled freely with the leading great men of his time,—at home and abroad, in public halls and private houses, on the platform and at the fireside,—and can remember no instance when among such men has he been made to feel himself an object of aversion. Men who are really great are too great to be small. This was gloriously true of the late Abraham Lincoln, William H. Seward, Salmon P. Chase, Henry Wilson, John P. Hale, Lewis Tappan, Edmund Quincy, Joshua R. Giddings, Gerrit Smith, and Charles Sumner, and many others among the dead. Good taste will not permit me now to speak of the living, except to say that the number of those who rise superior to prejudice is great and increasing.

Address Delivered on the Anniversary of Emancipation in Washington, DC, April 16, 1883 (excerpts)

Address by Hon. Frederick Douglass, Delivered in the Congregational Church, Washington, D.C., April 16, 1883, on the Twenty-First Anniversary of Emancipation in the District of Columbia **(Washington, DC: n.p., 1883)**

The amendments to the Constitution of the United States mean this [racial equality and the full rights of US citizenship], or they are a cruel, scandalous and colossal sham, and deserve to be so branded before the civilized world. What Abraham Lincoln said in respect of the United States is as true of the colored people as of the relations of those States. They cannot remain half slave and half free.[44] You must give them all or take from them all. Until this half-and-half condition is ended, there will be just ground of complaint. You will have an aggrieved class, and this discussion will go on. . . .

When the nation was in peril; when the country was rent asunder at the center; when rebel armies were in the field, bold, defiant and victorious; when our recruiting sergeants were marching up and down our streets from early morn till late at night, with drum and fife, with banner and badge, footsore and weary; when the fate of the Republic trembled in the balance, and the hearts of loyal men were failing them for fear; when nearly all hope of subduing the rebellion had vanished, Abraham Lincoln called upon the colored men of this country to reach out their iron arms and clutch with their steel fingers the faltering banner of the Republic; and they rallied, and they rallied, full two hundred thousand strong. Ah! then, my friends, the claims of the Negro found the heart of the nation a little more tender and responsive than now. But I ask Americans to remember that the arms that were needed then may be needed again;

and it is best that they do not convert the cheerful and loyal brows of six millions into a black Ireland.

A nation composed of all classes should be governed by no one class exclusively. All should be included, and none excluded. . . .

Here, to-night on the twenty-first anniversary of Emancipation in the District of Columbia, the capital of the grandest Republic of freedom on the earth, I kneel at the grave, amid the dust and shadows of bygone centuries, and offer my gratitude, and the gratitude of six millions of my race, to Morgan Godwin,[45] as the grand pioneer of Garrison, Lundy, Goodell, Phillips, Henry Wilson, Gerrit Smith, Joshua R. Giddings, Abraham Lincoln, Thaddeus Stevens, and the illustrious host of great men who have since risen to plead the cause of the negro against those who would oppress him. . . .

Among the great names which should never be forgotten on occasions like this, there is one which should never be spoken but with reverence, gratitude and affection, the one man of all the millions of our countrymen to whom we are more indebted for a United Nation and for American liberty than to any other, and that name is Abraham Lincoln, the greatest statesman that ever presided over the destinies of this Republic. The time is too short, his term of office is too recent to permit or to require extended notice of his statesmanship, or of his moral and mental qualities. We all know Abraham Lincoln by heart. In looking back to the many great men of twenty years ago, we find him the tallest figure of them all. His mission was to close up a chasm opened by an earthquake, and he did it. It was his to call back a bleeding, dying and dismembered nation to life, and he did it. It was his to free his country from the crime, curse and disgrace of slavery, and to lift millions to the plane of humanity, and he did it. Never was [a] statesman surrounded by greater difficulties, and never were difficulties more ably, wisely and firmly met. . . .

It is, however, consoling to think that this limitation upon human foresight has helped us in the past and may help us in the future. Could William the Silent have foreseen the misery and ruin he would bring upon his country by taking up the sword against the Spanish

Inquisition, he might have thought the sacrifice too great. Had William Lloyd Garrison foreseen that he would be hated, persecuted, mobbed, imprisoned, and drawn through the streets of his beloved Boston with a halter about his neck, even his courage might have quailed, and the native hue of his resolution been sicklied o'er with the pale cast of thought.[46] Could Abraham Lincoln have foreseen the immense cost, the terrible hardship, the awful waste of blood and treasure involved in the effort to retake and repossess the forts and arsenals and other property captured by the Confederate States; could he have foreseen the tears of the widows and orphans, and his own warm blood trickling at the bidding of an assassin's bullet, he might have thought the sacrifice too great.

"Mr. Douglass Interviewed: An Eloquent and Straightforward Statement of His Action," in the Parlor of His Home in Uniontown (Anacostia), Washington, DC, January 25, 1884 (excerpt)

***Washington Post*, January 26, 1884**

"The opinion has been expressed," said The Post, "that the colored people, who look to you as a leader, will consider your position in the light of your present action [his marriage to Helen M. Pitts, a white woman], as equivocal."

"I do not presume to be a leader," answered Mr. Douglass, "but if I have advocated the cause of the colored people it is not because I am a negro, but because I am a man. The same impulse which would move me to jump into the water to save a white child from drowning, causes me to espouse the cause of the downtrodden and oppressed wherever I find them. Mr. Lincoln and Mr. Sumner were leaders of the colored people, far greater than I, an humble citizen, can ever hope to be. They were both white men. What effect then can the affairs of my private life have upon my principles of justice. I want for the colored people equal rights and advantages of citizenship and for those objects I am still working just as earnestly and shall continue to do so until the end."

"The Nation's Great Act," Emancipation Day Speech at Lincoln Memorial Church, Washington, DC, April 16, 1885 (excerpts) Washington, DC, *National Republican*, April 18, 1885

Kentucky has done many evil things in her time, but she has also done many great and good things. . . . She has given us two of the largest hearts and broadest minds of which our country can boast, men who had the courage of their convictions, and who dared, at the peril of what men hold most dear, to be true to their convictions. These strong men, one dead and the other living, are Abraham Lincoln and John M. Harlan.[47] Abraham Lincoln is already enshrined in the hearts of the American people, and Justice John M. Harlan will hold a place beside him in the hearts of his countrymen.

Reminiscence of Abraham Lincoln, ca. 1886 Allen Thorndike Rice, ed., *Reminiscences of Abraham Lincoln by Distinguished Men of His Time* (New York: North American Publishing Co., 1886)

I do not know more about Mr. Lincoln than is known by countless thousands of Americans who have met the man. But I am quite willing to give my recollections of him and the impressions made by him upon my mind as to his character.

My first interview with him was in the summer of 1863, soon after the Confederate States had declared their purpose to treat colored soldiers as insurgents, and their purpose not to treat any such soldiers as prisoners of war subject to exchange like other soldiers. My visit to Mr. Lincoln was in reference to this threat of the Confederate States. I was at the time engaged in raising colored troops, and I desired some assurances from President Lincoln that such troops should be treated as soldiers of the United States, and when taken prisoners exchanged like other soldiers; that when any of them were hanged or enslaved the President should retaliate. I was introduced to Mr. Lincoln on this occasion by Senator Pomeroy, of Kansas; I met him at the Executive Mansion.

I was somewhat troubled with the thought of meeting one so august and high in authority, especially as I had never been in the White House before, and had never spoken to a President of the United States before. But my embarrassment soon vanished when I met the face of Mr. Lincoln. When I entered he was seated in a low chair, surrounded by a multitude of books and papers, his feet and legs were extended in front of his chair. On my approach he slowly drew his feet in from the different parts of the room into which they had strayed, and he began to rise, and continued to rise until he looked down upon me, and extended his hand and gave me a welcome. I began, with some hesitation, to tell him who I was and what I had been doing, but he soon stopped me, saying in a sharp, cordial voice:

"You need not tell me who you are, Mr. Douglass, I know who you are. Mr. Seward[48] has told me all about you."

He then invited me to take a seat beside him. Not wishing to occupy his time and attention, seeing that he was busy, I stated to him the object of my call at once. I said:

"Mr. Lincoln, I am recruiting colored troops. I have assisted in fitting up two regiments in Massachusetts, and am now at work in the same way in Pennsylvania, and have come to say this to you, sir, if you wish to make this branch of the service successful you must do four things:

"First—You must give colored soldiers the same pay that you give white soldiers.

"Second—You must compel the Confederate States to treat colored soldiers, when taken prisoners, as prisoners of war.

"Third—When any colored man or soldier performs brave, meritorious exploits in the field, you must enable me to say to those that I recruit that they will be promoted for such service, precisely as white men are promoted for similar service.

"Fourth—In case any colored soldiers are murdered in cold blood and taken prisoners, you should retaliate in kind."

To this little speech Mr. Lincoln listened with earnest attention and with very apparent sympathy, and replied to each point in his own peculiar, forcible way. First he spoke of the opposition generally to employing negroes as soldiers at all, of the prejudice against the race, and of the advantage to colored people that would result from their being employed as soldiers in defense of their country. He regarded such an employment as an experiment, and spoke of the advantage it would be to the colored race if the experiment should succeed. He said that he had difficulty in getting colored men into the United States uniform; that when the purpose was fixed to employ them as soldiers, several different uniforms were proposed for them, and that it was something gained when it was finally determined to clothe them like other soldiers.

Now, as to the pay, we had to make some concession to prejudice. There were threats that if we made soldiers of them at all white men would not enlist, would not fight beside them. Besides, it was not believed that a negro could make a good soldier, as good a soldier as a white man, and hence it was thought that he should not have the same pay as a white man. But said he,

"I assure you, Mr. Douglass, that in the end they shall have the same pay as white soldiers."

As to the exchange and general treatment of colored soldiers when taken prisoners of war, he should insist to their being entitled to all privileges of such prisoners. Mr. Lincoln admitted the justice of my demand for the promotion of colored soldiers for good conduct in the field, but on the matter of retaliation he differed from me entirely. I shall never forget the benignant expression of his face, the tearful look of his eye and the quiver in his voice, when he deprecated a resort to retaliatory measures.

"Once begun," said he, "I do not know where such a measure would stop."

He said he could not take men out and kill them in cold blood for what was done by others. If he could get hold of the persons who were guilty of killing the colored prisoners in cold blood, the case would be different, but he could not kill the innocent for the guilty.

Before leaving Mr. Lincoln, Senator Pomeroy said:

"Mr. President, Mr. Stanton is going to make Douglass Adjutant-General to General Thomas, and is going to send him down the Mississippi to recruit."

Mr. Lincoln said in answer to this:

"I will sign any commission that Mr. Stanton will give Mr. Douglass."

At this point we parted.

I met Mr. Lincoln several times after this interview.

I was once invited by him to take tea with him at the Soldiers' Home. On one occasion, while visiting him at the White House, he showed me a letter he was writing to Horace Greeley in reply to some of Greeley's criticisms against protracting the war.[49] He seemed to feel very keenly the reproaches heaped upon him for not bringing the war to a speedy conclusion; said he was charged with making it an Abolition war instead of a war for the Union, and expressed his desire to end the war as soon as possible. While I was talking with him Governor Buckingham sent in his card, and I was amused by his telling the messenger, as well as by the way he expressed it, to "tell Governor Buckingham to wait, I want to have a long talk with my friend Douglass."

He used those words. I said: "Mr. Lincoln, I will retire." "Oh, no, no, you shall not, I want Governor Buckingham to wait," and he did wait for at least a half hour. When he came in I was introduced by Mr. Lincoln to Governor Buckingham, and the Governor did not seem to take it amiss at all that he had been required to wait.

I was present at the inauguration of Mr. Lincoln, the 4th of March, 1865. I felt then that there was murder in the air, and I kept close to his carriage on the way to the Capitol, for I felt that I might see him fall that day. It was a vague presentiment.

At that time the Confederate cause was on its last legs, as it were, and there was deep feeling. I could feel it in the atmosphere here. I did not know exactly what it was, but I just felt as if he might be shot on his way to the Capitol. I cannot refer to any incident, in fact, to any expression that I heard, it was simply a presentiment that Lincoln might fall that day. I got right in front of the east portico of the Capitol, listened to his inaugural address, and witnessed his being sworn in by Chief Justice Chase. When he came on the steps he was accompanied by Vice-President Johnson. In looking out in the crowd he saw me standing near by, and I could see he was pointing me out to Andrew Johnson. Mr. Johnson, without knowing perhaps that I saw the movement, looked quite annoyed that his attention should be called in that direction. So I got a peep into his soul. As soon as he saw me looking at him, suddenly he assumed rather an amicable expression of countenance. I felt that, whatever else the man might be, he was no friend to my people.

I heard Mr. Lincoln deliver this wonderful address. It was very short; but he answered all the objections raised to his prolonging the war in one sentence—it was a remarkable sentence.

"Fondly do we hope, profoundly do we pray, that this mighty scourge of war shall soon pass away, yet if God wills it continue until all the wealth piled up by two hundred years of bondage shall have been wasted, and each drop of blood drawn by the lash shall have been paid for by one drawn by the sword, we must still say, as was said three thousand years ago, the judgments of the Lord are true and righteous altogether."

For the first time in my life, and I suppose the first time in any colored man's life, I attended the reception of President Lincoln on the evening of the inauguration. As I approached the door I was seized by two policemen and forbidden to enter. I said to them that they were mistaken entirely in what they were doing, that if Mr. Lincoln knew that I was at the door he would order my admission, and I bolted in by them. On the inside I was taken charge of by two other policemen, to be conducted as I supposed to the President, but instead of that they were conducting me out the window on a plank.

"Oh," said I, "this will not do, gentlemen," and as a gentleman was passing in I said to him, "Just say to Mr. Lincoln that Fred. Douglass is at the door."

He rushed in to President Lincoln, and almost in less than a half a minute I was invited into the East Room of the White House. A perfect sea of beauty and elegance, too, it was. The ladies were in very fine attire, and Mrs. Lincoln was standing there. I could not have been more than ten feet from him when Mr. Lincoln saw me; his countenance lighted up, and he said in a voice which was heard all around: “Here comes my friend Douglass.” As I approached him he reached out his hand, gave me a cordial shake, and said: “Douglass, I saw you in the crowd to-day listening to my inaugural address. There is no man’s opinion that I value more than yours: what do you think of it?” I said: “Mr. Lincoln, I cannot stop here to talk with you, as there are thousands waiting to shake you by the hand;” but he said again: “What did you think of it?” I said: “Mr. Lincoln, it was a sacred effort,” and then I walked off. “I am glad you liked it,” he said. That was the last time I saw him to speak with him.

In all my interviews with Mr. Lincoln I was impressed with his entire freedom from popular prejudice against the colored race. He was the first great man that I talked with in the United States freely, who in no single instance reminded me of the difference between himself and myself, of the difference of color, and I thought that all the more remarkable because he came from a State where there were black laws.[50] I account partially for his kindness to me because of the similarity with which I had fought my way up, we both starting at the lowest round of the ladder.

I must say this for Mr. Lincoln, that whenever I met him he was in a very serious mood. I heard of those stories he used to tell, but he never told me a story. I remember of one of Mr. Lincoln’s stories being told me by General Grant. I had called on him, and he said: “Douglass, stay here, I want to tell you about a little incident. When I came to Washington first, one of the first things that Lincoln said to me was, ‘Grant, have you ever read the book by Orpheus C. Kerr?’[51] ‘Well, no, I never did,’ said I. Mr. Lincoln said: ‘You ought to read it, it is a very interesting book. I have had a good deal of satisfaction reading that book. There is one poem there that describes a meeting of the animals. The substance of it being that the animals and a dragon, or some dreadful thing, was near by and had to be conquered, and it was a question as to who would undertake the job. By and by a monkey stepped forward and proposed to do the work up. The monkey said he thought he could do it if he could get an inch or two more put on his tail. The assemblage voted him a few inches more to his tail, and he went out and tried his hand. He was unsuccessful and returned, stating that he wanted a few more inches put on his tail. The request was granted, and he went again. His second effort was a failure. He asked that more inches be put on his tail and he would try a third time.' At last," said General Grant, "it got through my head what Lincoln was aiming at, as applying to my wanting more men, and finally I said: 'Mr. Lincoln, I don't want any more inches put on my tail.'" It was a hit at McClellan, and General Grant told me the story with a good deal of gusto. I got the book afterward and read the lines of Orpheus C. Kerr.

There was one thing concerning Lincoln that I was impressed with, and that was that a statement of his was an argument more convincing than any amount of logic. He had a happy faculty of stating a proposition, of stating it so that it needed no argument. It was a rough kind of reasoning, but it went right to the point. Then, too, there was another feeling that I had with reference to him, and that was that while I felt in his presence I was in the presence of a very great man, as great as the greatest, I felt as though I could go and put my hand on him if I wanted to, to put my hand on his shoulder. Of course I did not do it, but I felt that I could. I felt as though I was in the presence of a big brother, and that there was safety in his atmosphere.

It was often said during the war that Mrs. Lincoln did not sympathize fully with her husband in his anti-slavery feeling, but I never believed this concerning her, and have good reason for being confirmed in my impression of her by the fact that, when Mr. Lincoln died and she was about leaving the White House, she selected his favorite walking cane and said: "I know of no one that would appreciate this more than Fred. Douglass." She sent it to me at Rochester, and I have it in my house to-day, and expect to keep it there as long as I live.

Oration Commemorating Lincoln's Birthday, February 12, 1888

Services Commemorative of the Seventy-Ninth Anniversary of the Birth of Abraham Lincoln by the Republican National League, at the League House, 1401 Massachusetts Avenue, Washington, D.C., February 12th, 1888 (Washington, Gibson Bros., 1888)[52]

I could almost wish to be excused from offering a single remark after the able, eloquent, and comprehensive, and, I might say, faithful, address to which we have just listened.[53] It would, perhaps, have been much better that the meeting should disperse after hearing what we have heard. And yet I am not sure but there is a sort of propriety in my coming to you and saying a few words, at least, in respect to the great and the good man of whom we have heard so much and of whom nothing new can be said.

I think it may be safely affirmed that the moral and mental greatness of no character which has come upon the stage in our day and generation, and in modern times, has been more generally conceded, or more firmly established, than that great and good man whose birth we have assembled to-day to celebrate. A great cloud of witnesses,[54] which no man can number, composed of all classes and conditions of men, at home and abroad, everywhere, have recognized Abraham Lincoln as one of the greatest and best men ever produced by this country, if not ever produced by the world at large.

I, and those I represent in part, may well enough wish to share with you in your admiration of his character and in the perpetuation of his great memory. You may extol him as a statesman and a patriot: we may, and will, extol him as a man and a philanthropist. You may

Frederick Douglass and others standing outside his home, Cedar Hill, in Washington, DC. Walter O. Evans Collection of Frederick Douglass and Douglass Family Papers, Beinecke Rare Book and Manuscript Library, Yale University

honor his memory in that he saved your country when the light of its hope was going out, or seemed to be going out, in darkness, certainly in blood; we will cherish his memory in that he struck the galling fetters from four millions of the class to which we belong. You may honor him for the hope, aye, for the possibility, of a united country; we will honor him because he raised us from the depths, from the condition of chattelhood to the grand possibility of American citizenship. It was once said by Lamartine,[55] one of the most brilliant of all modern French writers, that "William Wilberforce went up to heaven with a million of broken fetters in his arms, as evidence of a life well spent." Four times more than this can we say of Abraham Lincoln. He went up before his Maker with four millions of broken fetters in his arms as evidence of a life well spent. Glorious man! He was a man so broad in his sympathy, so noble in his character, so just in his action, so free from narrow prejudice; he touched the world so completely at all sides that all classes, conditions, all nations, kindreds, tongues, and people could hail him as a countryman, a clansman, a kinsman, a brother beloved, a benefactor.

I knew Abraham Lincoln personally. To have known him as I knew him, I regard as one of the grandest privileges experienced by me during a considerable lifetime. I knew him. I would not part with that peep into that noble soul for all the wealth, as Clay once said, that could be bestowed upon the most successful conqueror.[56] It was a new revelation to me, my meeting with that great and good man. I saw him at a time of profound interest; a time when the fate of this Republic appeared to tremble in the balance. Men's hearts were failing them for fear of what was coming upon the land. I came down here from the North—I was not born in the North (Laughter)—but I went North on a mission some fifty years ago. It was not healthy for me to come down here for some twenty-five years after I went North. I came to him early in the year 1863, after the Emancipation Proclamation, of course, and I saw him to great advantage.

It was my first visit to Washington. First things are very important; and this was my first visit to Washington—the first time that I ever looked up and saw the Goddess of American Liberty on the lofty dome of yonder Capitol.[57] My eyes saw something then that thrilled me, for I saw it in the light of the liberty proclaimed by Abraham Lincoln. I saw it in the light of those stars (pointing to the American flag), and it filled me with hope and expectation. It was my first entrance, too, into the White House. No man who has never felt the yoke of American bondage on his neck; no one who has not felt the fetter on his heel can imagine and enter into the tumult of feeling with which I entered the White House. It was a great day for me, a very great day, to enter the Executive Mansion and to approach the President of the United States. I was a little disturbed and a great deal agitated, but there was no real cause for trepidation or for alarm. I was going to see a great man—a *great* man. It is always easier to see a great man than to see a little one. I have noticed that the higher we go up in the gradations of humanity and moral greatness the further we get from prejudices, from narrowness, from everything like pettiness. I found myself without excuse for being alarmed, for being disturbed; for I was in the presence of a great man. Mr. Lincoln was reading when I entered, and I hesitated to approach him until he raised his eyes from the paper he held in his hand. His face and features struck me. They bore the marks of care and toil and solemn responsibility. I think I never saw a face that had so much of the real, I was going to say, saintliness, combined with so much resolution, as I saw in that deeply-ridged forehead of Abraham Lincoln. I went up towards him, and as I came near him I began to tell him who I was and what I had been doing, and in his peculiar voice he stopped me. Said he, "I know who you are, Mr. Douglass, and I know what you have been doing; Mr. Seward has told me all about you." This put me at ease; but I had something to say to him. It was not mere courtesy. My mission to him was in regard to the enlistment and the treatment of colored troops. I had assisted in raising two regiments in the State of Massachusetts, and I was then engaged in the same work in the State of Pennsylvania, and I said to him, "I have come, Mr. Lincoln, to say to you three things, and only three things, and one of them is that I may be able to say to the colored soldiers at the North that they will be paid the same wages as the white soldiers.

"Secondly: when they perform brave and honorable deeds in the service of the country, on the battle-field, that you will promote them.

"Thirdly: when they are taken as prisoners and are killed, as the threat has been given that they shall be killed, that we shall retaliate." Those were the three things. I never shall forget how quietly and sympathetically Mr. Lincoln listened to what I had to say. I saw, when I came to the last proposition, the first he received with a smile of approval, the second also, but when it came to the third, that of retaliation, I got a peep into that good man's heart. There came over his face an expression of sadness, deep sadness, and he began to reply to the several propositions that I had made to him. He told me, "Mr. Douglass, you know that it was with great difficulty that I could get the colored soldiers, or get colored men, into the army at all. You know the prejudices existing against them; you know the doubt that was felt in regard to their ability as soldiers, and it was necessary at the first that we should make some discrimination in regard to them; they were on trial." And he argued the point as he only could argue.

I never heard a man that could make a statement which should be in itself an overwhelming argument, as Abraham Lincoln could. He argued the question fully, and I was made to see that it was something, whether with wages or without wages, money or without money, it was a grand triumph to get a blue coat on the back of a negro, and the eagle on his button, and the musket on his shoulder. I agreed with him. But he said, "Nevertheless, though we cannot offer them at present the same pay as we pay the white soldiers, that will be done, Mr. Douglass, and you may say to your people that they will eventually be paid," as they were eventually paid, "dollar for dollar, equal with other soldiers."

On the other point of promotion, he was equally willing, but on retaliation he asked, "Where will it stop?" I could see that there was a vista of blood opening to him from which his tender heart shrank. He said, "If I could get hold of the men that murdered your troops, murdered our prisoners of war, I would execute them, but I cannot take men that may not have had anything to do with this murdering of our soldiers and execute them. No, Mr. Douglass, I don't see where it would stop; besides, I understand they are beginning to treat our colored soldiers as prisoners of war."

But this was not all that I saw of Mr. Lincoln. After all perhaps I am taking up too much time (cries of go on; go on). I saw a good deal more of him during the war, and even down to his inauguration, his second inauguration. There, too, I think I caught a glimpse of the soul of this great man, a remarkable glimpse, a deep insight into his mind and his heart. I mean at his second inauguration. I felt at that time there was the spirit of murder here in the District of Columbia (I am glad it is not here now), and I watched his carriage when he was on his way down to the Capitol to be inaugurated, and to deliver his inaugural address. (I had had the pleasure of putting the gown on Chief-Justice Chase, who was to administer the oath on that occasion.) I got very near to Mr. Lincoln, for he did not hesitate, you know, to ask me to come even to his table, and ask me to eat with him, and ask me to the Soldiers' Home, dear man! Well, I say, I kept near to the carriage on his way to the Capitol. Pennsylvania avenue was not what it is now. Shepherd had not been along on the avenue.[58] (It was then a sheep without a Shepherd.[59]) I kept close to the carriage nearly up to the hub in mud, for I was afraid every step we took that something would happen to that good and glorious man. Well, when we got to the east portico of the Capitol, there I saw Mr. Lincoln in his true light. He had been abused. Oh, good men are apt to be abused. Men had been denouncing him on the right hand and on the left. Some of them blamed him very much that he hadn't brought the war to a close; another blamed him for not making the war an abolition war, and others blamed him for making it an abolition war, so he was blamed on all sides, and he answered them all in one sentence, and such a sentence I never heard from the lips of any man in his position before. He said: "Fondly do we hope, fervently do we pray, that this mighty scourge of war shall soon pass away; yet if God wills it continue till all the wealth piled up by two hundred years of bondage shall have been wasted, and each drop of blood drawn by the lash shall have been paid for one drawn by the sword, we must still say, as was said three thousand years ago, the judgments of the Lord are true and righteous altogether." Those words rang out over that throng, and they went over the country as never words went before, and they silenced all murmurs. They came down on the land like the summer's thunder shower on the parched ground, and a new life began.

But, my friends, I must not talk longer. I could talk all day about Abraham Lincoln.

Some people have said hard things about Mrs. Lincoln. For my part I take no stock in them. I loved Mrs. Lincoln. I loved her because Abraham Lincoln loved her. That was enough for me. And, besides, I don't take any stock in the stories of those who thought she was not in sympathy with him in his anti-slavery views. She was in sympathy with him. She used to say, when we abolitionists were very impatient with Mr. Lincoln, because he did not move fast enough, "Oh, yes, father is slow." Those words state what existed there. And when Mrs. Lincoln was leaving the White House, for Illinois, she said to her dressmaker [Elizabeth Keckley], who was near by when she was gathering up her things to go away: "Here is Mr. Lincoln's favorite cane (this is the identical cane that I now hold in my hand), and I know of no man who will value it more than Frederick Douglass." And she caused it to be sent to me at Rochester, N.Y., where I then lived; and I am the owner of this cane, you may depend on that; and I mean to hold it and keep [it] in sacred remembrance of Abraham Lincoln, who once leaned upon it.

Oration Commemorating the Twenty-Sixth Anniversary of Emancipation in the District of Columbia, Fourth Baptist Church, Washington, DC, April 16, 1888 (excerpt)
Washington, DC, *National Republican*, April 17, 1888

I admit that the negro, and especially the plantation negro, the tiller of the soil, has made little progress from barbarism to civilization, and that he is in a deplorable condition since his emancipation. That he is worse off, in many respects, than when he was a slave, I am compelled to admit, but I contend that the fault is not his, but that of his heartless accusers. He is the victim of a cunningly devised swindle, one which paralyzes his energies, suppresses his ambition, and blasts all his hopes; and though he is nominally free he is actually a slave. I here and now denounce his so-called emancipation as a stupendous fraud—a fraud upon him, a fraud upon the world. It was not so meant by Abraham Lincoln; it was not so meant by the Republican party; but whether so meant or not, it is practically a lie, keeping the word of promise to the ear and breaking it to the heart.[60]

"President Harrison and Our Colored Citizens" (excerpt)
The Independent (New York), April 21, 1892

It is not enough that the man at the head of this nation shall be a good man, he must be a strong man as well. It was the strength as well as the wisdom of Abraham Lincoln and General Grant that made them successful Presidents. No man in the country could forget for a moment who was President in the case of either.

Oration Commemorating Lincoln's Birthday, Delivered at the Annual Dinner of the Union League Club, Brooklyn, February 13, 1893
Brooklyn *Standard Union*, February 14, 1893

Gentlemen,—I beg to remind you at the outset that reminiscences are generally tedious. I hope you may find mine an exception to the general rule, though I fear the contrary, for speakers are often more interesting and eloquent about what they do not know, than about what they do know. (Applause.) It is impossible for me, and perhaps for anybody else, to say anything new about Abraham Lincoln. (Applause.) He is in the minds and hearts of all of us. We know him and know of him, as we know of no other great man of our century. (Applause.)

I had the good fortune to know Abraham Lincoln personally and peculiarly. I knew him, not on the side visible to the free, rich and powerful, but on the side which he presented to the unfortunate, the defenseless, the oppressed and the enslaved. (Applause.) It is something to know how a man will deport himself to his admitted equals, but more to know how he will bear himself to those who are recognized as his inferiors. (Applause.) It is this knowledge of Mr. Lincoln upon which I depend for any interest, value or significance of my story to you this evening.

Of course, and on general principles, it is a great thing for any man of whatever condition, to know a great man. For a truly great man is ever a rebuke to pride and selfishness in the strong, and a source of strength to the weak and unfortunate. The memory of such a great man is ennobling to men already noble, and we shall all feel better for reviving and keeping alive the memory of such a man to-night. (Applause.) We shall, I am sure, find this especially true when we shall have heard what my learned friend, Dr. Wayland,[61] shall say of Mr. Lincoln.

Gentlemen, let me be somewhat confidential and autobiographical. I have sometimes been held up as a man without friends or associates, but really I have been a very fortunate man during most of my life.

"Hon. Fred. Douglass on Platform in Pavilion" at Tuskegee Institute, March 26, 1892. Prints and Photographs Division, Library of Congress

Few men have had a chance to get more that is desirable and valuable out of this life, than I. I have seen both sides of this great world. I have seen men of all conditions. I have seen men high and low, rich and poor, slave and free, white and black, and hence I ought to be a broader, if not a better man, than most other men. I certainly have no excuse for narrowness or for race and color prejudice. I feel it more to be a man and a member of the great human family than to be a member of any one of the many varieties of the human race, whether Anglo-Saxon, Anglo-African, or any other.

Among the circumstances in which I deem myself most fortunate, is that of having seen many great men. They have not been of one country or of one continent alone. I have seen such men in England, and I have seen them in this republic. I have seen men of whom we have all heard; men who stood only a little lower than the angels.[62]

They were great and god-like men, divinely equipped and commissioned from on high to serve the highest needs of mankind. They were not only uplifted men, but they were uplifting men; men whose range was far above all that is little, low and mean; but I have met with no such man, at home or abroad, who made upon my mind the impression of possessing a more godlike nature, than did Abraham Lincoln. (Cheers and applause.)

Greater men than he intellectually there may have been, but to my mind, measuring him in the direction of the highest quality, of human goodness and nobility of character, no better man than he has ever stood or walked upon this continent. (Cheers.) But you did not ask me for my opinion of Mr. Lincoln. You asked me for my recollections of him, and these I shall proceed to give you.

It may be that the conditions surrounding Mr. Lincoln when I first met him had something to do with the exalted impression I received of him. It is one thing to see a man in prosperity, and another thing to see him in adversity. It is one thing to see him surrounded by hardships, difficulties and dangers, and it is another thing to see him in his hours of ease and prosperity.

The time to see a great captain is not when the wind is fair and the sea is smooth, and the man in the cross-trees or round-top can safely sing out, "All is well." At such a time a pigmy may seem a giant, and a poltroon, a hero. You must see him under other conditions. You must see him when the sky is dark; see him in rough weather; see him in the hour of danger, when he is far from land in mid-ocean, when his ship is in distress, tossed by the storm, engine disabled, rudder gone, sails blown away, stanchions staved in, mountain billows dashing over his deck. It is then, if ever, that you may know the true mettle of the man. If, then, you find him calm, collected, fearless and faithful, manly and undismayed, with no thought in his soul but the one thought of absolute and overmastering duty, and determined to do that duty, at whatever cost to himself or others, I say that you may then know that you are in the presence of a hero worthy of your highest human worship, and such a captain was ours.

The sea was not smooth, the sky was not bright, the wind was not fair, when I first met and measured Abraham Lincoln. It was in the darkest hours of the late war. There was much in the situation to make men anxious. It was a time to make the boldest hold his breath. No man could tell, at that time, whether the cause of the country would be saved or lost. I certainly was concerned, not only for the cause of the country, but for the cause of the slave; a cause for which I had given the best energies of my soul, the best years of my life, and the deepest longings of my heart. (Applause.)

The leaders of the rebellion were, at this time, especially fierce, bold and defiant. They had, in the pride of their power, scorned to accept the terms of peace that Mr. Lincoln had, a few months before, offered them, whereby they might have saved the lives of men on both sides, North and South, and their slavery in the bargain.

But it was not only the rebels in arms at the South, but also the disloyal men at the North, who complicated the problem, and gave Mr. Lincoln much cause for anxiety. Our forces in the field were diminishing. Recruiting was becoming difficult and well-nigh impossible. The draft was being resisted. Loyal black men were being murdered in the streets of New York. Asylums and houses of black people were being burned in resentment of the draft and of the continuance of the war. Besides, the Administration was being fiercely assailed by the press, the platform and the pulpit of the North. Out of this darkness and storm the soul of Lincoln shone with a light all the more clear, calm and steady. (Applause.)

I first saw Mr. Lincoln in the early summer of 1863. I had a special object in seeing him at this time. I had been engaged in raising two regiments of colored men in Massachusetts, the Fifty-fourth and Fifty-fifth. Two of my sons were in those regiments.[63] Jefferson Davis had taken notice of these colored soldiers and had notified the country that colored men taken in arms would not be treated as prisoners of war by the Confederate armies, but would be shot or hanged in cold blood, or sold into slavery. It was about this barbarous threat, in part, that I went to Washington to see Abraham Lincoln.

It required some nerve to approach the Chief Magistrate of the nation for such a purpose at such a time. I did not know how he would receive a man of my complexion, or whether he would receive me at all. I was not a member of Congress, a United States marshal, a Minister and Consul-General to Hayti, an elector at large, or even a citizen of the United States. I was still under the ban of the Dred Scott decision. So I felt it a bold thing for me to enter the White House and presume to talk with the President of the United States. Besides, I had no one to introduce me. Happily I was soon relieved at this point. I met with the late Senator Samuel Pomeroy (three cheers for Pomeroy), a good and true man, with whom I had become acquainted during the border ruffian war in Kansas, and he kindly consented to accompany me to the White House and introduce me to Mr. Lincoln. It was a daring thing even for him, Senator though he was, to walk the streets of Washington with me at that time. To do so was to invite insult.

This done I went to the Executive Mansion, not however, without much solicitude as to how I should deport myself: how I should order my speech, and how this great man in his exalted office would be likely to receive and treat a man of my condition. The result was altogether at variance with my fears. I had not been an instant in the presence of this great man before all apprehensions were dispelled.

I saw before me a man, a great man, a tall man physically, and I was not long in discovering that I was in the presence of a great man mentally. I also made the discovery that it is much easier to see and converse with a great man than with a small man; with a big man than with a little one. (Laughter and applause.)

I found Mr. Lincoln seated in a low chair and surrounded on all sides by unbound books and papers which I thought he had been overhauling.

As I approached, he began to rise to receive me, and he continued to rise, higher and higher, till I found myself looking up to him, and he looking down upon me. He gave me a welcome which was none too much nor too little; but just enough to make me at ease.

First, I began to talk of myself, as I have been doing this evening. I told him what I had been doing. He blandly put an end to it all by saying: "Mr. Douglass, you need not tell me who you are. I know who you are. Mr. Seward has told me all about you." Brought thus to a standstill, I proceeded with the object of my visit:

I said: "Mr. President, I have been recruiting colored troops; and if you want me to succeed, I must be able to assure them that colored soldiers while in the service shall have pay equal to that of white soldiers. Secondly, that when they shall perform acts of bravery in battle, which would secure promotion to white soldiers, the like promotion shall be accorded colored soldiers. Thirdly, that if the threat of Jefferson Davis is carried out, you, President Lincoln, will retaliate in kind." (Good! Good!)

Feeling myself now perfectly free to say to Mr. Lincoln all that I thought on the subject, I supported my demands, as best I could, with arguments to which he calmly and patiently listened, not once interrupting me, and, when I had finished, he made a careful reply, covering each proposition that I had submitted to him.

He admitted the justice of the demand for equal wages and equal promotion to colored soldiers; but reminded me that, for the moment, there were causes for delay in its execution. He called my attention to the necessity, at that critical time, of avoiding any shock to the prejudices of the white soldiers, and told me of the many objections there were to making colored men soldiers; of the doubts entertained of them; of how it was first proposed that they should be employed simply as laborers; that they should be clothed in a peculiar and inferior uniform; that they should not bear arms, but that they should work in trenches, with pickax and shovel; that, as time went on, they were thought worthy to be soldiers, but were not to take the field like other soldiers. They were only to hold fortified positions in sickly places, after those places should be captured by white soldiers. He thought it was a great thing that they could be armed and uniformed as soldiers at all. He held, however, that in time, the first two points I had insisted upon would be conceded; that colored soldiers would be equally paid and equally promoted.

But when it came to the matter of retaliation, the tender heart of the great President appeared in the expression of his eyes, and in every line of his careworn countenance, as well as in the tones of his appealing voice. "Ah!" said he, "Douglass, I cannot retaliate. I cannot hang men in cold blood. I cannot hang men who have had nothing to do with murdering colored prisoners. Of course, if I could get hold of the actual murderers of colored prisoners, I would deal with them as they deserve; but I cannot hang those who have had no hand in such murders." (Applause.) I was not convinced that Mr. Lincoln's logic was right; but I was convinced that Mr. Lincoln himself, was right. (Applause.)

I could, and did, answer Mr. Lincoln's arguments; but I was silenced by his overmastering mercy and benevolence. I had found a President with a heart—one who could, even in war, love his enemies;[64] and that was something. In parting, he said: "Douglass, never come to Washington without calling upon me." And I never did.

Though neither of the objects sought were immediately obtained, I was full of faith in the man, and felt sure that he would do what he could to secure justice to our soldiers, and protection to the lives of colored prisoners. I saw Mr. Lincoln several times after this interview and found him ever the same large-hearted man as when I first met him. At one time during the war he sent for me, to consult as to how to get more slaves into our lines. He had offered them freedom and protection, but he said that they were not coming in fast enough.

While we were talking over the matter, Gov. Buckingham, the war Governor of Connecticut (applause), was announced, and I at once arose, and asked leave to withdraw, saying to Mr. Lincoln: "I must not stay to prevent your interview with Gov. Buckingham." Instead of allowing me to leave, he said to the messenger, in his peculiarly high and honest voice: "Tell Gov. Buckingham to wait. I am talking with my friend, Douglass." (Applause).

In this interview President Lincoln told me to devise some plan by which to get more slaves within our lines, and to submit my plan to him. I did so;[65] but it was never after necessary to put the plan into operation. Our rapid successes, and the increasing intelligence of the slaves concerning the new departure of the loyal people and Government, in their favor, brought the free[d]men into our lines much faster than the means we had could care for them.

I have often said that Mr. Lincoln was the first great man with whom I could talk for hours without being once reminded, either by way of compliment or condescension, of my color.

Perhaps this statement was a little too strong; but it seemed true when I made it. The impression I designed to make was that Mr. Lincoln said and did nothing during our interview that reminded me in any way of our difference in color. He not only invited me to see him at the White House, but he invited me to tea with him at the Soldiers' Home (applause); and convinced me that he was far above the prevailing prejudices of his countrymen.

I found Mr. Lincoln different from my expectation of him, not only in his kindness to me, but also in his manners, which were very different from the current representation of them. He had been described as wanting in dignity; as jocose, and fond of telling witty stories. This description of him doubtless has some foundation, for—

"A little nonsense, now and then,
Is relished by the best of men."[66]

But I am bound to say of President Lincoln that it was never my lot to find him in any such mood. His whole deportment was a contradiction and a rebuke to everything like levity or merrymaking. He was not only intensely in earnest, but sadly in earnest.

The dimmed light in his eye, and the deep lines in his strong American face, told plainly the story of the heavy burden of care that weighed upon his spirit. I could as easily dance at a funeral as to jest in the presence of such a man. I felt that his heart was occupied with the thought of his imperiled country and of its brave sons, imperiled and dying on the battle-field. I was present at the beginning of President Lincoln's second term, and witnessed his second inauguration. I saw and followed his carriage that day from the White House to the Capitol. Pennsylvania avenue had not then felt the energy of Gov. Shepherd. It was a thoroughfare of mud. The wheels of Mr. Lincoln's carriage sank in it nearly to the hubs, and it was easy to keep pace with his horses. For some reason, or for no reason, I was oppressed with a dread foreboding as I followed his carriage. The fear was upon me that Mr. Lincoln might be shot down on his way to the Capitol, and it was a great relief to me when the trip was safely ended. I know not why, but I felt that there was murder in the air of Washington. No hint had then been given that an organized band of assassins was hiding in the dark places of the city, seeking the life of Mr. Lincoln.

I stood near the steps of the east front of the Capitol when Mr. Lincoln appeared and had the oath of office administered to him by Chief Justice Chase. I heard his remarkable, memorable, and I might say, wonderful speech on that occasion. To me he seemed more the saint and prophet, in his appearance as well as in his utterance, than he did the President of a great nation, and the Commander-in-Chief of its army and navy. To understand that brief speech of Mr. Lincoln's we must remember that he had been fiercely and bitterly criticised from at least three different quarters. He had been assailed by Northern Democrats for making the war an abolition war. He had been denounced by the Abolitionists for not making it an abolition war. He was denounced for not making peace at any price, and again, for not prosecuting the war with more vigor. He answered all his critics with the following brief sentence: "Fondly do we hope, fervently do we pray, that this mighty scourge of war will soon pass away. (Applause.) Yet, if God wills that it continue until all the wealth piled by the bondsman's two hundred and fifty years of unrequited toil shall be sunk, and until every drop of blood drawn by the lash shall be paid by another drawn with the sword, as was said three thousand years ago, so still it must be said, 'The judgments of the Lord are true and righteous altogether.'" (Applause.) This was said in a voice of deep solemnity, bordering upon inconsolable sadness; but a voice as firm as the everlasting hills, and as pure and clear as the "brave old overhanging sky."[67] There seemed at the time to be in the man's soul the united souls of all the Hebrew prophets. I was much relieved when the President returned in safety to his room in the Senate, for I was, all through his speech, haunted with the thought that he might be murdered before he could finish what he had to say.

In the evening I attended Mr. Lincoln's inaugural reception. It was a new experience for Washington, a new experience for me, and a new experience for the country, to see a person like myself present on such an occasion. (Applause.)

I was once in Albany, in company with that princely philanthropist, the late Hon. Gerrit Smith, and was invited with him to dine with E. C. Delavan,[68] an eminent gentleman of that city. I was about declining to accept this invitation, when the greathearted Gerrit Smith said, "Oh yes, Douglass, go! Some one must break the ice!" (Laughter.) Well, I did go, and did break the ice, and I have been breaking ice ever since (laughter), and some of it pretty hard and thick ice. Having witnessed the inauguration of Mr. Lincoln in the morning, my colored friends urged me to attend the inauguration reception at the Executive Mansion in the evening. Here, indeed, I found solid ice to break, for no man of my "race, color, or previous condition,"[69] had ever attended such a reception, except as a servant or waiter. I did not look upon the matter lightly, either subjectively or objectively. To me it was a serious thing to break in upon the established usage of the country, and run the risk of being repulsed; but I went to the reception, determined to break the ice, which I did in an unexpectedly rough way.

When myself and companion presented ourselves at the door of the White House, we were met by two sturdy policemen, who promptly informed us that we could not be allowed to enter, and when we attempted to enter without their consent, they pushed us back with some violence. I was, however, determined not to be repulsed, and forced myself and lady inside the door, despite the guard. But my trouble was not ended by that advantage. A policeman inside met us and, with a show of friendliness, said to us, "Oh, yes; come this way! come this way!" Thinking that he was about to conduct us to the famous East Room, where the reception was proceeding, we followed the lead of our new, red faced, burly, blue-coated friend; but just when we thought that we were entering, we found ourselves being conducted through an outside window on a plank for the exit of visitors. (Laughter.)

I never before knew so exactly what is meant by "walking the plank." (Laughter.) I said, "This will not do!" To a gentleman who was passing at the moment I said, "Tell Mr. Lincoln that Frederick Douglass is at the door and is refused admission." I did not walk the plank, and, to the policeman's astonishment, was especially invited into the spacious East Room, and we found ourselves in a bewildering sea of beauty and elegance (applause), such as my poor eyes had never before seen in any one room, at home or abroad. High above every other figure in the room, and overlooking the brilliant scene, stood the towering form of Mr. Lincoln, completely hemmed in by the concourse of visitors passing and taking his hand as they passed. The scene was so splendid, so glorious, that I almost repented of my audacity in daring to enter.

But as soon as President Lincoln saw me I was relieved of all embarrassment. In a loud voice, so that all could hear, and looking towards me, he said, "And here comes my friend, Frederick Douglass!" (Good! Good!) I had some trouble in getting through the crowd of elegantly dressed people to Mr. Lincoln.

When I did succeed, and shook hands with him, he detained me and said, "Douglass, I saw you in the crowd to-day, listening to my inaugural address. How did you like it?" I replied, "Mr. Lincoln, I must not stop to talk now. Thousands are here, wishing to shake your hand." But he said, "You must stop. There is no man in the United States whose opinion I value more than I do yours. How did you like it?" (Applause.) I said, "Mr. Lincoln, it was a sacred effort," and passed on, amid some smiles, much astonishment and some frowns. And this was the last time that I heard the voice and saw the face and form of honest Abraham Lincoln.

A few weeks later he fell before the bullet of the assassin. His murder was the natural outcome of a war for slavery. He fell a martyr to the same barbarous and bloody spirit which now pursues, with outrage and vengeance, the people whom he emancipated and whose freedom he secured. Did his firm hand now hold the helm of state; did his brave spirit now animate the nation; did his wisdom now shape and control the destiny of this otherwise great Republic; did he now lead the once great Republican party, we should not, as now, hear from the nation's capital, the weak and helpless, the inconsistent and humiliating confession that, while there are millions of money and ample power in the United States Government to protect the lives and liberties of American citizens in the republics of Hayti and far off Chili, and in every other foreign country on the globe, there is no power under the United States Constitution to protect the lives and liberties of American citizens in any one of our own Southern States from barbarous, inhuman and lawless violence. (Applause.)

"Self-Made Men," Address Delivered to the Students of the Indian Industrial School, Carlisle, Pa., on April 6, 1893 (excerpt) Frederick Douglass Papers, Manuscript Division, Library of Congress

Side by side with the great Hungarian [Lajos Kossuth], let me name the King[70] of American self-made men; the man who rose highest and will be remembered longest as the most popular and beloved President since Washington—ABRAHAM LINCOLN. This man came to us, not from the schools or from the mansions of ease and luxury, but from the back woods. He mastered his grammar by the light of a pine wood torch. The fortitude and industry which could split rails by day, and learn grammar at night at the hearthstone of a log hut and by the unsteady glare of a pine wood knot, prepared this man for a service to his country and to mankind, which only the most exalted could have performed.

"Why is the Negro Lynched?" Address Delivered at the Metropolitan A.M.E. Church in Washington, DC, January 9, 1894[71] (excerpts) *Lessons of the Hour* (Baltimore: Thomas and Evans, 1894)

I come now to the question of negro suffrage. It has come to be fashionable of late to ascribe much of the trouble at the South to ignorant negro suffrage. The great measure according suffrage to the negro [the 15th amendment] recommended by General Grant and adopted by the loyal nation is now denounced as a blunder and a failure. They would, therefore, in some way abridge and limit this right by imposing upon it an educational or some other qualification. . . . It is as good against our Republican form of government as it is against the negro. The wonder is that its votaries do not see its consequences. It does away with that noble and just idea of Abraham Lincoln, that our government should be a government of the people, by the people, and for the people, and for *all* the people.[72] . . .

[Later in the speech, Douglass discussed colonization and racial prejudice during the Civil War, including the New York City draft riot of 1863.] Even the noble and good Mr. Lincoln, one of the best men that ever lived, told a committee of negroes who waited upon him at Washington, that "they were the cause of the war." Many were the men who accepted this theory, and wished the negro in Africa, or in a hotter climate, as some do now.

Frederick Douglass had this photograph made when he visited Hillsdale College in Michigan on January 21, 1863. Hosted by the Ladies' Literary Union, his speech at the college chapel was titled "Popular Error and Unpopular Truth." Hillsdale College

Appendix 1
Douglass's Letters to Lincoln

On August 29, 1864, Douglass sent two letters to Lincoln. The first followed up on his second meeting with Lincoln, to offer a strategy for freeing as many slaves as possible if Lincoln failed to be reelected. The second note regarded his son, Charles R. Douglass, who was serving in the 5th Massachusetts Cavalry.

Letter to Abraham Lincoln, August 29, 1864
Abraham Lincoln Papers, Manuscript Division, Library of Congress

Rochester: N.Y. August 29th 1864

Hon Abraham Lincoln: President of the United States:

Sir: Since the interview with wh. Your Excellency was pleased to honor me a few days ago, I have freely conversed with several trustworthy and Patriotic colored men concerning your suggestion that something should be speedily done to inform the slaves in the Rebel states of the true state of affairs in relation to them and to warn them as to what will be their probable condition should peace be concluded while they remain within the Rebel lines: and more especially to urge upon them the necessity of making their escape. All with whom I have thus far spoken on the subject, concur in the wisdom and benevolence of the Idea, and some of them think it practicable. That every slave who escapes from the Rebel states is a loss to the Rebellion and a gain to the Loyal cause, I need not stop to argue the proposition is self evident. The negro is the stomach of the rebellion. I will therefore briefly submit at once to your Excellency—the ways and means by which many such persons may be wrested from the enemy and brought within our lines:

1st Let a general ag[en]t be appointed by your Excellency charged with the duty of giving effect to your Idea as indicated above: Let him have the means and power to employ twenty or twenty five good men, having the cause at heart, to act as his agents: 2d Let these agents which shall be selected by him, have permission to visit such points at the front as are most accessible to large bodies of slaves in the Rebel states: Let each of the said agts have power—to appoint one sub agent or more in the locality where he may be required to operate: the said sub agent shall be thoroughly acquainted with the country—and well instructed as to the representations he is to make to the slaves:—but his chief duty will be to conduct such squads of slaves as he may be able to collect, safely within the Loyal lines: Let the sub agents for this service be paid a sum not exceeding two doll[ar]s—per day while upon active duty.

3dly In order that these agents shall not be arrested or impeded in their work—let them be properly ordered to report to the Generals commanding the several Departments they may visit, and receive from them permission to pursue their vocation unmolested. 4th Let provision be made that the slaves or Freed men thus brought within our lines shall receive subsistence until such of them as are fit shall enter the service of the country or be otherwise employed and provided for: 5thly Let each agent appointed by the General agent be required to keep a strict acc[oun]t of all his transactions,—of all monies received and paid out, of the numbers and the names of slaves brought into our lines under his auspices, of the plantations visited, and of everything properly connected with the prosecution of his work, and let him be required to make full reports of his proceedings—at least, once a fortnight to the General Agent.

6th Also, Let the General Agt be required to keep a strict acct of all his transactions with his agts and report to your Excellency or to an officer designated by you to receive such reports: 7th Let the General Agt be paid a salary sufficient to enable him to employ a competant clerk, and let him be stationed at Washington—or at some other Point where he can most readily receive communications from and send communications to his Agents: The General Agt should also have a kind of roving commission within our lines, so that he may have a more direct and effective oversight of the whole work and thus ensure activity and faithfulness on the part of his agents.

This is but an imperfect outline of the plan—but I think it enough to give your Excellency an Idea of how the desirable work shall be executed.

Your Obedient Servant

Fred[k] Douglass

Letter to Abraham Lincoln, August 29, 1864
RG 94 (Records of the Adjutant General's Office), Entry 360 (Colored Troops Division, Letters Received, 1863-1888), National Archives

Private

Now, Mr President—I hope I shall not presume to[o] much upon your kindness—but I have a very great favor to ask. It is not that you will appoint me General Agent to carry out the Plan now proposed—though I would not shrink from that duty—but it is, that you will cause my son Charles R Douglass. 1st Sergeant of Company I 5th Massachusetts dis-mounted Cavalry—now stationed at "*Point Look out*" to be dis-charged—He is now sick. He was the first colored volunteer from the state of New York—having enlisted with his Older Brother [Lewis] in the Mass. 54th partly to encourage enlistments—He was but 18. when he enlisted—and has been in the service 18. months. If your Excellency can confer this favor—you will lay me under many obligations

Again Your Obedient Servant

Fredk Douglass

[Lincoln endorsed the back of the letter on September 1, 1864, "Let this boy be discharged." In accordance with Lincoln's endorsement, Charles R. Douglass was discharged at Point Lookout, Maryland, on September 15.]

Sgt. Charles R. Douglass. Courtesy of Swann Auction Galleries

Appendix 2
Undated Drafts of Speeches

Undated Manuscript (likely a draft of the June 1, 1865, eulogy) Frederick Douglass Papers, Manuscript Division, Library of Congress

The people who always love and admire themselves saw themselves reflected in Abraham Lincoln. He was their typical man—their national representative and as such they loved him. He was a better representative of American Institutions than were the men who made them—because he was the natural child of those institutions. Washington, Adams, Jefferson, Madison, sprung from Monarchical and Aristocratical Institutions—and their lives were tinged by those influences—but here was a man who swung clear of all such bias. There was about him none of the formalities and authorities, which surround all approach to Aristocratic and Monarchical rulers. To an extent almost incredible he made himself accessible to the people.

It was my exceeding great privilege to know Abraham Lincoln personally. I saw and conversed with him freely at different times during his administration and at various turns of the fortunes of war—and always at his invitation.[1]

The fact that he could so invite a colored man to the executive Mansion, though small in itself[,] is one of some significance as indicating the broad and manly character which distinguished him.

He was the first American President, who in this respect, rose above the customs and prejudices of his country. Some men there are who can face death and dangers—but have not the moral courage to contradict a prejudice or face ridicule. In daring to admit, nay in daring to invite a Negro to an audience at the white house, Mr Lincoln did that which he knew would be offensive to the crowd and excite their ribaldry. It was saying to the country, I am President of the black people as well as the white—and I mean to respect their rights and feelings as men and as citizens.

In my interviews with him, I found him as I have already described him, a plain man. There was neither paint nor varnish about him. His manners were simple, unaffected, unstudied. His language, like himself, was plain[,] strong and sinewy, just as it appears in his written productions. He spoke as he wrote, without ornament. Earnest always but never extravagant. I never met a man who could state more clearly and forcibly, just what he wished to make apparent.

Conscious always of the tremendous responsibility which the crisis devolved upon him—and of his own insufficiency, he was still resolved to do what he could to save the country—and to receive counsel from even the humblest quarter to that end. He felt himself to be the President of the United States; but the great dignity of the presidency never stood in the way of his amiability as a man. From which ever side the observer beheld him, he was always the same man—animated by the same great purpose.

Undated Manuscript (excerpts)[2]
Frederick Douglass Papers, Manuscript Division, Library of Congress

[Regarding the August 19, 1864, meeting:] This interview was if possible more gratifying than the one of which I have already spoken. . . . [Douglass here described his conversation with Lincoln about Horace Greeley's meeting with Confederate envoys at Niagara Falls.] I was all the more impressed by this benevolent solicitude of his because he had already said in answer to this clamor that his object was to save the union with or without slavery. What he had to say to day showed that he knew how, when, and *to whom* to speak. . . . In this interview with President Lincoln I was made to feel an absolute freedom: That the man was greater than the President. I felt myself in the peaceful atmosphere of a great soul—one altogether too great to remind me of my humble condition or my inferiority as to race or color. . . .

I hope I did not take his attentions to me altogether as due to my personal qualities—while the fact of my having been a slave, having gained my freedom and having by my own industry and perseverance picked up some sort of an education, in fact being like himself after fashion a self made man, gave me some hold upon the friendship—the main thing that gave me consideration in his eyes doubtless was that I represented in some measure the colored people of the Republic and could help in his great work of suppressing rebellion and restoring the American Union.

Undated Typescript with Handwritten Emendations Frederick Douglass Papers, Manuscript Division, Library of Congress

No higher eulogy can any bestow, no higher eulogy ought any to desire than to be honestly accorded the title of an honest man. Than the word honest no other word in the English language holds more of what our world stands in need, and of which it cannot well do without. It is the solid foundation without which no structure can stand the test of time. Human character, no less than human creations must stand on this basis or perish. It was the good fortune of Mr. Lincoln to have his name prefixed by the great word honest and this too, by common consent. No man yet has robbed him of this high honor. When the torrent of treason roared loudest and dashed highest, and passion poured out upon him its bitterest epithets, this title, like a rainbow of promise spanned his horizon, undimmed and unbroken. Whatever else was thought or said of him, no man said or thought of him as other than an honest man and as honestly endeavoring to do the right as "God gave him the ability to see the right."[3] He made no boast of his courage, but was courageous. He professed no special patriotism, but was a patriot. He claimed no eminence in statesmanship, but was a statesman. He made no show of philanthropy, but was a philanthropist, and is acknowledged today to have been among the wisest and best of all the class who have earned such fame. As a man of the race he emancipated, and one who knew Mr. Lincoln personally, I am glad of this and all other opportunities to bear testimony to his great qualities. To my mind, he was brave among the bravest, as a statesman, he was among the wisest, as a patriot, he was among the noblest and as a philanthropist he was among the best.

Nothing new need be said of him, and nothing new can be said of him. His name is illustrated and rendered illustrious in all the annals of the country. All that this occasion requires is to keep in mind what manner of man he was and what manner of man history has handed him down to us. Time will do for him what it has done for great men in all ages. Each decade will add something to his renown and render some element of his great character more conspicuous.

If I were called upon to single out one of his many noble qualities, for special thought, it would not be his patriotism, his wisdom, his patience or his philanthropy (though in all these he lacked nothing) but I would call attention to his invincible[4] courage. Though great in all else, here he certainly was a true hero. No man can weigh and measure Abraham Lincoln properly, who does not call to mind the stormy events in the midst of which he dared to enter upon his career as the president of this Republic, and the perils he encountered in reaching his post of duty at its capital. When he took charge of the Government, he found a country with an empty treasury, a disbanded army, a scattered navy, a ruined credit, a divided people, a nation threatened by a fierce and protracted fratricidal war, the end of which the wisest were unable to tell. His advent here, was like a man setting sail for sea on a sinking ship, one that was already abandoned by her former captain as not only unseaworthy, but incapable of repair. It is doubtful if any other statesman in this whole country could have stepped on the deck of our ship of State, with a courage as strong and a faith as sublime at that perilous time, as did Abraham Lincoln. More than the courage of the battle-field where bullets fly and bayonets gleam, was his when even the oldest and greatest of American warriors then living quailed before the rising storm of wrath and fire; when every rib, every beam, every bar, every bolt and brace of the Ship of State creaked with the dreadful signs of dissolution; Abraham Lincoln bravely took the helm and with a courage that never quailed, a faith that never doubted, a skill that never failed[,] and a patience that never wearied, conducted her safely through the storm.

Abraham Lincoln engraving by William Marshall, circa 1894, described by Douglass on page 190. Prints and Photographs Division, Library of Congress

Appendix 3
Recollected Words

Several memoirs published by people who knew Douglass recounted words he had said about Abraham Lincoln. These are reproduced here in the order in which they were published.

Recollection of Lincoln's Second Inaugural Reception at the White House
Elizabeth Keckley, *Behind the Scenes; Or, Thirty Years a Slave, and Four Years in the White House* (New York: G. W. Carleton, 1868)

Many colored people were in Washington, and large numbers had desired to attend the levee, but orders were issued not to admit them. A gentleman, a member of Congress, on his way to the White House, recognized Mr. Frederick Douglass, the eloquent colored orator, on the outskirts of the crowd.

"How do you do, Mr. Douglass? A fearful jam to-night. You are going in, of course?"

"No—that is, no to your last question."

"Not going in to shake the President by the hand! Why, pray?"

"The best reason in the world. Strict orders have been issued not to admit people of color."

"It is a shame, Mr. Douglass, that you should thus be placed under ban. Never mind; wait here, and I will see what can be done."

The gentleman entered the White House, and working his way to the President, asked permission to introduce Mr. Douglass to him.

"Certainly," said Mr. Lincoln. "Bring Mr. Douglass in, by all means. I shall be glad to meet him."

The gentleman returned, and soon Mr. Douglass stood face to face with the President. Mr. Lincoln pressed his hand warmly, saying: "Mr. Douglass, I am glad to meet you. I have long admired your course, and I value your opinions highly."

Mr. Douglass was very proud of the manner in which Mr. Lincoln received him. On leaving the White House he came to a friend's house where a reception was being held, and he related the incident with great pleasure to myself and others.

On the Monday [March 6] following the reception at the White House, everybody was busy preparing for the grand inaugural ball to come off that night. I was in Mrs. Lincoln's room the greater portion of the day. While dressing her that night, the President came in, and I remarked to him how much Mr. Douglass had been pleased on the night he was presented to Mr. Lincoln. Mrs. L. at once turned to her husband with the inquiry, "Father, why was not Mr. Douglass introduced to me?"

"I do not know. I thought he was presented."

"But he was not."

"It must have been an oversight then, mother; I am sorry you did not meet him."

Recollection of Douglass's Second White House Meeting with Lincoln

John Eaton, *Grant, Lincoln, and the Freedmen: Reminiscences of the Civil War* (New York: Longmans, Green, and Co., 1907)

Immediately after the interview [between Lincoln and Douglass on August 19, 1864] I called upon Douglass, and found him pacing the long, old-fashioned parlors in a state of extreme agitation. He did not know that I was in Washington, and greeted me in surprise; but nothing could distract his mind for long from that interview. "I have just come from President Lincoln," he said, making no attempt to suppress his excitement. "He treated me as a man; he did not let me feel for a moment that there was any difference in the color of our skins! The President is a most remarkable man. I am satisfied now that he is doing all that circumstances will permit him to do. He asked me a number of questions, which I am preparing to answer in writing," and he pointed to the writing materials on a table near him. There was never any doubt afterwards of Mr. Douglass's enthusiastic regard for the President. He had seen the situation for the first time as it appeared to Mr. Lincoln's eyes; he discovered Mr. Lincoln's masterly power in dealing with it,—and, parenthetically it might be remarked, with him,—and ever after, as is evidenced by informal testimony as well as by the orations which he delivered over the country, he told the story of Mr. Lincoln's greatness and excellence. . . . This little story, insignificant perhaps in itself, illustrates the President's skill in handling the men who were inclined to find fault with his policy.

Statement of John W. Cromwell on Douglass's 1876 Monument Dedication Speech

Freeman Henry Morris Murray, *Emancipation and the Freed in American Sculpture* (Washington, DC: Published by the Author, 1916)

I have before me the oration of Mr. Douglass on the occasion of the unveiling of the monument in Lincoln Park, Washington, April 14, 1876.

I find, however, no criticism of the group in the published address; evidently it was an *extempore* utterance brought out by the occasion and the environment. He did, however, make the criticism and I was about fifteen feet—not more—from him during the entire address. He was very clear and emphatic in saying that he did not like the attitude; it showed the Negro on his knees, when a more manly attitude would have been more indicative of freedom.

Frederick Douglass in Boston, ca. 1879. Lincoln Financial Foundation Collection, Allen County Public Library, Fort Wayne, Indiana

Endnotes

Introduction (pages xi–xx)

1 *New-York Tribune*, February 7, 1863.

2 Quoted in David W. Blight, *Frederick Douglass: Prophet of Freedom* (New York: Simon & Schuster, 2018), 114.

3 New York *Anglo-African*, February 13, 1864.

4 Emancipation Day Address at Poughkeepsie, August 2, 1858, in part 1.

5 Address Delivered at Rochester, April 15, 1865, in part 4.

6 We excluded a previously unpublished letter to Crofts, dated December 29, 1863, which appeared in the *Leeds Mercury* on January 21, 1864, because it does not mention Lincoln. Crofts acknowledged publishing it in a letter to Douglass, February 5, 1864, Douglass Papers.

7 Blight, *Frederick Douglass*, 202–27; Leigh Fought, *Women in the World of Frederick Douglass* (New York: Oxford University Press, 2017).

8 Letter to Crofts, April 20, 1865, in part 5.

9 Crofts to Douglass, May 19, 1865, Douglass Papers. Other times Crofts acknowledged receiving Douglass's letters are noted with the letter.

10 Russell L. Carpenter to Douglass, n.d., and March 28, [1865], Douglass Papers.

11 Letter to Carpenter, September 1, 1864, in part 3.

12 Letter to Crofts, April 20, 1865, in part 5.

13 Ibid.

14 "Assassination and Its Lessons," February 13, 1866, in part 7. Douglass alluded to a comment made by Andrew Johnson on October 24, 1864, when he told an audience of black Americans in Tennessee, "I will indeed be your Moses." See Robert S. Levine, *The Failed Promise: Reconstruction, Frederick Douglass, and the Impeachment of Andrew Johnson* (New York: W. W. Norton, 2021). In his postwar recollections, Douglass seemed to have forgotten his initial high hopes for Johnson's presidency. See Douglass's descriptions of Lincoln's second inauguration in parts 6 and 7.

15 *Leicester Chronicle*, September 3, 1864.

16 *Narrative of the Life of Frederick Douglass, an American Slave* (Boston: Anti-Slavery Office, 1845), 71–73.

17 Douglass, *My Bondage and My Freedom* (New York: Miller, Orton, and Mulligan, 1855), 247.

18 John Stauffer makes this observation in *Giants: The Parallel Lives of Frederick Douglass and Abraham Lincoln* (New York: Twelve, 2008), xii, 27–66.

19 *The Liberator*, July 7, 1854.

20 "Speech of Frederick Douglass," May 11, 1847, reported in the *National Anti-Slavery Standard*, May 20, 1847.

21 James Oakes, *The Radical and the Republican: Frederick Douglass, Abraham Lincoln, and the Triumph of Antislavery Politics* (New York: W. W. Norton, 2007), 20; Douglass, "The Constitution of the United States: Is It Pro-Slavery or Antislavery?" speech at Glasgow, Scotland, March 26, 1860, in Philip S. Foner, ed., *The Life and Writings of Frederick Douglass*, 5 vols. (New York: International Publishers, 1950–1955 and 1975), 2:469.

22 *Oration Delivered in Corinthian Hall, Rochester, By Frederick Douglass, July 5th, 1852* (Rochester: Lee, Mann & Co., 1852), 9–10, 36–37.

23 Douglass, "Constitution of the United States," *Life and Writings of Frederick Douglass*, 2:472, 473, 475. For further elaboration of Douglass's change of mind about the Constitution, see Peter C. Myers, *Frederick Douglass: Race and the Rebirth of American Liberalism* (Lawrence: University Press of Kansas, 2008), 88–99. On the development of antislavery and abolitionist constitutional traditions, see James Oakes, *The Crooked Path to Abolition: Abraham Lincoln and the Antislavery Constitution* (New York: W.W. Norton, 2021).

24 Douglass, "Reconstruction," *Atlantic Monthly* 18 (December 1866): 765.

25 Douglass, "The Color Question: An Address Delivered in Washington, DC," July 5, 1875, in John W. Blassingame and John R. McKivigan, eds., *The Frederick Douglass Papers, ser. 1, vol. 4: Speeches, Debates, and Interviews, 1864–1880* (New Haven, Conn.: Yale University Press, 1991), 420.

26 *The National Leader*, April 27, 1889; "The Nation's Problem," April 16, 1889, *Frederick Douglass Papers*, 5:412.

27 Douglass, "Colored Churches," *The North Star*, February 25, 1848.

28 Douglass, "Why Should a Colored Man Enlist?" *Douglass' Monthly*, April 1863.

29 "Speech of Frederick Douglass on the War," February 12, 1862, *Douglass' Monthly*, March 1862.

30 Ibid.

31 Douglass, "Constitution of the United States," *Life and Writings of Frederick Douglass*, 2:478–79.

32 Lincoln, "Speech at Peoria, Illinois," October 16, 1854, *CWL*, 2:276.

33 Lincoln to Albert G. Hodges, April 4, 1864, *CWL*, 7:281.

34 Sean Wilentz, *No Property in Man: Slavery and Antislavery at the Nation's Founding* (Cambridge, Mass.: Harvard University Press, 2018), 97.

35 Lincoln, "Speech at Peoria," October 16, 1854, *CWL*, 2:274.

36 Lincoln, "Speech at Chicago, Illinois," July 10, 1858, *CWL*, 2:501.

37 Lincoln, "Speech at Springfield, Illinois," June 26, 1857, *CWL*, 2:406.

38 Lincoln, "Speech at New Haven, Connecticut," March 6, 1860, *CWL*, 4:22.

39 Lincoln, "First Inaugural Address," March 4, 1861, *CWL*, 4:264.

40 James Oakes, *Freedom National: The Destruction of Slavery in the United States, 1861–1865* (New York: W. W. Norton, 2013), 238–39, 259, 275–76, 434–35; Eric Foner, *The Fiery Trial: Abraham Lincoln and American Slavery* (New York: W. W. Norton, 2010), 176, 194–95, 201–2.

41 Speech at Rochester, April 18, 1865, in part 4.

42 "Oration in Memory of Abraham Lincoln," April 14, 1876, in part 7.

Part 1: Pre-Civil War Commentary (pages 1–36)

1 "Slavery, Freedom, and the Kansas-Nebraska Act: An Address Delivered in Chicago, Illinois, on October 30, 1854," *Frederick Douglass' Paper*, November 24, 1854.

2 Douglass to Gerrit Smith, July 2, 1860; "The Chicago Nominations," June 1860.

3 "Emancipation Day at Geneva," October 1860.

4 "The Abolition Movement Re-Organized," October 1860; "Political Anti-Slavery Convention," *Douglass' Monthly*, November 1860. Smith ran a highly unsuccessful campaign, winning only 176 votes, one of which was cast by Douglass.

5 "The Late Election," December 1860 (emphasis in original).

6 "Dissolution of the American Union," January 1861.

7 "The Inaugural Address," April 1861.

8 Lincoln, "First Inaugural Address," March 4, 1861, *CWL*, 4:264.

9 "The Inaugural Address," April 1861.

10 "The Chicago Nominations," June 1860.

11 At his fourth debate with Lincoln in Charleston, Illinois, on September 18, 1858, Stephen Douglas cited Frederick Douglass's Poughkeepsie speech as proof of Lincoln's "perfect embodiment" of "negro equality and negro citizenship." *CWL*, 3:171–72.

12 In 1854, Sen. Stephen A. Douglas ushered the Kansas-Nebraska Act through Congress. The controversial bill repealed the Missouri Compromise of 1820 and opened up the Kansas and Nebraska territories to "popular sovereignty"—meaning that the white settlers who moved there could vote to decide whether to permit slavery. This law angered Lincoln and roused him back into politics.

13 On June 16, 1858, Lincoln received the nomination of the Republican Party of Illinois to contest the Senate seat held by Stephen A. Douglas. His acceptance speech quoted Mark 3:25: "And if a house be divided against itself, that house cannot stand." *CWL*, 2:461–69.

14 This was a reference to the repeal of the Missouri Compromise of 1820 with the passage of the Kansas-Nebraska Act.

15 William H. Seward, a US senator from Auburn, New York, was the frontrunner for the Republican nomination in 1860. He would go on to serve as Lincoln's secretary of state.

16 Daniel Webster of Massachusetts and Henry Clay of Kentucky were Whig leaders in the Senate. Silas Wright, a Democrat, served as governor of New York (1845–1846).

17 William Henry Harrison, James K. Polk, Zachary Taylor, and Franklin Pierce served as presidents from 1841 to 1857 (Douglass left Millard Fillmore off this list).

18 In 1858, Seward delivered a speech in which he stated that the North and South were engaged in "an irrepressible conflict between opposing and enduring forces, and it means that the United States must and will, sooner or later, become entirely either a slave-holding nation, or entirely a free-labor nation."

19 Horace Greeley initially supported Edward Bates, a conservative Whig from Missouri, for the Republican nomination for president in 1860. Bates would go on to serve as Lincoln's attorney general.

20 John Bell of Tennessee and Edward Everett of Massachusetts ran on the Constitutional Union ticket in 1860. They carried the states of Virginia, Kentucky, and Tennessee.

21 "ALL RIGHTS FOR ALL!" was one of the slogans of *Frederick Douglass' Paper.*

22 On July 23, 1860, the *New York Herald* published extracts of a letter from Smith to Douglass, concluding, "Lincoln is no more satisfactory to Mr. Smith than Breckinridge, Bell, Douglas or [Sam] Houston. They all stop short at some recognitions of slavery, while Smith, 'constitution or no constitution, would have the North vote slavery to death,' or ask permission of the South peaceably to leave the Union."

23 Lincoln's running mate, Hannibal Hamlin, was a US senator from Maine.

24 The vehemence of Douglass's characterization of Lincoln ("Its candidate") owes to Lincoln's and the Republican Party's commitment to upholding the US Constitution in its entirety, including the fugitive slave clause (and corresponding Fugitive Slave Act of 1850).

25 John C. Breckinridge, a Kentucky slaveholder, served as vice president under James Buchanan and was the southern Democratic candidate for president in 1860. He eventually served as a Confederate general and secretary of war.

26 In *Somerset v. Stewart* (1772), English jurist Lord Mansfield held that slavery "is of such a nature that it is incapable of being introduced on any reasons, moral or political, but only by positive law, which preserves its force long after the reasons, occasions, and time itself from whence it was created, is erased from memory. It is so odious, that nothing can be suffered to support it, but positive law."

27 In a speech on "Colonial Slavery" in the House of Commons on July 13, 1830, Lord Henry Brougham said that slavery violated God's eternal law and that it was a "wild and guilty fantasy, that man can hold property in man!"

28 An allusion to Shakespeare's *Othello*, act 1, scene 3.

29 Douglass quotes Hamlet's famous "To be or not to be" soliloquy in Shakespeare's *Hamlet*, act 3, scene 1.

30 Benjamin Lundy was an early abolitionist who had died in 1839.

31 Federal authorities had pursued several fugitive slaves in Boston, including Shadrach Minkins (1851) and Anthony Burns (1854).

32 In 1856, John C. Frémont ran as the first Republican candidate for president.

33 "Black Republican" was a popular epithet Democrats used to tar Republicans as favoring freedom and equality for African Americans.

34 Slaves overthrew French colonial rule in Saint-Domingue during the Haitian Revolution (1791–1804).

35 Douglass loosely quotes Lincoln's "House Divided" speech.

36 Although President James Buchanan rejected a state right of secession, in his fourth annual message to Congress, December 3, 1860, he denied that the president or Congress possessed any right to preserve the Union by force.

37 Winfield Scott, a native of Virginia, was the commanding general of the Union army at the beginning of the Civil War.

38 An allusion to Lincoln's Cooper Union speech of February 27, 1860, when Lincoln said to southern Democrats who threatened disunion if a Republican were elected president, "You will rule or ruin in all events." *CWL*, 3:543.

39 Douglass again quotes Lincoln's "House Divided" address.

40 "Doughface" signified a northern Democrat with pro-slavery principles, like James Buchanan.

41 Following the English Civil War, Oliver Cromwell ruled the Commonwealth of England as Lord Protector from 1653 to 1658.

42 An allusion to the moneylender Shylock's demand for security in Shakespeare's *Merchant of Venice*, act 4, scene 1.

43 Sara Lucy Bagby (Douglass misspelled her surname) was a fugitive slave from Wheeling, Virginia, who was captured in Cleveland, Ohio, and convicted under the Fugitive Slave Act of 1850.

44 In his *Commentaries on the Laws of England* (1765), English jurist William Blackstone wrote that civil law "command[s] what is right, and prohibit[s] what is wrong."

45 On March 7, 1850, Daniel Webster delivered an address in the Senate supporting the Compromise of 1850. The speech was highly unpopular in his home state of Massachusetts.

46 An allusion to Roger B. Taney's dictum in *Dred Scott v. Sandford* that African Americans had no rights that white people were "bound to respect."

47 Confederate president Jefferson Davis.

48 Montgomery, Alabama, the first Confederate capital.

49 An allusion to the inscription on the Liberty Bell, "Proclaim Liberty Throughout All the Land Unto All the Inhabitants thereof" (from Leviticus 25:10), which was a slogan of abolitionists in the 1830s.

50 On April 14, 1842, in a speech in the House of Representatives, Adams argued that during a war, "military authority takes . . . the place of all municipal institutions," including slavery. The former president rejected the idea that "the States where slavery exists have exclusive management of the subject," and maintained that "*not only the President of the United States, but the Commander of the Army, has power to order the universal emancipation of the slaves.*"

51 Douglass likely meant "Constitution."

52 Lincoln called for 75,000 militiamen on April 15, 1861.

53 A quotation from Rev. William A. Scott, *Daniel, a Model for Young Men* (1854).

54 A quotation from Shakespeare's *A Midsummer Night's Dream*, act 5, scene 1.

55 Albany newspaperman Thurlow Weed—a close associate of Seward's—published an editorial in the *Albany Evening Journal* in December 1860 calling for the passage of "an *efficient*, but not *revolting*, Fugitive Slave law . . . followed by a repeal of Personal Liberty laws." Meanwhile, in March 1861, Rep. Thomas Corwin of Ohio proposed an unamendable amendment to the Constitution that would prevent Congress from abolishing slavery in the states where it existed. Lincoln supported the Corwin Amendment because he did not believe it conceded anything that the South did not already have under the Constitution.

56 Allusions to Isaiah 10:12 and 2:12.

57 Sen. Jesse D. Bright, a Democrat from Indiana, claimed that senators like Charles Sumner, John P. Hale, and Salmon P. Chase, who were associated with the Free Soil movement in 1852 (and would later become Republicans), were excluded from committees because "they were outside of a healthy political organization."

Part 2: Civil War Commentary: Pre-Emancipation (pages 37–78)

1 "Change of Opinion Announced," *The North Star*, May 15, 1851, as reported in *The Liberator*, May 23, 1851.

2 Both Lincoln and Douglass supported Frémont in his presidential bid in 1856. Lincoln delivered more than 50 speeches in Illinois for Frémont, and Douglass announced publicly his shift from supporting Gerrit Smith, the candidate of the Radical Abolition Party, to the Frémont-Dayton ticket.

3 "General Fremont's Proclamation to the Rebels of Missouri," October 1861.

4 "The Slave Democracy Again in the Field," November 1862.

5 Lincoln, "Address on Colonization to a Deputation of Negroes," August 14, 1862, *CWL*, 5:370–75.

6 Lincoln, "Emancipation Proclamation," January 1, 1863, *CWL*, 6:29.

7 Letter to Samuel J. May, January 28, 1863.

8 Douglass published a letter to the editor, dated New York, April 20, 1861, by a correspondent calling himself "Immaterial," that advocated for the recruitment of black soldiers into the Union army. He then added these "remarks."

9 In his July 4, 1861, message to Congress in special session, Lincoln mentioned the slave states only one time. *CWL*, 4:421–41.

10 Cabinet members in the Lincoln Administration: Secretary of State William Seward, Secretary of the Treasury Salmon P. Chase, Secretary of War Simon Cameron, and Postmaster General Montgomery Blair.

11 On July 25, 1861, Lincoln appointed John C. Frémont to command the Department of the West. On August 30, 1861, Frémont issued a proclamation of martial law to quell the civil unrest in Missouri. It also authorized the confiscation of the property of rebels, "and their slaves, if any they have, are hereby declared freemen."

12 Missouri, Kentucky, Maryland, and Delaware were slave states that did not secede from the Union.

13 An allusion to Matthew 18:6.

14 On September 2, Lincoln requested that Frémont, "of your own motion, modify" the proclamation to comply with Congress's Confiscation Act of August 6, which authorized the liberation of slaves of rebels only if they had "been employed in hostile service against the Government of the United States." Frémont refused, telling Lincoln, "If . . . your better judgement still decides that I am wrong in the article respecting the liberation of slaves, I have to ask that you will openly direct me to make the correction." On September 11, Lincoln "very cheerfully" ordered Frémont to do so. *CWL*, 4:506–7.

15 Lincoln removed Frémont from his command on November 2, 1861. He would be reinstated in March 1862.

16 Smith's December 6, 1861, letter to Pennsylvania Rep. Thaddeus Stevens, a Radical Republican, was published as a broadside. For more information, see John R. McKivigan, ed., *The Frederick Douglass Papers*, ser. 3, vol. 2: Correspondence, 1853–1865 (New Haven, Conn.: Yale University Press, 2009), 325.

17 Illinois Republican Owen Lovejoy introduced a resolution in the US House of Representatives to instruct the judiciary committee to report a bill for the "confiscation of all property of all citizens who shall be found engaged in armed rebellion against the government of the United States, and . . . also, for the unconditional liberation of their slaves."

18 The possibility of war with England arose on November 8, 1861, when a US navy vessel captured two Confederate envoys on the British ship *Trent*. The interception of the envoys violated Great Britain's declared neutrality in the American Civil War. Lincoln was reported to have said, "One war at a time," and in January released the Confederate envoys.

19 Allusions to Matthew 10:16 and Proverbs 28:1.

20 Isaiah 1:5–6.

21 On March 6, 1862, Lincoln sent a message to Congress recommending compensation for any state that adopted gradual emancipation. *CWL*, 5:144–46.

22 Ibid.

23 Thomas Carlyle was a Scottish writer of the Victorian era.

24 An allusion to Shakespeare's *Macbeth*, act 3, scene 2.

25 Thomas Perronet Thompson, a radical reformer in England, had served as governor of Sierra Leone (1808–1810), as an army officer in the Middle East and India (1818–1821), and as a member of Parliament for several nonconsecutive terms between 1835 and 1859.

26 Secretary of the Treasury Howell Cobb of Georgia and Secretary of War John B. Floyd of Virginia used their positions within the Buchanan administration to aid the nascent Confederacy before the Civil War began.

27 On November 20, 1861, Maj. Gen. Henry Wager Halleck, a conservative Democrat in command in Missouri, issued General Orders No. 3, excluding fugitive slaves from coming into Union lines.

28 Congress passed the First Confiscation Act on August 6, 1861, and the Second Confiscation Act on July 17, 1862, about two weeks after Douglass's essay was published.

29 Section 6 of the Second Confiscation Act authorized Lincoln to issue a proclamation that would lead to the confiscation of property owned by persons in rebellion. Douglass was likely unaware when he wrote this that Lincoln had issued a proclamation on July 25. *CWL*, 5:341.

30 Section 9 of the Second Confiscation Act authorized Lincoln "to employ as many persons of African descent as he may deem necessary and proper for the suppression of this rebellion."

31 Edwin M. Stanton became secretary of war on January 20, 1862, replacing Simon Cameron. Lincoln delivered his speech in front of the US Capitol on August 6, 1862. *CWL*, 5:358–59.

32 During the August 14 meeting, Lincoln said that "without the institution of Slavery and the colored race as a basis, the war could not have an existence. It is better for us both, therefore, to be separated." *CWL*, 5:370–75.

33 Douglass was unaware that the very day he wrote this letter, Lincoln would issue his Preliminary Emancipation Proclamation, which the newspapers published the following day. The bribe remark is a barbed allusion to the song "I Spurn the Bribe" from an 1860 Republican songbook, which tells of a man who would not allow his vote to be bought.

34 Douglass quotes Lincoln's Preliminary Emancipation Proclamation of September 22, 1862. The October 1862 *Douglass' Monthly* also printed the entire proclamation along with Lincoln's August 22 public letter to Horace Greeley, which Douglass said "should be read again" to understand "in the most clear and concise words the reasons for issuing the late Proclamation." In that letter, Lincoln said, "My paramount object in this struggle *is* to save the Union, and is *not* either to save or to destroy slavery. If I could save the Union without freeing *any* slave I would do it, and if I could save it by freeing *all* the slaves I would do it; and if I could save it by freeing some and leaving others alone I would also do that." The letter concludes, "I have here stated my purpose according to my view of *official* duty; and I intend no modification of my oft-expressed personal wish that all men every where could be free." *CWL*, 5:388–89. It should be noted that Douglass did not know that the true purpose of Lincoln's letter to Greeley was to generate public support for emancipation because Lincoln had already decided to issue an emancipation proclamation.

35 A Democratic mantra during the war was, "The Constitution as it is and the Union as it was"—meaning, restore the Union with slavery intact.

36 Dixon Stansbury Miles, a West Point graduate and native of Maryland, was outmaneuvered by Confederate General "Stonewall" Jackson at Harpers Ferry, Virginia, in mid-September 1862. His surrender of over 12,000 men led some to surmise foul play.

37 On December 5, 1862, Crofts mailed Douglass two copies of the *Mercury* containing "the long & interesting extract from your last letter to me that you thought might be published with advantage." Crofts to Douglass, December 5, 1862, Douglass Papers.

38 An allusion to Psalm 33:10.

39 Democrats made great gains in the elections of 1862. In New York, Democrat Horatio Seymour defeated Republican James Wadsworth in the gubernatorial race.

40 An allusion to Jesus feeding the five thousand in Matthew 14:13–21.

41 Edward Gibbon, author of *The History of the Decline and Fall of the Roman Empire*, 6 vols. (1776–1789).

42 In Shakespeare's *Othello*, Iago is the villainous antagonist of Othello.

43 Roundheads were supporters of Parliament and constitutional monarchy during the English Civil War.

44 In 1845, James Russell Lowell wrote these opening lines to "The Present Crisis," a poem protesting the annexation of Mexico as an expansion of slavery.

45 Lincoln, Annual Message to Congress, December 1, 1862, *CWL*, 5:518–37.

46 The Democratic Party won significant gains in the elections of 1862, picking up nearly 30 seats in the House of Representatives as well as several important state seats, including the governorship in New York.

Part 3: Civil War Commentary: Post-Emancipation (pages 79–124)

1 "The Slaveholders Rebellion," August 1862, in part 2.

2 Letter to Crofts, January 28, 1863.

3 "The Slaveholders Rebellion," August 1862.

4 "The Work of the Future," *Douglass' Monthly*, November 1862.

5 Jonathan W. White, *A House Built By Slaves: African American Visitors to the Lincoln White House* (Lanham, Md.: Rowman and Littlefield, 2021), 85–99.

6 Jefferson Davis, General Orders No. 111, December 24, 1862.

7 Letter to Stearns, August 1, 1863.

8 See "Secession and War" in part 6.

9 Letter to Carpenter, September 1, 1864.

10 Address Delivered in Rochester, April 15, 1865, in part 4.

11 The February 1863 *Douglass' Monthly* reprinted the *Chicago Tribune*'s account of the speech.

12 Samuel J. May was a Unitarian minister, Garrisonian abolitionist, and member of the Syracuse Freedmen's Aid Society.

13 Isaiah 51:3.

14 The first line of the refrain in "The Jubilee," a hymn by Charles Wesley.

15 Douglass made minor alterations when he reprinted this speech in *Douglass' Monthly* in March 1863. We have silently incorporated Douglass's corrections.

16 In November 1862, Attorney General Edward Bates issued an opinion that African Americans were citizens of the United States, ignoring the primary holding of the *Dred Scott* decision.

17 Theodore Parker was a Unitarian minister, Transcendentalist, social reformer, and radical abolitionist.

18 The 1829 Catholic Emancipation Act secured civil rights for Catholics and permitted them to serve as ministers of parliament. The 1832 British Reform Bill redistributed political representation in the House of Commons from small "rotten" boroughs controlled by the nobility and gentry to heavily populated industrial towns. The 1846 Importation Act (Prime Minister Robert Peel's Bill of Repeal) repealed the Corn Laws by removing protectionist measures and enabling free trade to lower the cost of imported food to commoners in England.

19 Shakespeare's *Henry VI*, part II, act 3, scene 2.

20 Douglass changed "everywhere" to "anywhere" in *Douglass' Monthly*.

21 An allusion to Shakespeare's *As You Like It*, act 2, scene 7.

22 Douglass changed this word to "almost" in *Douglass' Monthly*.

23 The *Tribune* mistakenly said this was "Graves" church, but it was actually Leonard A. Grimes.

24 A pamphlet version of this speech in the African American Pamphlet Collection at the Library of Congress adds that there were "Cheers and long-continued applause" here.

25 The pamphlet version adds that there were "Cries of That's the question."

26 The Lincoln administration offered diplomatic recognition to Haiti and Liberia, and in February 1863, Haitian diplomat Ernest Roumain arrived in Washington, DC, where he met with Lincoln, Secretary of State William H. Seward, and other national leaders.

27 The pamphlet version adds, "Cheers and cries of We will."

28 George L. Stearns, an abolitionist from Massachusetts who had supported John Brown in the 1850s, engaged Douglass in early 1863 to recruit black soldiers.

29 Unbeknownst to Douglass when he wrote this letter and his editorial, "The Commander-In-Chief and His Black Soldiers," which appeared on the same page of *Douglass' Monthly*, Lincoln had already issued an order of retaliation on July 30, 1863, that pledged to execute one Confederate soldier for every black soldier "killed in violation of the laws of war," and to place a Confederate "at hard labor on the public works" for "every one enslaved by the enemy or sold into slavery." According to Lincoln, the rules of civilized warfare "permit no distinction as to color in the treatment of prisoners of war as public enemies." *CWL*, 6:357.

30 The 54th Massachusetts Infantry, a black regiment, was raised soon after Lincoln's Emancipation Proclamation and achieved fame through their assault on Fort Wagner in Charleston, South Carolina, on July 18, 1863.

31 Douglass added this editorial note at the end of the letter.

32 Term for Peace Democrats, northern opponents of the Civil War who sought immediate cessation of hostilities regardless of the impact on southern slavery.

33 In July 1863, a mostly Irish mob protested the draft by rioting in the streets of New York City. Over the course of several days, the mob killed unarmed African Americans and burned the Colored Orphan Asylum to the ground. More than 100 people died in the violence.

34 In November 1862, Gen. Nathaniel P. Banks was appointed commander of the Army of the Gulf and led Lincoln's Reconstruction efforts in Louisiana.

35 From the poem "Stanzas for the Times" by abolitionist author John Greenleaf Whittier, published in 1835 in the *Boston Courier.*

36 Douglass had met Lincoln for the first time earlier that day.

37 Assistant Adjutant-General, US Volunteers.

38 Samuel C. Pomeroy was a Republican senator from Kansas.

39 The original manuscript says "his his bill."

40 Lorenzo Thomas was adjutant general of the US army.

41 Republican senator John Sherman, Ohio.

42 The *Inquirer* stated that this letter was addressed to the secretary of the Halifax Ladies' Emancipation Society. According to Crofts, Mary Carpenter held that position until early 1865. See Crofts to Douglass, February 23, [1865], Douglass Papers.

43 Bartholomew Fussell was a founding member of the American Anti-Slavery Society in 1833 and active in the Underground Railroad in Pennsylvania.

44 Lincoln's August 22, 1862, public letter to Horace Greeley (see part 2, note 34).

45 Annual Message to Congress, December 8, 1863, *CWL*, 7:49.

46 Lincoln was working behind the scenes to abolish slavery in Maryland. In October, voters in Maryland ratified a new antislavery state constitution that officially abolished slavery in the state on November 1.

47 Tennessee was exempted from the Emancipation Proclamation because it was under Union control. However, after the War Department created the Bureau of Colored Troops in May 1863, both free and enslaved black men in Tennessee were recruited into the Union army.

48 The Willey Amendment to the West Virginia statehood bill provided for gradual manumission of enslaved minors. Its passage in early 1863 enabled the statehood bill to pass on June 20, 1863.

49 In June 1863, a Missouri state constitutional convention approved an ordinance for gradual, compensated manumission. Slavery would finally be abolished in the state in January 1865.

50 Although the Emancipation Proclamation did not apply to Kentucky because it remained loyal to the United States, Douglass expected slavery to collapse there because it was doing so in the bordering states of Tennessee, West Virginia, and Missouri. By early summer of 1864, Camp Nelson, Kentucky, would become a major recruiting center for the US Colored Troops.

51 This phrase originated from a 1677 play called *The Rival Queens; Or the Death of Alexander the Great.* The original phrase, which appears in act 4, was, "When Greeks joyn'd Greeks, then was the tug of War."

52 Crofts told Douglass that she had an extract of this letter published in the *Leeds Mercury*, "as I did before." See Crofts to Douglass, April 14, [1864], Douglass Papers.

53 On January 29, 1863, Banks issued General Orders No. 12, which mandated "a yearly system of negro labor" (a form of sharecropping) that many interpreted as slavery by other means. Douglass would hold Lincoln partly responsible for this development.

54 While the Democratic convention would not meet until late August, most political observers expected the Democrats to nominate the pro-war, pro-slavery Maj. Gen. George B. McClellan for president.

55 On August 5, 1864, Mary Carpenter acknowledged this letter, telling Douglass, "I have been copying out a great part of your very interesting letter which we shall send to the Inquirer." See Mary Carpenter to Douglass, August 5, 1864, Douglass Papers.

56 William Lloyd Garrison published an excerpt from this letter in *The Liberator* on September 16, 1864, under the headline, "Frederick Douglass on President Lincoln." Douglass responded to this letter on September 17.

57 Douglass contrasts Lincoln's lenient Amnesty Proclamation of December 8, 1863, with the Wade-Davis Bill of July 2, 1864, which the president pocket-vetoed.

58 At their national convention in Baltimore in June 1864, the Republicans dumped Vice President Hannibal Hamlin from the ticket and placed Andrew Johnson, a War Democrat and military governor of Tennessee, as Lincoln's running mate.

59 Since McClellan was pro-war, the Democrats sought to balance their ticket by nominating George H. Pendleton, Peace Democrat and Ohio congressman, for vice president.

60 While the minutes of the convention do not indicate that Douglass wrote this address, he claimed authorship in his letter to Tilton, October 15, 1864, reprinted below.

61 On April 12, 1864, Confederate forces under Nathan Bedford Forrest and James R. Chalmers captured Fort Pillow on the Tennessee River and massacred the black Union soldiers who occupied the fort when they tried to surrender. The battle was reported as a "massacre" and "butchery." Of about 300 Union deaths, almost 200 were US Colored Troops, compared with only 16 Confederates killed in the battle.

62 Following a disastrous diplomatic mission between Horace Greeley and Confederates in Canada in July 1864, Lincoln released a public letter addressed "To whom it may concern" informing the Confederates that he would entertain "Any proposition which embraces the restoration of peace, the integrity of the whole Union, and the abandonment of slavery, and which comes by and with an authority that can control the armies now at war against the United States." *CWL*, 7:451.

63 While the Senate had approved the 13th amendment by the necessary two-thirds majority in April 1864, the House of Representatives failed to meet that constitutional threshold until January 31, 1865.

64 Theodore Tilton, an abolitionist from New York City, was editor of *The Independent*.

65 On August 17, 1864, Lincoln drafted a public letter to Charles D. Robinson, a War Democrat and Wisconsin editor, in the aftermath of Greeley's ill-considered diplomatic mission to Canada. In the letter, Lincoln spoke of his commitment to preserving the Union and destroying slavery, but he closed with an ambiguous line: "If Jefferson Davis wishes, for himself, or for the benefit of his friends at the North, to know what I would do if he were to offer peace and re-union, saying nothing about slavery, let him try me." *CWL*, 7:499–501.

66 Lincoln's "To whom it may concern" letter.

67 See the Address of the Colored National Convention in Syracuse, October 4, 1864.

68 On April 16, 1862, Lincoln signed a law banning slavery in the District of Columbia, and on June 19, 1862, he signed a law prohibiting slavery in all federal territories.

69 Chief Justice Roger B. Taney, the author of the infamous *Dred Scott* decision, had died in Maryland on October 12, 1864. Lincoln replaced him with Salmon P. Chase.

70 An allusion to Taney's opinion in the *Dred Scott* case.

71 Crofts told Douglass that she "speedily made lengthy extracts" from this letter and sent them to the editor of the *Leeds Mercury* and that "they were immediately published." See Crofts to Douglass, February 23, [1865], Douglass Papers.

72 An allusion to the parable of the rich man and Lazarus in Luke 16.

Part 4: Eulogies (pages 125–158)

1 Remarks at City Hall, Rochester, April 15, 1865.

2 Speech in Rochester, April 18, 1865.

3 Eulogy at Cooper Union, June 1, 1865.

4 Earlier in the proceedings, Rev. Ezekiel Robinson, a professor at Rochester Theological Seminary, said, "If treason expected to reap any advantage from this foul and unnatural murder, never would treason be more disappointed."

5 Alexander Pope, "Essay on Man" (1734).

6 This word may be "tears," but the Rochester *Democrat*, which also covered the speech, reported it as "fears."

7 This quote aligns with what Lincoln said elsewhere. For instance, in his 1854 Peoria Address, Lincoln used the word "hate" four times to express his feelings toward slavery. *CWL*, 2:255, 270.

8 Douglass replaced "great" with "good."

9 After Secretary of War Edwin M. Stanton intervened, African Americans received permission to march.

10 An allusion to Roger Taney's dictum in *Dred Scott v. Sandford* that African Americans had no rights that white people were "bound to respect."

11 An allusion to Luke 7:47.

12 An allusion to Job 13:15.

13 An allusion to the closing of Lincoln's second inaugural address.

14 This line suggests that Douglass was still optimistic about Andrew Johnson.

15 Mary Surratt, one of the Lincoln assassination conspirators, would become the first woman executed by the federal government when she was hanged along with three other conspirators on July 7, 1865.

16 An allusion to God's promise to Noah in Genesis 9 that He would not flood the entire earth again. The covenant sign would be a "bow," meaning rainbow.

17 Douglass compares the nation's travail to Jesus in the Garden of Gethsemane the night he was betrayed in Matthew 26:39, when Christ prays: "O my Father, if it be possible, let this cup pass from me: nevertheless not as I will, but as thou *wilt*."

18 "Know thyself" is a famous inscription on the Temple of Apollo at Delphi.

19 The success of Lincoln and loyal Americans in preserving the Union gave hope to Mexico's Republican forces that they would, with American assistance, be able to repel the French invasion by Archduke Maximilian.

20 Douglass had originally written "nearly ninety years ago," but he revised it to allude to the opening of Lincoln's Gettysburg Address: "Four score and seven years ago," which dated the birth of the United States to 1776, the year of the Declaration of Independence.

21 An allusion to words spoken by Henry Clay during a debate in Congress in 1813.

22 Booth shouted "*Sic semper tyrannis*," the state motto of Virginia, after jumping to the stage at Ford's Theatre. It means, "Thus always to tyrants." Douglass may have meant "motto of defiance."

23 In November 1864, Confederate saboteurs attempted to start fires in New York City hotels as well as P. T. Barnum's Museum.

24 P. G. T. Beauregard was a Confederate general who commanded the defenses around Charleston during the firing on Fort Sumter in 1861, and whose defense of Petersburg, Virginia, slowed the Union advance toward Richmond at the end of the Civil War.

25 Lewis Powell (aka Payne) was a Confederate soldier who attempted to kill William H. Seward as part of Booth's conspiracy.

26 Booth tasked George Atzerodt with killing Vice President Andrew Johnson, but Atzerodt did not follow through with the plan.

27 An allusion to Shakespeare's *Richard III*, act 1, scene 1.

28 Douglass originally wrote "struck dumb."

29 Douglass quotes from the closing sentence of Lincoln's second inaugural address.

30 "Sheeted dead" is a phrase from Shakespeare's *Hamlet*, act 1, scene 1.

31 Douglass appears to have written "lost" here, but he almost certainly meant "loss."

32 Douglass appears to have inadvertently omitted a word or phrase from this sentence, but he appears to be referring to Lincoln's meeting with the black delegation in August 1862.

33 William A. Buckingham was Republican governor of Connecticut.

34 This undated manuscript largely aligns with the report of Douglass's speech that appeared in the *Portland Daily Press*, December 9, 1865; however, the newspaper report does include some material that may be from pages of this speech that are missing.

35 Douglass refers to support for the abolitionist Liberty Party candidate for president, James G. Birney, which increased from 7,453 votes in 1840 to 62,103 in 1844.

36 The Kansas-Nebraska Act of 1854, which opened up federal territories to popular sovereignty.

37 In *Notes on the State of Virginia* (1785), Jefferson speculated that American slavery might invite divine punishment: "Indeed I tremble for my country when I reflect that God is just: that his justice cannot sleep for ever."

38 An allusion to Lincoln's April 4, 1864, public letter defending emancipation to Kentucky newspaperman Albert G. Hodges: "I claim not to have controlled events, but confess plainly that events have controlled me." *CWL*, 7:281–83.

39 This manuscript appears to be incomplete. We have also omitted one page from the file that appears to be from another speech.

Part 5 Postwar Correspondence (pages 159–170)

1 *The Liberator*, November 11, 1864.

2 This is a quote by Horatio in Shakespeare's *Hamlet*, act 1, scene 2.

3 Soldiers used cartridge boxes to store and carry ammunition.

4 Wilson's response, dated September 6, 1865, appeared in *The Liberator* on October 27, 1865.

Part 6 Autobiography (pages 171–190)

1 This is actually a paraphrase of Lincoln's 1858 "House Divided" address, not something Lincoln said in 1854 at the time of the Kansas-Nebraska Act.

2 While Douglass was traveling in Europe in 1860, his 10-year-old daughter Annie died of a brain hemorrhage.

3 An allusion to Shakespeare's *Macbeth*, act 4, scene 5.

4 Letter to Stearns, August 1, 1863, in part 3.

5 Shakespeare's *As You Like It*, act 2, scene 7.

6 Lincoln's Preliminary Emancipation Proclamation of September 22, 1862, gave the Confederate states 100 days to cease their rebellion against the United States or he would issue a final proclamation freeing the slaves in areas of rebellion.

7 While McClellan was removed from command in November 1862, Grant did not assume overall command of the armies until March 1864.

8 Grant engaged Lee's Army of Northern Virginia at the Wilderness on May 5–7, 1864, near Fredericksburg, Virginia. Following the bloody engagement, Grant continued to advance against Lee until he ultimately laid siege near Petersburg.

9 An allusion to Lincoln's August 22, 1862, public letter to Horace Greeley (see part 2, note 34).

10 See appendix 1.

11 It was actually Sherman's capture of Atlanta in September and Sheridan's victories in the Shenandoah Valley of Virginia—not the Wilderness, which was a devastating Union defeat—that secured Lincoln's electoral victory in November.

12 William P. Dole, commissioner of Indian Affairs.

13 From the late 1850s until the 1890s, Douglass frequently delivered an address called "Self-Made Men" (an excerpt is reproduced in part 7).

14 A day after receiving the Republican nomination for president in June 1864, Lincoln told a delegation of Republicans that he was reminded "of a story of an old Dutch farmer, who remarked to a companion once that 'it was not best to swap horses when crossing streams.'" *CWL*, 7:383–84.

15 In a final act of desperation, in 1865, the Confederacy offered freedom to slaves who would join the Confederate army.

16 This recollection conflicts with what Douglass wrote in the April 1865 letters in part 5, in which he showed great optimism for Johnson's presidency.

17 Luke 14:18.

18 James Abram Garfield (not Abraham) was assassinated in 1881, while Douglass was writing *Life and Times.*

19 Remarks at City Hall, Rochester, April 15, 1865, in part 4.

20 An allusion to Shakespeare's *Troilus and Cressida*, act 3, scene 3.

Part 7: Remembrances (pages 191–246)

1 Letters to Carpenter, April 18, 1865, and Crofts, April 20, 1865, in part 5.

2 "Inauguration of Douglass Institute: Lecture by Fred'k Douglass, Esq.," September 29, 1865, *The Liberator*, October 13, 1865; Robert S. Levine, *The Failed Promise: Reconstruction, Frederick Douglass, and the Impeachment of Andrew Johnson* (New York: W. W. Norton, 2021), 54–55.

3 Jonathan W. White, *A House Built By Slaves: African American Visitors to the Lincoln White House* (Lanham, Md.: Rowman and Littlefield, 2022), 197.

4 "Oration in Memory of Abraham Lincoln," April 14, 1876.

5 Ibid.

6 "Oration Commemorating Lincoln's Birthday," February 13, 1893.

7 Lincoln, "Speech at Peoria, Illinois," October 16, 1854, *CWL*, 2:276.

8 Douglass, "Oration Commemorating the Twenty-sixth Anniversary of Emancipation in the District of Columbia," April 16, 1888.

9 The report in the Washington *Daily National Intelligencer*, February 8, 1866, contained several differences; we will note the most significant. It added "to your favorable consideration" at the end of this sentence.

10 The *National Intelligencer* added "—I mean our whole race" at the end of this sentence.

11 The *National Intelligencer* added "able" before "successor."

12 The *National Intelligencer* added "that we should ask" after "improper."

13 When Douglass delivered this speech in Chicago on February 28, 1866, he commented, "It is said that Andrew Johnson is following in the footsteps of Abraham Lincoln. It is a foul and black slander on the dead." Douglass added that if Lincoln were "living now, he would stand to-day with the men who go farthest in asserting equal rights to all the people." *Chicago Tribune*, March 1, 1866. According to a Vermonter in the audience, Douglass had said, "He who says President Johnson is following in the footsteps of his predecessor, *casts foul dishonor on the name of Abraham Lincoln!*" Bellows Falls *Vermont Chronicle*, March 31, 1866. Douglass also delivered a version of this speech at the state capitol in Springfield, Illinois, on April 3, 1866, in the same room in which Lincoln had delivered his "House Divided" address. Springfield *Daily Illinois State Journal*, April 4, 1866.

14 Douglass used these same allusions to Shakespeare's *Hamlet*, act 1, scene 1, and Matthew 27:51–53 in his June 1865 eulogy.

15 At the request of Congress, historian George Bancroft delivered an address "on the Life and Character of Abraham Lincoln" in the House of Representatives on Lincoln's birthday, February 12.

16 Ermine was the white fur on robes traditionally worn by justices.

17 An allusion to Andrew Johnson's "Moses" speech in Nashville on October 24, 1864.

18 Lincoln advocated for these two groups to be enfranchised in a letter to Louisiana governor Michael Hahn on March 13, 1864, and in a speech at the White House on April 11, 1865. *CWL*, 7:243, 8:403–4. Following Lincoln's death, black leaders pointed to these statements in their fight for the right to vote.

19 James M. Mason, a Confederate emissary to England, sent a public letter to a London newspaper on April 27, 1865, denying that the assassination of Lincoln was part of a rebel plot. "Letter from Mr. Mason," *New York Times*, May 11, 1865.

20 For this speech, we relied on Robert S. Levine, *The Failed Promise: Reconstruction, Frederick Douglass, and the Impeachment of Andrew Johnson* (New York: W. W. Norton, 2021), 237–59.

21 In 1872, Sen. Charles Sumner endorsed the Liberal Republican (and Democrat-endorsed) Horace Greeley for president against the incumbent, U.S. Grant. In this public letter, Douglass urged black voters to reject Greeley because he had become a vocal critic of Reconstruction.

22 An allusion to Confederate Vice President Alexander H. Stephens's claim that slavery and white supremacy were the "cornerstone" of the Confederacy.

23 The money for the statue was donated entirely by African Americans—a movement that started with a $5 donation by a former slave named Charlotte Scott.

24 Thomas Jefferson to Jean Nicolas Démeunier, June 26, 1786.

25 Lincoln said this to the black delegation that came to the White House in August 1862. *CWL*, 5:370–75.

26 An allusion to Lincoln's August 22, 1862, letter to Horace Greeley (see part 2, note 34).

27 An allusion to Shakespeare's *Hamlet*, act 5, scene 2.

28 An allusion to Shakespeare's *Julius Caesar*, act 3, scene 2.

29 On February 21, 1862, Nathaniel Gordon became the only American executed for transatlantic slave trading.

30 The Constitution of the Confederate States of America stated that "No . . . law denying or impairing the right of property in negro slaves shall be passed" (art. 1, sec. 9).

31 In the pamphlet edition of this speech, Douglass footnoted Lincoln's April 4, 1864, letter to Kentucky newspaperman Albert G. Hodges: "I am naturally anti-slavery. If slavery is not wrong, nothing is wrong. I cannot remember when I did not so think and feel."

32 Douglass quotes Lincoln's second inaugural address.

33 An allusion to the moneylender Shylock's demand for security in Shakespeare's *Merchant of Venice*, act 4, scene 1.

34 An allusion to Zechariah 13:6.

35 This stanza comes from Thomas Hood's 1844 poem "The Lay of the Laborer."

36 The pamphlet mistakenly says "where."

37 In 1855, Nathaniel Banks of Massachusetts said "Let the Union slide" in a speech in Maine. The phrase was widely repeated in the 1850s and during the war.

38 Thomas Ball's "Freedmen's Memorial" or "Emancipation Group" that Douglass had dedicated five days earlier.

39 In *Life and Times* (1881), Douglass mistakenly said Madison Square was the venue of this speech.

40 The Grand Army of the Republic was a Union veterans' organization founded in Illinois in 1866. Local chapters, like the Abraham Lincoln Post No. 13 in New York City, were established throughout the country in the years after the war.

41 In a May 29, 1868, telegram accepting the Republican nomination for president, Ulysses S. Grant concluded, "Let us have peace," which became the unofficial slogan of his successful campaign.

42 In the *Slaughter-House Cases* (1873) and *U.S. v. Cruikshank* (1876), the Supreme Court interpreted the 14th amendment so narrowly that it undermined the rights of black Americans, thereby weakening Reconstruction in the former Confederate states.

43 This was later published in Osborn H. Oldroyd, ed., *The Lincoln Memorial: Album-Immortelles* (New York: G. W. Carleton, 1882), 265.

44 An allusion to Lincoln's 1858 "House Divided" address.

45 Morgan Godwyn was a 17th-century Anglican priest who served as a missionary to colonial Virginia and Barbados and preached that it was not a sin to baptize black people.

46 Shakespeare's *Hamlet*, act 3, scene 1.

47 Although he was raised in a slaveholding family, John Marshall Harlan rose to become one of the great voices for black rights on the US Supreme Court, writing powerful dissenting opinions in *The Civil Rights Cases* (1883) and *Plessy v. Ferguson* (1896).

48 The 1886 edition mistakenly says "Sewell"; this was corrected in subsequent editions.

49 This was actually the draft of Lincoln's public letter to Charles D. Robinson. See Douglass to Tilton, October 15, 1864, in part 3.

50 In the 1850s, Illinois law prohibited interracial marriage, black testimony in court against whites, black militia or jury service, and black voting. Moreover, in 1853, Illinois enacted a law that prohibited the migration of free African Americans into the state.

51 Robert Henry Newell wrote a series of satirical pieces under the pseudonym "Orpheus C. Kerr"—a play on the phrase "office seeker." Lincoln was very fond of reading these writings and sharing them with others.

52 This pamphlet appears to have accidentally duplicated words and phrases in various parts of the speech. For the sake of clarity, we omitted these duplicates.

53 Sen. Shelby M. Cullom of Illinois delivered the first speech.

54 An allusion to Hebrews 12:1.

55 Alphonse Marie de Lamartine, author of *Les Méditations Poétiques* and a key figure in the 1848 Revolution in France.

56 An allusion to an 1827 speech delivered by Henry Clay before the American Colonization Society in the House of Representatives chamber at the US Capitol.

57 Douglass may have been conflating his two visits to the White House. The Statue of Freedom on the Capitol dome was not completed until December 1863, a few months after Douglass's first visit with Lincoln.

58 As vice chair of Washington's Board of Public Works in the early 1870s, Alexander Robey Shepherd carried out massive public improvements in the District of Columbia.

59 This phrase was used several times in the Bible, including Matthew 9:36 and Mark 6:34.

60 An allusion to Shakespeare's *Macbeth*, act 5, scene 8.

61 Immediately following Douglass's address, the Rev. Henry L. Wayland delivered remarks in response to a toast of "What We May Learn from Abraham Lincoln."

62 An allusion to Psalm 8:5.

63 Charles Remond Douglass and Lewis Henry Douglass both served in the 54th Massachusetts Infantry.

64 An allusion to Matthew 5:44.

65 See appendix 1.

66 This nursey rhyme dates back at least to the mid-18th century.

67 An allusion to Shakespeare's *Hamlet*, act 2, scene 2.

68 Edward Cornelius Delavan was a wealthy temperance advocate in New York.

69 An allusion to the 13th amendment.

70 A manuscript draft in the Douglass Papers says "prince."

71 The speech was covered in the *Washington Post*, January 10, 1894. The title used here comes from an 1895 printing of the speech.

72 An allusion to Lincoln's Gettysburg Address.

Appendix 2: Undated Drafts of Speeches (pages 251–256)

1 Only the August 19, 1864, meeting was at Lincoln's invitation.

2 This four-page manuscript largely repeats what is in *Life and Times* and other speeches. We therefore include only excerpts that offer different perspectives.

3 An allusion to Lincoln's second inaugural address.

4 This word may be "invisible."

Index